Strategic Leadership for Medical Groups

Strategic Leadership for Medical Groups

Navigating Your Strategic Web

John D. Blair
Myron D. Fottler

Jossey-Bass Publishers
San Francisco

Sponsored by
The Center for Research
in Ambulatory Health Care
Administration

Jossey-Bass books and products are available through most bookstores. To contact Jossey-Bass directly, call (888) 378-2537, fax to (800) 605-2665, or visit our website at www.josseybass.com.

Substantial discounts on bulk quantities of Jossey-Bass books are available to corporations, professional associations, and other organizations. For details and discount information, contact the special sales department at Jossey-Bass.

For sales outside the United States, please contact your local Simon & Schuster International Office.

 Manufactured in the United States of America on Lyons Falls Turin Book. This paper is acid-free and 100 percent totally chlorine-free.

Library of Congress Cataloging-in-Publication Data

Blair, John D. (John David), date.
Strategic leadership for medical groups : navigating your strategic web / John D. Blair, Myron D. Fottler. — 1st ed.
p.   cm.
Includes bibliographical references and index.
ISBN 0-7879-0853-3
1. Group medical practice.   2. Integrated delivery of health care.
3. Business networks.   I. Fottler, Myron D.   II. Title.
[DNLM: 1. Group Practice—organization & administration.
2. Leadership.   3. Delivery of Health Care, Integrated—trends.
W92 B635s 1998]
R729.5.G6B56   1998
610'.65—dc21
DNLM/DLC
for Library of Congress   97-50436

FIRST EDITION
HC Printing
10 9 8 7 6 5 4 3 2 1

CONTENTS

LIST OF TABLES,
FIGURES, AND TOOLS

TABLES

FIGURES

TOOLS

PREFACE

The American healthcare industry—including its medical group segment—is currently undergoing a revolution that is unprecedented in both magnitude and velocity. The old healthcare system is being rapidly dismantled, and restructuring is under way. One example of the change is that, under the old system, strategies were formulated in response to the latest regulatory and payor initiatives aimed at controlling quality and cost. Now, the hyperturbulent environment has forced medical group leaders to find more global strategies. They can no longer set policy on an ad hoc basis. They must, among other things, identify, assess, and manage their relationships with other organizations.

This book introduces four new concepts and a number of toolkits that will help leaders address these changes for medical groups. The concepts are as follows:

- A *strategic web* describes the complex interplay of the many supportive and nonsupportive relationships that a medical group has with the stakeholders in its strategic environment.

- *Strategic navigation* refers to medical group leaders' attempts to position their group within a competitive environment.

- *Web navigation* refers to the way medical group leaders set their priorities in managing their group's relationships with the stakeholders who can either be supportive or threatening.

- *Strategic web navigation* refers to leaders' efforts to integrate strategic and web navigation in order to successfully navigate their own strategic web.

Another change is that contemporary organizational culture has shifted. It no longer favors *independence;* rather, *interdependence* is a fact of life. Our concept of the strategic web emerged from our thinking about this interdependence. The strategic web is that complex set of strategic relationships within which health-care organizations find themselves. Every organization's strategic web is being fundamentally restructured as a result of the accelerating move to organized delivery systems that aspire to be truly integrated delivery systems/networks (IDS/Ns). We call these evolving systems *integrating systems,* a term suggesting that systems are in the process of integration. Few (if any) have achieved true clinical and managerial integration.

Strategic relationships for a healthcare organization are external relationships with the organizations and key stakeholders who control significant economic and noneconomic resources. The focus of our work is the medical group practice; we examine other organizations, such as hospitals, as they relate to the medical group. Key individual and organizational stakeholders for medical groups include employers, competitors, and patients, as well as those that are now—or could become—the professional and organizational components of an IDS/N. These are hospitals, physicians, managed care organizations, and a new addition: the central headquarters or systems office. This last key stakeholder not only controls the network or system but may itself be controlled by a key stakeholder partner that initiated or funded the system's formation—a hospital, a managed care organization, or the system's physicians. The executive team of the medical group faces the challenge of eliciting the necessary economic and noneconomic resources from their relationships with these key stakeholders. Their success in the endeavor will increasingly determine the success or failure of the medical group.

This hyperturbulent environment has caused the strategic web of relationships to shift continuously. Some stakeholders are becoming more important to the medical group; others are becoming less so. Some relationships are becoming more positive; others are becoming more negative. More resources (time, effort, and money) must be devoted to the stakeholders who are becoming more important to the medical group, whereas conflicts with those becoming less important must be avoided. Enhancing relationships with key existing stakeholders may also be required.

Even though a number of challenges face the executive and physician leadership teams of medical groups, the most fundamental challenge is to simultaneously manage traditional strategic management issues, such as the pursuit of market share or becoming the low-cost leader, with the management of a strategic web of relationships. Strategic web navigation is organizational adaptation to the evolving environment through the simultaneous management of strategy and the new web of relationships with key stakeholders.

BACKGROUND

Whereas in 1993 and 1994 much attention in the media and among healthcare policy analysts was focused on the government's role in healthcare, fundamental healthcare reform was already taking place with the integration of healthcare delivery and financing. These market reforms were influenced, of course, by the perceived promise—or threat—of governmental reform, but reforms have developed a life and power of their own as the strategic web for healthcare organizations becomes restructured. In 1997, we see "still integrating" networks and systems rather than integrated systems per se.

The only constant in the healthcare industry is change itself. Consequently, vertically integrated systems with tightly linked hierarchies of physician, managed care organization (MCO), and hospital may no longer be feasible or desirable. *Traditional vertical integration* meant that healthcare integration needed interorganizational relationships that were tightly linked or coupled. Alternatively, *virtual integration* has taken place when vertical integration is attempted through loosely linked or coupled relationships. Such organizations are highly flexible, with lower hierarchical overhead in terms of both cost and flexibility in decision making. However, problems of coordination and control are frequent. Strategies for navigating a web of network relationships are needed to replace the hierarchical control (and the apparent effectiveness) of traditional vertical integration.

Vertically integrated systems are feasible to design and develop in industries with stable environments where change is modest and incremental. Although they provide an appearance of efficiency and strategic control, we do not believe that tightly integrated systems can be successfully sustained in an environment with constant and significant change. Constant organizational restructuring due to changing environmental threats and opportunities implies the need for navigation skills and flexible web management.

Consequently, truly integrated systems with full coordination and control, as they have been conceived, may be unrealistic. If our perspective is correct, medical groups must address a host of possible forms of quasi- or virtual integration with other partners. These relationships have varying commitments, investments, power balances, sharing of rewards, and durations.

Our method of identifying, assessing, and navigating an organization's strategic web requires us to look in detail at the organization's relationships with the key potential components of any network or system that provides them either tight or loose vertical (or horizontal) integration. In addition, strategic web navigation looks inside the organization itself. Given that new, large composite medical groups have been formed from existing solo practices joined together with small groups, there may be significant internal cultural clashes, as well as political, professional, or specialty-group and personality conflicts that need to be managed.

Also, strategic web navigation looks beyond the organization and its network or system partners to the wider arena, which includes competitors, potential allies, and the potential prizes of competition: patients to care for and the resources with which to do so. Finally, we examine the extended web in which national contracting and political lobbying by organizations and their professional and trade associations are important.

The concept of strategic web navigation provides both a complement to traditional ways of managing hierarchical, tightly vertically integrated organizations and the needed fundamental approach for the effective management of new forms of virtual integration. In investigating these issues, we have been able to create and study a joint quantitative and qualitative database. These two sources are rich in information about the uncertain future of medical groups—a growing and increasingly important category of healthcare organizations. Such information includes the challenges and opportunities that await medical practice executives and the appropriate strategies for these healthcare executives to employ. These strategies enable executives to effectively facilitate their management of stakeholder relationships in the uncertain future.

Our first source of information is the "Facing the Uncertain Future" (FUF) study, which was based on an extensive questionnaire we administered in 1995 to physician and nonphysician medical practice executives. In that study, we looked at the fundamental changes that were creating a growing feeling of uncertainty about the future of healthcare in the United States. When we report specific quantitative results, such as percentages, they are taken from this study. Details concerning the 686 executive respondents are provided in Resource A.

It should be noted here that the sixteen-page questionnaire took over an hour to complete. At the time we administered the questionnaire, we knew the length would reduce our response rate and our ability to generalize our results to *all* group practices. However, our purpose was to gather more comprehensive, in-depth information from a smaller number of medical groups rather than more statistically powerful information from a larger database. As a result, the 686 medical group respondents (27 percent response rate) tended to overrepresent medical groups that were larger, multispecialty, and located in areas with high managed care penetration. The results also overrepresented more highly educated respondents. In sum, we had in-depth responses from a relatively sophisticated sample of medical group executives representing organizations that are more likely to be affected by the changing healthcare environment.

Our second source of information was the "Strategy in Action" (SIA) study, an ongoing, multiyear, qualitative study of one integrating organization as it attempted to adapt and thrive in the uncertainties of the mid-1990s. This second source provides some unique insights because it grounds the general realities experienced by many organizations in a specific case study of a single, multiunit organization with numerous relationships, which we call Integrating System A. This case study is particularly interesting because of its increasingly complex sets of strategic and operational relationships that illustrate the types of relationships many integrating systems need to manage. When we show strategic web figures and report findings from Integrating System A, the information is primarily from this second study. More details about the study are provided in the Resource at the end of the book.

PURPOSES OF THE BOOK

There are several major purposes of this book. First, we hope to provide a complement to what has been learned about IDS/Ns, the process of integration, and the results of integration through several excellent, in-depth case studies of a limited number of integrated systems such as those by Coddington, Moore, and Fischer (1996) and Shortell and others (1996). We did not want to rely on case studies, however. That is why we conducted the national survey of medical groups to determine the perceptions of their physician and nonphysician executives of their present and intended strategies.

These groups were not preselected to be examples of existing integration but fall along the entire continuum from full independence to high levels of integration with other medical groups or with hospitals and managed care organizations. To understand the current challenges and to predict the future choices that will need to be made, it is important to examine the entire range of situations facing healthcare organizations today. Such data allow us to model a wide range of possibilities along the broad and varied continuum of integration rather than to merely reflect the experiences of organizations that are already integrated.

Second, we focus on medical groups as a focal point for increasing our understanding of integrated healthcare. Physicians who were formerly solo practitioners are consolidating into medical groups, and existing groups are becoming larger. Medical groups will play an increasingly important role in providing coordinated, cost-effective, high-quality medicine to the covered lives (the number of individual enrollees covered by a managed care plan) so cherished in the growing managed care environment. Medical groups will be a significant starting point for integrated healthcare in many settings. In others, they are (and will be) essential partners for emerging systems. For example, many hospital-based systems are creating their own composite medical groups to harness and coordinate the energy of physicians whose practices have been acquired. In addition, looking at networks/systems from this focus provides fundamentally different perspectives than are available with hospitals or managed care organizations as the focus.

Third, to better understand the complicated realities of medical groups, we present the first typology of the key ingredients of the strategic web concept for an integrating system and its component organizations. These types are the *organizational web,* the *network/system web,* the *competitive web,* and the *extended web.* We identify and discuss the specific leadership challenges and strategic choices each presents.

Fourth, we apply and modify our own theory, as well as those of others, to issues of effectively navigating the changing strategic web. Specifically, we identify four types of organizations that represent an extension and refinement of two key strategic issues identified by Miles and Snow (1978), whose concepts have been used extensively in healthcare. Their strategic types are the Analyzer, the Prospector, the Defender, and the Reactor. By contrast, our organizations fall into four categories that are both similar and different from theirs: the Strategic Navigator, the Strategic Entrepreneur, the Strategic Engineer, and the Strategic Ostrich. We also examine to what degree there is a fit between what medical practice executives report their strategic intentions to be and the tactics they actually follow; we examine whether that makes a difference and whether that fit will increase or decrease as integrating proceeds. We examine organizations in terms of their priorities in managing their webs of relationships. These organizations appear to fall into four types: the Web Navigator, the Web Optimist, the Web Pessimist, and the Web Ostrich. We look at the degree of fit between what medical group leaders report their strategic intentions to be with their priorities in managing relationships with key stakeholders, and whether that fit will increase or decrease in the future. We call these integrated types that combine strategic and web navigation the Strategic Web Navigator, the Strategic Navigator Only, the Web Navigator Only, the Limited Navigator, and the Strategic Web Ostrich. And we look at navigating the emerging integration by examining the major IDS/N players in detail, with a focus on future key strategic relationships within the evolving healthcare web. These major players are physicians, hospitals, managed care organizations, and the IDS/Ns themselves. We also examine web relationships with key stakeholders outside the IDS/N, such as patients and competitors.

Finally, the orientation of our analyses allows us to provide practical and prescriptive guidelines for managing the strategic web in the emerging healthcare environment. For example, we look at both the big picture and the requirements for effective implementation to see whether organizations with different types of integration or strategic and tactical types actually perform better. In other words, both a purpose and a contribution of this book is that we apply our theoretical insights, supported by our unique database, to the challenging world of leadership and managerial practice.

OVERVIEW OF THE CONTENTS

We begin the book with an overview of the types of leadership challenges healthcare executives face as they attempt to manage the emerging and future strategic web. Medical group practices are used as the entry point to look at the web of relationships in the emerging and still uncertain future of integrated healthcare. Then, we provide examples of what a strategic web looks like for one large system; we identify its components.

In Chapter One, we use the medical group as the focal organization. Then, we provide a complex but simplified example of what the strategic web looks like for one integrating system and its component organizations within a strategic web. The four levels of the strategic web are defined, illustrated, and explained. Chapter One ends with the first of ten toolkits that are designed to permit leaders of medical groups to identify and assess stakeholders who matter to their group—now and in the future.

Chapter Two predicts the emerging healthcare environment and the key stakeholders in that changing environment. We identify the major leadership challenges facing healthcare executives as they attempt to manage the emerging and future strategic web. Toolkit 2 is designed to permit the leaders of medical groups to identify and assess their strategically important goals and relationships and assess the impact the changing environment has on those relationships.

In Chapter Three, we explore medical group leaders' strategic thinking and actions now and in the future by examining the organization's goals, business strategies, tactics, and the stakeholders necessary to implement them. We identify four strategic types of organizations in terms of their fundamental strategic intentions and actions, as well as the relative significance of each type in the past and into the future. We also assess the degree of fit between strategy and tactics. Toolkit 3 will permit medical groups' leaders to determine who they are in terms of their strategies and priorities in confronting their strategic web.

Chapter Four explores the impact of the four strategic types on various dimensions of organizational performance relative to local competitors. We also consider the impact of other medical practice characteristics such as size and academic practice on performance. Because Strategic Navigators perform better than the other three strategic types, Toolkit 4 will help medical practice leaders identify the strategies and tactics that will help them become Strategic Navigators.

Chapter Five identifies the key web relationships and how a medical practice executive might analyze and classify them from the perspectives of reducing threat and enhancing cooperation. Toolkit 5 provides guidance on assessing and classifying various external stakeholders in their strategic web.

Chapter Six outlines and defines a series of tactical actions for medical practice executives to use in managing their web of relationships. The need to fit web diagnoses and tactics is also discussed. Finally, the relationship between the four web navigation types and navigators, along with various dimensions of performance, is discussed. Toolkit 6 outlines a process for navigating the web of relationships for a medical practice.

Chapter Seven examines the medical group's organizational web internal to the system. Our discussion encompasses relationships with system headquarters, hospitals within the system, health plans that are part of the system, and primary care and specialist physicians within the system. Our emphasis in this chapter is on physician integration and its challenges. We discuss the managerial challenges, the potential barriers and facilitators in relating to each, and managerial choices. Toolkit 7 is targeted to assessing and navigating the medical group's organizational web, which is made up of often-problematic relationships among multiple physician subgroups and between administrative and physician leaders at different levels.

Chapter Eight focuses on how the medical group relates to other internal stakeholders, as discussed in Chapter Seven, and to external stakeholders who support or collaborate with the medical group practice and other organizations in the system. Examples of the latter include other external IDS/Ns, health plans, and hospitals. Again, the managerial challenges, barriers, facilitators, and choices are addressed. Toolkit 8 provides tools to go outside the medical group itself and assess and navigate the medical group's network/system web made up of partner relationships with allied managed care organizations and hospitals, as well as other aligned physicians and medical groups.

Chapter Nine examines the competitive web of the medical group. The competitive web includes all competitive systems and their component organizations, including competitive hospitals and group practices. This web also includes actual or potential partners (such as employers) and customers (such as Medicare or Medicaid patients). Chapter Nine also examines the extended web, which includes external stakeholders who are not part of the organizational, system, or competitive webs but who influence the medical group or the system. These include public officials, agencies, and programs that are not part of the first three webs, even though they may affect the focal group practice for better or worse. Examples come from all levels of government and from various roles (for example, legislator, regulator, or payor), as well as professional associations, national employers or coalitions, regional or national physician management companies, pharmaceutical firms, voluntary hospital buying groups, national for-profit health systems or hospitals, and national HMOs (health maintenance organizations) or PPOs (preferred provider organizations).

Managerial barriers, facilitators, and choices in relating to their competitors and potential collaborators are discussed. Toolkit 9 is focused on worksheets for understanding and effectively navigating the medical group's competitive web made up of direct and indirect competitors, as well as the buyers of physician services that are provided by the leaders' medical group.

Chapter Ten pulls together the theoretical and practical implications of our analyses of all four levels of the strategic web. Because we see that the pace of change in the health services industry requires flexibility, no structures or strategies are always appropriate; nor could any be considered ideal. As a result, *virtual integration* is our preferred strategy rather than *vertical integration* or *structural integration*. We conclude with a discussion of what strategic navigation really means and what should and should not be done in navigating the strategic web so critical to the future survival and effectiveness of all healthcare organizations.

Chapter Ten ends with the last of ten toolkits. These tools provide the leaders of medical groups with guides to navigating the extended web and to integrating their strategies and priorities for navigating the entire complex of important relationships that make up their strategic web.

AUDIENCES FOR THE BOOK

Our primary audience consists *of medical group leaders—both executives and physicians.* The members of this leadership group are both similar and dissimilar. All are in medical groups, but their roles in the groups are different. Executive and physician leadership roles create different challenges and choices, but unless everyone involved can create an effective strategic leadership team, groups will not be effective in the long run. In addition, there are many kinds of medical groups, varying in size and complexity and in whether they have primarily a patient care mission or the multiple missions of academic medical groups. Further, some of these medical group leaders are already involved in a tightly linked system; others are in a loosely linked network that is in the process of further vertical integration; still others are in free-standing groups that may or may not remain that way. For these medical group leaders, the toolkits provided at the ends of the chapters should help to make the text materials practical and relevant to their particular organizations.

Other healthcare executives who will benefit from this book operate in different segments of the overall healthcare industry—in hospitals, managed care organizations, insurance companies, and (a new but growing group) in the headquarters of integrated systems and networks, including partially integrated ones such as independent practice associations (IPAs), physician-hospital organizations (PHOs), and management services organizations (MSOs).

This audience also includes physician leaders within all the organizations mentioned who are interested in better understanding and in playing a leadership role in the emerging, highly restructured strategic web. For all healthcare executives, the toolkits provide new ways to assess and plan for a successful future.

Board members of hospitals, managed care organizations (MCOs), insurance companies, IPAs, PHOs, MSOs, and IDS/Ns play an increasingly important role in healthcare leadership. Board members who wish to further their own understanding of the increasingly complex relationships that healthcare executives in their organizations are attempting to manage will find this book useful. Together, executives and board members can be more sophisticated in their strategy development and implementation.

Our secondary audience includes health policy makers, suppliers, and researchers. Policymakers have had and will continue to have significant consequences for medical groups, hospitals, insurance companies, and the systems and networks that are emerging. The integration of the healthcare strategic web has to a great extent been encouraged by governmental policy because of the predicted elimination of service and technology duplication and their attendant costs. These pressures have created incentives for clinical and other forms of integration, along with high hopes for enhanced organizational synergy. Whether these outcomes were intended or unintended or whether they are beneficial or detrimental (and to whom) is unclear. Our analysis suggests caution, quasi-integration, and a go-slow approach. Bigger and fully integrated is not necessarily better than smaller and quasi-integrated.

Suppliers to the healthcare industry will also benefit from this book. These suppliers include vendors such as medical equipment suppliers and pharmaceutical firms, professional and trade associations, consultants, and the investment community. Executives in these industry-supplier organizations will find this work helpful in understanding the rapidly evolving healthcare system and its web of strategically important relationships.

Researchers in medical group management or healthcare management and health services generally, as well as those in strategic management outside the healthcare industry, will also find value in what is discussed here, particularly the new concepts of the strategic web and its strategic navigation. Our work not only contributes to the knowledge base on integrated delivery systems and networks but also provides the first systematic measurement instrument for examining relationships with key stakeholders from a strategic perspective.

Finally, all parties involved in organizing and conducting strategic planning retreats will find useful information and agendas for determining their own organizations' operational and strategic webs, how those webs are changing, what strategic choices they must make to navigate without floundering, and what tactics and resources—including strategic vision and leadership—it will take to make their intended strategic choices work.

This book is the first to be developed as part of the new strategic alliance between Jossey-Bass Publishers and the Medical Group Management Association.

This alliance permits both parties to better serve the needs of practicing medical group administrative and physician leaders who are facing their own organizations' uncertain futures and increasingly challenging strategic webs.

March 1998   JOHN D. BLAIR
                                      Lubbock, Texas

                                      MYRON D. FOTTLER
                                      Birmingham, Alabama

The mission of the Center for Research in Ambulatory Health Care Administration (CRAHCA) is to advance the art and science of medical group practice management to improve the health of our communities through health services research based largely in group practices and other health care delivery settings. As the research and development arm of the Medical Group Management Association (MGMA), CRAHCA conducts health services research, develops measurement tools, and conducts educational seminars for the benefit of the entire health care industry.

Founded in 1926, MGMA is the leading organization representing medical group practice. More than 8,900 group practices and 19,900 individuals are MGMA members, representing nearly 199,400 physicians. MGMA executive offices are in Englewood, Colorado.

ACKNOWLEDGMENTS

Many people contributed their vision, leadership, and technical skills to make this book possible. In particular, we are indebted to Rebecca L. McGovern, the past editor of the Jossey-Bass Health Series, who initiated this project, as well as Andrew Pasternack, the current Jossey-Bass editor who has guided our completion of this book. We also extend special appreciation to Andrea R. Paolino of the Center for Research in Ambulatory Care Administration and Timothy M. Rotarius, now at Central Florida University, who worked hand-in-computer with us on the "Facing the Uncertain Future" (FUF) study as the co-project directors for the Medical Group Management Association and Texas Tech University, respectively. Special thanks go also to William M. Dwyer, senior director of strategic marketing, Abbott Laboratories, Abbott Park, Illinois, who recognized the potential of the FUF study and, as a representative of Abbott Laboratories, offered to fund it.

We would like to recognize several staff members of the Medical Group Management Association (MGMA), the Center for Research in Ambulatory Health Care Administration (CRAHCA), and the American College of Medical Practice Executives (ACMPE). For their vision and leadership in supporting and developing this study, we would like to thank Frederick J. Wenzel, former executive vice president/chief executive officer, and Fred E. Graham, II, former senior vice president/chief operating officer at MGMA. For helping us promote this study and win the support of ACMPE members, we would like to thank Andrea Rossiter, MGMA senior vice president for the college.

We thank Barry R. Greene, senior vice president for research and education and co-principal investigator of the FUF study, for his theoretical contributions and for managing both internal and external organizational issues. We extend our appreciation to John M. Greaves, research intern, who offered his technical expertise and worked tirelessly on data analysis issues of our survey; David N. Gans, survey operations director, and Miriam L. Fultz, survey operations project director, for providing insightful comments on the survey instruments; Dawn I. Lewis, data technician, for her technical expertise in compiling data for this study; Donna L. Burman, CRAHCA research associate, for contributions related to the survey instrument; Cyndy L. Redmiles, CRAHCA administrative coordinator, for her continuing administrative support through the end of the study; and Jana J. Harkrider, CRAHCA administrative support assistant, for providing ongoing administrative support. Cynthia Kiyotake, director of the MGMA Library, provided us with extensive reference sources and help.

We also would like to thank Steven S. Lazarus, president of MSA Corporation, Denver, Colorado, for his leadership and support and for his contributions in the development of the second-round survey instrument. And a special thanks to members of MGMA's research committee, who acted as pretesters for the survey instrument. These included Marshall M. Baker, executive director of physician services, St. Luke's Regional Medical Center, Boise, Idaho; Paul H. Barrett, Jr., associate medical director, Colorado Permanente Medical Group, Denver, Colorado; and William R. Nicholas, associate professor and assistant chairman, College of Human Medicine, department of surgery, Michigan State University, East Lansing, Michigan.

The initiation of the "Strategy in Action" study was made possible by two uniquely strategic leaders: William D. Poteet, III, currently president, North Texas division of Columbia/HCA, and Paul Schilder, director of specialty services at the Austin Regional Medical Clinic.

Others who could envision healthcare's changing strategic webs and shared their insights with us include Robert Smithee, administrator, Cardiovascular Institute of Texas; Dana Rains, vice president, Lubbock Methodist Hospital; Robert Salem, chairman and chief medical officer of the Methodist Medical Group; James Burrell, president and CEO of St. Mary Medical Group; Gena Bosse, director of operations for the Diagnostic Clinic of San Antonio and an employee of PhyCor; Karol Shepherd and Ray Reynolds, both former directors of Methodist Practice Management; Matt Driskill, founding executive director of Methodist Medical Group; and Bill Davis, president and CEO of Peak Systems, the management systems organization for Hermann Hospital in Houston.

Finally, special thanks to the brave and visionary members of the stealth think-tank known only as the "Knipling Group."

We would like to acknowledge the support provided by several Texas Tech University research colleagues. Our appreciation goes to Grant T. Savage, associate professor of management and health organization management and current director of the M.B.A. and Ph.D. programs in health organization management (HOM), who helped us develop a theoretically meaningful questionnaire; Timothy W. Nix, who provided theoretical and developmental support for the first questionnaire and graciously performed some data analysis, writing, graphics support, and copyediting for this report; Susan B. Dymond, for her guidance and insight involving the practical value of the FUF study and for always ensuring that we never forgot the operational side of healthcare delivery; and Pamela Kiecker, of Virginia Polytechnic Institute, for expert support when we were designing our sampling methodology.

Special appreciation goes to John A. Buesseler, founding dean of the Texas Tech University School of Medicine, who provided his far-ranging medical and managerial knowledge to us and who critically analyzed, and thereby improved, drafts of both questionnaires. As the visionary "godfather" of the HOM program, he had led us years earlier to recognize the need to focus on the strategic future of medical groups and the challenges facing their administrative and physician leaders.

In addition, we could not have succeeded with this project without the support of Cathryn A. Buesseler, for providing meticulous copyediting and rewriting; Terence T. Rock, a doctoral student at Texas Tech University, for his theoretical and methodological insights; Todd Lipscomb, for providing statistical and analysis support at various times throughout this study; Bonny M. McMurrough, for valuable assistance in the development of the second questionnaire; Kristi Morse, Farinaz Wigmans, and Sonya Castro—health organization management students and strategic analysts—for their administrative support during the many periods of intense writing, data analysis, and toolkit development.

We also owe special thanks to G. Tyge Payne, for his insights and efforts to developed the linked strategic webs found in this book and for his creativity and perseverance in the development of the toolkits, which make navigating the strategic web more practical.

To Carlton Whitehead, professor of management and health organization management and associate dean of the College of Business Administration, who was one of the two researchers who started the strategic stakeholder management program of research for healthcare organizations, goes special appreciation for his theoretical contributions and vision. Further unselfish collegial support was provided by Kimberly Boal, associate professor of management and strategic management scholar, and Alex Stewart, associate professor of management, network expert, and strategic ethnographer.

We also wish to acknowledge and thank several individuals at the University of Alabama at Birmingham (UAB). Donna Malvey, doctoral candidate in administration-health services and now assistant professor at the University of South Florida, deserves special thanks for her contributions to the design of the second-round survey instrument, her data analysis, and her critical reading of the original manuscript; Susan Cleghorn and Gayla Schultz, administrative assistants for the Ph.D. program in administration-health services, were crucial in coordinating and facilitating communication between researchers at UAB, Texas Tech University, and MGMA. In addition, Keisa Daniels typed two drafts of several chapters. Contessa Fincher and Beth Woodard, both doctoral students, read the book manuscript critically and provided valuable insights. Charles Zabada provided research assistance in the development of literature reviews and examples used in several chapters.

Finally, we conclude with a special note of thanks to our wives, Starr and Carol, for their support of this research and publication endeavor. Their understanding of the time required for this activity and their patience are truly appreciated.

THE AUTHORS

JOHN D. BLAIR holds the Trinity Company Professorship in management and healthcare strategy and serves as coordinator of the management area (and chair of the management department) in the College of Business Administration at Texas Tech University. From 1984–94, he was associate chair of the department of health organization management in the Texas Tech School of Medicine. He was formerly a member of the graduate faculty at the University of Maryland at College Park, having received his Ph.D. from the University of Michigan in 1975.

Since the fall of 1997 he has served as director of the Center for Healthcare Strategy (CHS), which he founded at the Texas Tech College of Business Administration. From 1994–97, he directed the Institute for Management and Leadership Research (IMLR), after having directing the institute's specialized research programs in health organization management and strategic studies for much of a decade.

Blair was the founding director of the M.B.A. and Ph.D. programs in health organization management, which are based on a joint venture of the College of Business Administration and the Texas Tech School of Medicine. The M.B.A. (HOM) program is dual-accredited as a graduate business program by AACSB and as a health services administration program by ACEHSA.

Blair's book (with M. D. Fottler) *Challenges in Health Care Management: Strategic Perspectives for Managing Key Stakeholders* (San Francisco: Jossey-Bass Management Series and Health Series) appeared in the fall of 1990. In 1992, the best books committee of the American College of Healthcare Executives selected

Challenges as one of four books to be recommended to their practitioner members. In addition, the Academy of Management chose it as one of six finalists for the 1992 George R. Terry Book Award that is given for the most significant new scholarly book in the field of management.

In 1993, he edited (with Jay Stanley) *Challenges in Military Health Care: Perspectives on Health Status and the Provision of Care* (New Brunswick, N.J., Transaction Publishers). This book combines his long-term interests in military and healthcare organizations. In 1995 (with M. D. Fottler, A. R. Paolino, and T. M. Rotarius), he published the research monograph *Medical Group Practices Face the Uncertain Future: Challenges, Opportunities and Strategies* published by the Center for Research in Ambulatory Health Care Administration (CRAHCA).

In 1994, he was presented the Senior-Level Healthcare Executive Regents Award by the American College of Healthcare Executives "for building bridges between theory and practice." The healthcare management division of the Academy of Management recognized him as the senior author for the three papers that won the division's 1997, as well as the 1995 and 1994 "Best Theory to Practice Paper" awards, sponsored by *Health Care Management Review.* He was elected the 1991–92 chair of the healthcare management division.

In 1995–1996, Blair received both the Texas Tech University Outstanding Researcher Award and the College of Business Administration Research Award "for outstanding research accomplishments." From the university, he had earlier received the President's Award for Academic Achievement "for distinguished teaching, research and service" in 1991 and the President's Award for Excellence in Teaching in 1984.

MYRON D. FOTTLER is professor and director of the Ph.D. program in administration-health services, with a joint appointment in the School of Business and the department of health services administration in the School of Health Related Professions at the University of Alabama at Birmingham. He received his B.S. degree (1962) from Northeastern University in industrial relations, his M.B.A. degree (1963) from Boston University in human relations, and his Ph.D. degree (1970) from the Graduate School of Business at Columbia University in business, with concentration in management and industrial relations.

Fottler is a frequent presenter at academic meetings and currently serves on the editorial review boards of *Health Care Management Review, International Journal of Quality Management,* and *Medical Care Research and Review;* he has served as a reviewer for most of the major healthcare and management journals. He is the 1996 winner of the Edgar C. Hayhow Award for the outstanding article published in *Hospital and Health Services Administration,* sponsored by the American College of Healthcare Executives, as well as "The Best Paper Based on a Dissertation," sponsored by the healthcare management division of the Academy of Management. His main interests in recent years have included integrated delivery systems, managed care, strategic human resources management, job design, corporate reorganization, and stakeholder management. He has published extensively in these and related areas in most of the major management and healthcare journals.

Fottler's previous books include *Manpower Substitution in the Hospital Industry* (1972), *Prospective Payment* (1985, with H. L. Smith), *Challenges in Health Care Management* (1990, with J. D. Blair), *Assessing Health Manpower Shortages* (1992, with K. D. Blayney and R. M. Bamberg), *Strategic Management of Human Resources in Health Services Organizations,* second edition (1994, with S. R. Hernandez and C. L. Joiner), *Medical Groups Face the Uncertain Future* (1995, with J. D. Blair, A. R. Paolino, and T. M. Rotarius), and *Applications in Human Resource Management,* third edition (1996, with S. M. Nkomo and R. B. McAfee).

Fottler is a past program chair and past division chair of the healthcare management division of the Academy of Management. He also serves as a site visitor for the Accrediting Commission for Graduate Education in Health Services Administration and has served as founding chair of the Doctoral Education Forum of the Association of University Programs in Health Administration.

Strategic Leadership for Medical Groups

CHAPTER ONE

THE EVOLVING STRATEGIC WEB
FOR MEDICAL GROUPS

Healthcare in the United States is changing. Demands on providers have continued to increase, and concern with continued profitability and even survival has continued to grow (Blair, Fottler, Paolino, and Rotarius, 1995). Previously, the U.S. healthcare industry was made up of individual, free-standing providers; it now has become a complex web of systems, alliances, and networks. The provision of care has been evolving from individual units to multiprovider units. The emergence of integrated, multiprovider systems that address the continuum of healthcare needs at a local or regional level has become necessary (Kaluzny, Zuckerman, and Ricketts, 1995; Fottler and Malvey, 1995; Coddington, Moore, and Fischer, 1996; Shortell and others, 1996).

These new, loosely integrated networks and more tightly integrated systems are (1) the *response to change* that is driven by forces such as threatened governmental healthcare reform and the growing prevalence and power of managed care and (2) the *source of change,* or much of it, as integrating activities and organizations themselves have great impact on the strategic realities of the local, regional, (and increasingly) the national marketplace.

As a result, leaders of provider organizations—whether inside or outside the systems/networks—must manage relationships with a growing number of active, powerful, and sometimes competing stakeholders. These are not just any stakeholders. They represent key competitive forces underpinning the profitability of the healthcare industry.

Types of provider organizations include hospitals, long-term care facilities, home healthcare agencies, solo or limited partnership physician practices, and medical groups. Change can produce considerable threats and can also lead these organizations to new opportunities.

Currently (in 1997), the healthcare industry is characterized by many integrating systems and networks rather than by fully integrated systems. Executives must assess which stakeholders will be crucial to the move to fully integrated delivery systems and what strategies and tactics will be necessary to the integration process. They must also raise questions and provide at least tentative answers to many questions regarding their organization's future. Our focus is more on the process of answering these questions than on providing answers that may not be appropriate in all cases.

Specifically, in this chapter we will

- Introduce the concept of the *strategic web* and discuss its growing importance.

- Use the metaphorical term *strategic navigation* to combine traditional strategic management issues with the management of web relationships among key stakeholders.

- Present the first typology of the key components of the strategic web concept for an integrating system and its component organizations.

- Introduce the four web types—the organizational web, the network/system web, the competitive web, and the extended web.

- Identify and discuss the leadership challenges and strategic choices each type presents.

CHANGE IN KEY STAKEHOLDERS

All medical groups have stakeholders (Blair and Fottler, 1990). Indeed, all organizations have stakeholders (Mason and Mitroff, 1981; Freeman, 1984; Fottler, 1987; Savage, Nix, Whitehead, and Blair, 1991), that is, individuals, groups, or organizations who have a stake in the decisions and actions of an organization and who attempt to influence those decisions and actions. Stakeholders exert an influence on every issue and must be recognized and evaluated for their potential to support or threaten the organization and its competitive goals. Stakeholders try to affect those decisions and actions so the organization will be more consistent with the stakeholders' needs and priorities.

Nearly a decade ago, we laid out a managerial approach that could help executives in healthcare organizations meet certain types of challenges (Blair and Fottler, 1990). For example, they could be more effective in managing their organization's relationships with the individuals, groups, and organizations that have a stake in what the organization does or fails to do. Today, the need for understanding how to manage stakeholder relationships in a systematic and strategic manner is even more crucial because those relationships are changing. Often, they are becoming more threatening and uncertain.

A medical group usually cannot choose a given category of stakeholder; in managed care organizations, stakeholders provide needed resources. However, a medical group can choose among individuals *within* each stakeholder category (that is, in a particular managed care organization).

Typically, a stakeholder decides to exercise its right to "protect its stake" on an issue-by-issue basis. For example, employees are usually thought of as supportive stakeholders to the employer on most organizational issues. However, regarding the issue of increasing employees' contributory share of health benefits, employers would likely find that their usually supportive stakeholder has just become less supportive. In other words, a stakeholder's view of an organization and its degree of supportiveness or nonsupportiveness for the organization's decisions depends on the issue at hand.

THE STRATEGIC WEB

The web of stakeholder relationships in healthcare is being fundamentally restructured as a result of the accelerating move to organized delivery systems that aspire to be truly integrated delivery systems. This emergence of rapidly growing IDS/Ns (integrated delivery systems/networks) has changed the situations and circumstances within which healthcare organizations find themselves.

The *strategic web* is made up of a complex set of interrelated strategic relationships. Strategic relationships are those with organizations and other types of stakeholders that control key resources—resources needed for the organization to complete its mission in a turbulent, rapidly changing environment. As Porter (1980) reminds us, the extent of economic and noneconomic resources provided through these relationships will increasingly determine the fundamental success or failure of the organization.

Support reflects the degree of potential threat or cooperation from each category of stakeholder (such as patients) and from the individuals, groups, and organizations (such as Medicare risk-contract patients, indemnity-insured patients, patients from a specific health maintenance organization [HMO], CHAMPUS patients, county indigent patients) that form the stakeholder group. These often-fluid and frequently conflicted constituencies are in the process of change themselves, so it follows that the degree of support in the web of stakeholder relationships is likely to be continually changing.

Strategic navigation refers to the way managers adapt to a changing environment by formulating and implementing a business strategy that is based on identifying and managing key stakeholders at all levels of their organization's strategic web. Although strategic thinking and action are important, we must remember that skilled implementation is needed if the promise of brilliant strategic ideas is to be fulfilled. The management of web stakeholder relationships is the heart and soul of implementation.

The term *strategic web* is based on a metaphor, as is *strategic navigation*; the latter may need more elaboration. The challenges and demanding actions of navigation provide an appropriate image of what healthcare leaders must do if their organizations are to succeed in an uncertain future. In its traditional sense, *navigation*, stemming from the Latin "to sail," implies directing a vessel, perhaps one with limited ability to maneuver through a raging storm. This picture aptly describes the traditional healthcare organization as it faces a turbulent, economically threatening environment.

In its modern sense, the metaphor is linked to the concept of a web of electronic linkages in cyberspace (through the World Wide Web). *Navigating the Web*, in that sense, implies finding one's way through a complex set of Web sites in search of key resources—in this case, information. Again, this might be an apt description of a healthcare organization that must make the correct linkages among many potential partners within many webs of formal and informal relationships.

Each organization's strategic web must provide key resources needed for the organization to complete its mission within a rapidly changing environment. The extent of economic and noneconomic resources provided through these relationships will increasingly determine the fundamental success or failure of the organization. The degree of support found in the web of relationships is likely to be in transition.

Our understanding of the emerging and evolving strategic web is built on our study of a real-world composite medical group—nearly one hundred physicians brought together by a hospital system in the process of integrating to include physicians and managed care organizations. We call that system Emerging System A, and it is shown in Figure 1.1. The focal organization here is the composite, multispecialty group called System A Medical Group (SMG).

SMG represents an increasingly typical medical group within the evolving strategic web for the medical group industry. Composite medical groups are constructed of several existing medical groups, some limited partnerships, and a large number of solo practitioners. The strategic impetus—and the capital—may well come, not from the physician owners of the original practices but from local, regional, or national hospitals, hospital systems, insurance companies, large existing medical groups, or integrating health systems.

The strategic web we have studied is for a geographical region consisting of an urban city and its surrounding rural region, including the regional providers.

Figure 1.1. The Evolving Strategic Web for an Integrating System: A Simplified Model.

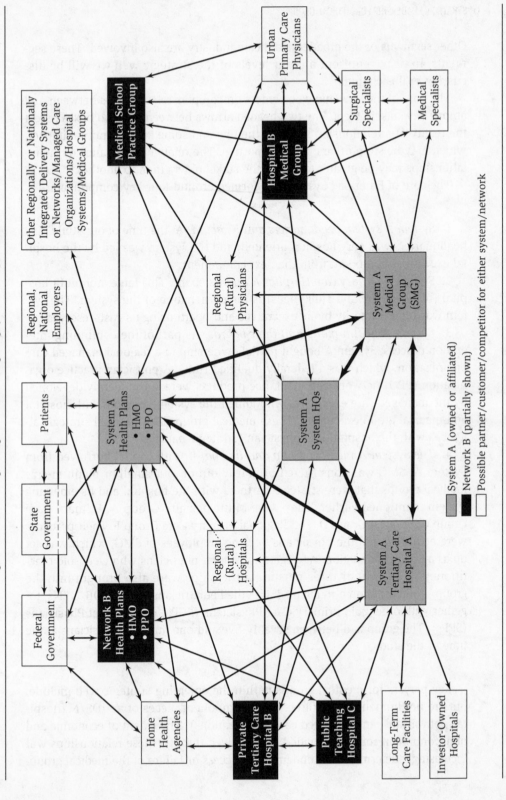

System A (owned or affiliated)

Network B (partially shown)

Possible partner/customer/competitor for either system/network

Other segments of the broader healthcare industry are also involved. These segments, in turn, represent all four levels of the strategic web we will be discussing in this chapter.

The core of the strategic web centers on complex relationships between and among key stakeholders. The two-headed arrows between any two boxes reflect the reality of a relationship between the two and some kind of mutual impact, which may be supportive or nonsupportive. The relative importance of the relationships may be greater to one of the stakeholders than to another.

The core of Emerging System A is formed around four key components:

1. *System A system headquarters and its board.* At the time of our study, this headquarters was very hospital-oriented, and the system was led by the hospital executives and board from the next component.

2. *System A tertiary care Hospital A and its board.* This large, nonprofit hospital (between 750 and 1,000 beds) is the cornerstone of the system. The system was built primarily by its executives and board using its cash reserves.

3. *System A health plans and their boards.* As part of the continuing integration process, System A bought partial ownership in a regional managed care organization, which was a federally qualified HMO. A physician practice organization (PPO) network and insurance products were subsequently developed by the managed care executives who joined the system, together with hospital and medical group executives. These medical groups had informal strategic alliances with the hospital—its physician "strategic partners."

4. *The System A medical group and its board.* With capital borrowed from System A, SMG was constructed primarily out of four small or medium-size medical groups that were strategic partners with the hospital and its emerging system mentioned earlier. They were Multispecialty Group A, Primary Care Group C, Surgical Group D, and Regional Primary Care Group F. Their practices were acquired, and the physicians became employees of SMG, which was set up as a 501(a) foundation. Aggregates of similar physicians who were solo practitioners or in two- or three-person partnerships were also brought into the group. They are shown in Figure 1.1 as the Pediatricians and the OB/GYNs, together with other solo Primary Care Physicians (PCPs) or Specialist Physicians (SPPs). The group had between seventy-five and one hundred physicians at the time of the study.

Key players for medical groups within the emerging strategic web include, but are not limited to, the three major component pieces of an IDS/N (hospitals, physicians, and managed care organizations). The extent of economic and noneconomic resources provided and received through these relationships will increasingly determine the fundamental success or failure of the medical group.

CORE ELEMENTS OF INTEGRATED DELIVERY SYSTEMS

Figure 1.2 illustrates the core elements of the evolving system shown in Figure 1.1. In addition to the three components noted earlier (hospitals, health plans, and medical groups), we have added a fourth one: the system headquarters or parent company.

Even with this extensive simplification, the multitude of relationships shown point to a very problematic issue: Who will control the IDS/N? A pure "network of equals" with no governance structure is unlikely to exist for very long. Will this governance structure continue to be balanced equitably among all three components and their many organizational subcomponents (such as medical groups of different sizes and specialties), or will IDS/Ns be dominated and controlled by their insurance, acute care, or physician components (Coile, 1994)?

In our case study, the controlling organization is the acute care hospital, which poses significant issues for its new medical group—a composite of small groups and individual practices. These issues are indicated by the question

Figure 1.2. The Integrating Core of the Strategic Web for the System Medical Group.

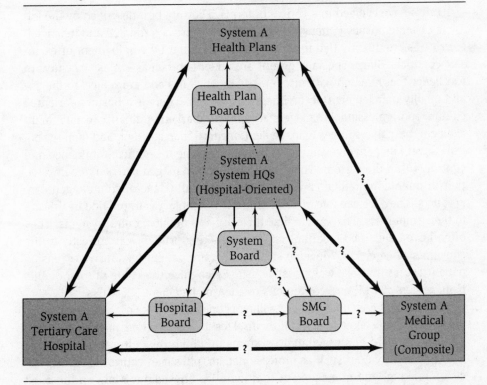

marks in Figure 1.2. At this time, many models exist. Which (if any) will become the dominant control structure regionally or nationally—or in your market area?

Integrated delivery systems/networks (related to or competitive with your medical group) would not have appeared in a model of the strategic web of only a few years ago. IDS/Ns are complex, multifaceted organizations that are growing in importance in the constantly changing healthcare industry. Within this emerging strategic web, other key players are the needed component pieces of the internal IDS/N (hospitals, other medical groups, managed care organizations, and the central headquarters or system office). Note: our position is that more integration will be required in the future so that employers, third-party payors, and other payors may purchase health benefits through one-stop shopping. However, nothing requires that the components of such a system be owned by a single entity. *Virtual integration*, with separately owned components linked by contract, can accomplish the same thing.

The emergence of these multiorganizational structures requires that all healthcare industry organizations—medical group practices, hospitals, payor organizations, suppliers—adapt to the ever-increasing demands being placed on them as the industry experiences revolutionary changes. However, IDS/Ns are not the only organizational stakeholders that have emerged or changed in importance.

IDS/Ns have evolved in a variety of forms. They are best described by the following characteristics (Ottensmeyer, 1993). They are coordinated and managed. Physicians are directly tied to the organization either by employment or exclusive contracts. Single-specialty groups are under contract as exclusive centers of excellence that function with discounted fee schedules and are subject to the use and quality management of the integrated system. There is a business-oriented culture, and professional managers accomplish marketing, finance, capital management, human resources management, medical management, and quality control. Governance involves physicians and allows them significant influence and control within the system. They work well with managed care service lines either through commercial carriers or with internally developed managed care products. They are capable of contracting with employers to provide healthcare to their employees. They internalize their use and quality control systems. They often have diversified locations capable of taking primary care directly to the consumer of care. They develop systems that are patient-responsive by easing patient access in every way possible. They recognize the value of total quality management (TQM) and continuous quality management (CQM).

The IDS/N is dependent on the willing cooperation of physicians. Predictably, physicians will be slow to commit themselves to organizations they do not trust. They will reward and gravitate to systems in which the culture is compatible with physician values such as professionalism, physician control of clinical decision making, and management that includes physicians. Many of the most successful and most competitive organizations today are physician-governed and physician-managed.

An emerging IDS/N was recently formed in Minneapolis by the merger of two separate entities. On one side of the merger was Health Partners, the state of Minnesota's largest HMO (Sommers, 1994). On the other, was Ramsey Health Care, which had previously consolidated physician and hospital services into a nationally recognized physician-hospital organization (PHO). This merger set the stage for a strict control of costs from its physicians, hospital, and health plan network providers and staff.

Such cost control was expected to be accomplished by redirecting care from inpatient to outpatient services, emphasizing the primary care gatekeeper approach, hospitalizing patients only when necessary, case managing each patient carefully during hospitalization, using hi-tech and specialty services only when needed, setting and sticking to financial and utilization targets, and downsizing and reengineering selectively.

Note that the *potential* benefits just mentioned will only be achieved if the different partners can overcome their cultural differences and the differences in their incentives. For example, the HMO has an incentive to restrict access to services that may alienate patients and reduce income for the merger partners. However, the HMO provides the medical groups and the hospital a steady flow of patients. These providers need to manage carefully through an effective, efficient delivery system. Whether they will be able to put the goals of the system ahead of their own goals is uncertain.

There are potential downsides to IDS/Ns from the viewpoint of medical groups. Futurist Jeff Goldsmith, president of Health Futures, has warned of the inherent discord in vertically integrated systems (Slomski, 1995). He believes it is folly to expect medical groups, hospitals, and health plans to exist harmoniously when they continue to have conflicting motives and incentives. Integrating systems vertically does not necessarily provide cheaper care. Such systems are often hampered by layers of management, painfully slow decision making, reliance on expensive consultants, and arms-length relationships with physicians.

Because IDS/Ns usually pay salaries to physicians, they reduce their physicians' share of financial risk (Slomski, 1995). At the same time, system hospitals remain preoccupied with filling beds and increasing revenue rather than improving the quality of care. The managed care organization attempts to reduce "unnecessary" use in order to make money on its capitated payments (fixed prospective reimbursement paid to providers per HMO member, per month, that obligates them to provide all contracted care). There is a dynamic tension between medical groups, hospitals, and insurers that is lost when their activities are combined into one organization. Under these conditions, internal conflict and misunderstanding become the norm.

According to Goldsmith:

The largest vertically integrated healthcare system in the United States is the Veterans Administration. . . . What every proprietor of vertically integrated system will have to worry about is how to prevent the hospital from being run like the post office and how to prevent the physicians from behaving like cranky civil servants who go home at 4 o'clock and let the boss worry about whether patient needs are being met (Slomski, 1995, p. 56).

An example of a failing, vertically integrated system cited by Goldsmith is Kaiser Permanente, which is losing market share in all of its western markets (Slomski, 1995). It is no longer cheaper than other plans. As a result, PacifiCare, FHP International, and Health Net are gaining market share at Kaiser's expense. Instead of being vertically integrated and owning hospitals and medical groups, these other plans are virtually integrated. They have contractual relations with hospitals and capitated networks of doctors.

Many medical groups have had to deal with the results of failed mergers with vertically integrated systems, including the ultimate failure—divorce. When the 250–doctor Guthrie Clinic in Sayre, Pennsylvania, merged with the Robert Packer Hospital in 1990, the clinic and hospital administrators thought they understood each other's culture because they had existed on the same campus for eighty years (Slomski, 1995). But after four years of intense wrangling over control, they called it quits.

The clinic physicians expected to have better access to capital, reduced overhead costs, and more managed care contracts (Slomski, 1995). After two years of struggling for control, the clinic was in shambles. All of its midlevel administrators had left, and their jobs were being done on a part-time basis by hospital personnel. Economies of scale were not achieved, as administrative expenses doubled. No new managed care contracts were acquired. Gastroenterologist Kevin V. Carey, vice president of the Guthrie Clinic, expressed doubt that physicians and hospitals can ever truly align their incentives. Now that it is again independent, Guthrie plans to seek managed care contracts with multiple hospitals.

Despite this example, it would be a mistake to conclude that any particular approach to integration will *always* be successful or unsuccessful. There is no one set of rules for the way integration can and should be accomplished. However, there is a growing realization that the process of system integration needs to be physician-led (Montague, 1994). A physician leader can help assure physicians that the organization will be quality- and delivery-oriented, as opposed to just being concerned with the bottom line.

In sum, integrated systems (vertical or virtual) offer the potential advantages of increased efficiency, economies of scale, improved utilization control, and improved leverage in market negotiations. However, potential disadvantages include high initial costs, physician resistance, physician loss of individual autonomy, and difficulty overcoming cultural differences and differences in incentives. Vertically integrated systems have performed well relative to fee-for-service systems but not against virtually integrated networks that coordinate medical group, physician, hospital, and insurance functions through contractual rather than ownership linkages (Robinson, 1996). This phenomenon mirrors larger trends away from corporate hierarchies and toward network forms of organization in the non-health economy (Robinson and Casalino, 1996). In addition, performance of a given system also depends on the leadership of the system and how the system is managed. The latter will be discussed in Chapter Four.

Nevertheless, seeking the best model for integration among those currently available and visible may not be productive. Although it may be tempting to emulate an organization that appears to be successful, such success is often difficult to repeat. A system that has achieved success at a given time and place may not achieve a similar result under other circumstances. Although elements of some existing models may be worthy of emulation, modeling current efforts on those that were effective in the past may not be effective.

Success in the evolving healthcare market may not depend entirely in the structure of a system. Rather, it may lie in the ability of medical groups, hospitals, and insurers to agree on objectives and to work cooperatively toward achieving them. The ultimate requirements for such an integration are a complete alignment of objectives, complete economic unification, and a greater concern for the system as a whole than for the individual components. Because these requirements are difficult to fulfill and may require many years to do so, virtual integration may be more realistic and appropriate than vertical integration in the late 1990s.

MULTIPLE INTERRELATED CHALLENGES FOR MULTIPLE WEBS

As Jeff Goldsmith has noted, "Health care should be organized as a dense *web of networks and contractual alliances* that require all players to share risk" (Slomski, 1995, p. 56). Indeed, as the integration of delivery and financing proceeds (Coddington, Moore, and Fischer, 1996; Shortell and others, 1996), we have discovered four kinds of strategic webs that leaders of medical groups and other healthcare organizations see as challenges they must confront and learn to navigate in new ways. The four types are the *organizational web*, the *network/system web*, the *competitive web*, and the *extended web*.

Organizational Web

The organizational web consists primarily of the internal components of an organization. If a medical group, a hospital, and a health plan are all parts of an IDS/N, each is also a separate "organization" or strategic business unit. When we refer to the organizational web in our examples, we will be assuming that the organization is part of an IDS/N, and we will be focusing on the medical group that is part of the vertically or virtually integrated core of the system. Key stakeholders in the organizational web are primarily internal stakeholders within the particular medical practice.

Horizontal integration among physicians is occurring as well (Coddington, Moore, and Fischer, 1996). For example, the large, multispecialty medical group that is part of an emerging integrated system may itself be made up of many small, formerly independent, primary and specialty care medical groups, as well as loosely integrated aggregates of individual primary care physicians and specialists. We have called this relatively new but increasingly common form of organization a *composite medical group*.

For the organization to operate effectively, the internal organizational structure and support systems must be developed. Examples include a common management information system and common human resource management policies and procedures. Even more important, administrative and physician leadership must be acquired or developed to deal with a new level of administrative and managerial complexity that may be foreign to any of the existing leaders from the organizations that were brought together; each leader is likely to see the world from his or her own group's or specialty's perspective.

Key leadership challenges for the organizational web are as follows:

- Reducing the composite medical group's costs
- Enhancing the group's income
- Reducing internal conflict within the medical group
- Increasing satisfaction of the group's patients
- Enhancing internal cooperation
- Assuring the group's quality of patient care
- Enhancing the organizational synergy of the composite group's components (small preexisting physician groups and individual practices)

Network/System Web

The network/system web consists primarily of the internal organizational components of the integrated system itself. This may include one or more of each of the following: medical groups, hospitals, and health plans.

If each of these component organizations is a separate organization or strategic business unit, the system itself is a multidivisional corporation. Because insurance companies, physician practices, and inpatient hospitals have operated in separate parts of the healthcare industry, this represents a new phenomenon, except for some of the longstanding integrated systems such as those discussed by Coddington, Moore, and Fischer (1994, 1996).

When we refer to the network/system web, we mean the necessary interrelationships of the different organizational parts of the integrated system. The key stakeholders in the network/system web are the internal stakeholders that make up the integrated system.

It is unlikely that any executives from the components that have formed (or been formed into) one system have experience in managing all of the pieces. It is most likely that the system leadership has come from the dominant or initiating component of the network/system. In our case example, the system was initiated and governed by the leaders (including the board) of a large, tertiary care hospital.

Thus, the challenges are likely to be great, as organizations from three related but unique segments of the industry are brought together. Perhaps even worse, many leaders in these organizations see the other two types as untrustworthy or even hostile, if not as outright enemies. Pressures for integration do, indeed, make for interesting bedfellows.

Key leadership challenges for the network/system web are as follows:

- Reducing network/system overhead and coordination costs
- Enhancing network/system income
- Reducing conflict among network/system component organizations
- Enhancing cooperation among network/system components
- Increasing systemwide patient satisfaction
- Assuring systemwide quality of patient care
- Enhancing the operational synergy of network/system components

Competitive Web

The competitive web consists primarily of external stakeholders who determine competitive success—its direct or indirect competitors, its suppliers, and its buyers (Porter, 1980), as well as partners and potential partners. The competitive web can be defined either from the point of view of one of the internal organizational components (who may be in competition with similar system components) or from the perspective of the integrated system itself. The operational web may, in the real world, be a part of the competitive context.

The competitive strategic web consists of competitors and potential customers (or partners), along with those components of the system itself that have their own strategic impact on any of the system's separate component organizations. For example, system health plans may or may not facilitate the strategic success of the system hospitals and medical groups. In addition, the competitive success of one component, such as the system medical group (which is a separate strategic business unit), might be sacrificed for the success of another one, such as the hospital. For example, to fill empty, system-owned, inpatient hospital beds, the system managed care organization may be directed to sign capitated contracts that are below the costs its medical group will incur to provide the physician services to support the contract and, eventually, fill many of those empty beds.

This becomes even more messy when the system is made up, at least in part, of loosely integrated network components such as affiliated hospitals and physicians. Thus, the challenge of determining who is successful and why becomes more complex, as it is likely that newly emerging integrated systems have neither the integrated MIS (management information system)capability nor the conceptual ability nor the political will to fully sort this out.

Key leadership challenges for the competitive web are as follows:

- Acquiring more covered lives
- Identifying and reducing competitive threats
- Creating and sustaining competitive advantage, if possible, or competitive parity, as a minimum
- Enhancing competitive synergy of system components
- Discovering targets of opportunity for collaboration on competitive issues, programs, or product-service lines
- Meeting employers' needs for high-quality, cost-effective services

Extended Web

The extended web consists primarily of stakeholders who determine organizational success over the long term, especially the federal government and major healthcare systems, as well as national direct or indirect competitors, national buying groups for similar types of organizations, and national suppliers such as international pharmaceutical or hospital supply companies and buyers such as national employers or employer groups.

The extended web can have an impact on both the internal organizational components and the integrated system itself. All of these do or could control necessary economic or noneconomic resources.

Key leadership challenges for the extended web are as follows:

- Reducing overall system risks and costs
- Pursuing or resolving legislative reform
- Identifying and reducing regional and national threats
- Enhancing synergy of system or other systems/networks
- Discovering opportunities for regional and national collaboration

LEADERSHIP IMPLICATIONS

Physician and nonphysician leaders in medical groups need to either understand and reaffirm their organization's mission and goals or redefine the mission and goals to achieve a better fit with the changing environment in the local market. This requires a thorough understanding of that environment and of what its future demands might be on the medical group. Although the environmental trends that will be identified in Chapter Two apply to most market areas, the level and intensity of future change will vary. Once the medical group's mission and goals, along with the environment's changes and demands, have been identified, internal stakeholders must be educated so they can understand and accept the need for change. Then, the medical group leaders and other organizational members need to work together to create a clear vision of a more desirable future.

Development and implementation of this vision will require the medical group leadership team to make strategic and informed choices in forming interorganizational relationships with hospitals, other medical groups, managed care organizations, and IDS/Ns. In many markets, being part of an IDS/N may be a necessary prerequisite to achieving competitive advantage because many purchasers of health services prefer one-stop shopping.

However, success of a particular IDS/N or its components is not assured. Success depends upon how well the particular IDS/N meets the needs of the local market, overcomes cultural differences among its component parts, builds trust among its components, aligns incentives among its components, and emphasizes the needs of the system, as opposed to the components. It also depends on the willing cooperation of physicians, the quality and role of physician leadership, and physician control of clinical decision making—all of which are difficult conditions to achieve.

Given the inherent difficulties in making an IDS/N work, medical group leaders may want to consider partial IDS/N partners rather than permanent ones. This means virtual integration via contracts rather than vertical integration through outright merger with single ownership. Given the pace of change, permanent relationships through single ownership may not serve the medical group or its physicians and patients as well as being part of a virtually integrated system would serve them. Admittedly, this approach has disadvantages. Members sometimes have less commitment and communicate less effectively than members of a loosely coupled system do. However, this approach is more flexible and allows the medical group more options as the environment changes (Weick, 1982).

The IDS/N and its component parts are only one element in the strategic and organizational webs that medical group leaders must navigate to successfully maneuver their organizations through difficult straits. The navigation metaphor points to the direction-setting nature of strategic leadership, including paying attention to the challenges facing the organizational ship that is attempting to navigate in a hyperturbulent environment. Navigators on ships face storms and treacherous waves. Navigators on planes face storms and treacherous winds. Organizational navigators face uncertainty and change as well. Medical group leaders must either adapt and learn to manage uncertainty and change or leave it to others.

Navigators of the World Wide Web attempt to identify information that will be helpful in their decision making. To achieve this goal, they often start with broad, generic categories like "travel and leisure." Then, they click on specific categories at various levels on the Web page until they find the specific information they seek. Medical group leaders who must navigate the four levels of the strategic and operational webs are seeking to manage their key stakeholders at each of these levels so that needed economic and noneconomic resources will be forthcoming.

Thomas Chapman points to two other metaphors for what navigating the four levels of the web of relationships entails (Chapman, 1993, p. 10). The first is Peter Drucker's image of the *leader as symphony conductor,* who both chooses and communicates a splendid musical score and calls forth the gifts of trained and talented professionals. The second metaphor, used by business executive Max Du Pere, likens the organizational leader to the jazz musician.

Four levels in the strategic web have been identified: the organizational web, the network/system web, the competitive web, and the extended web. The key stakeholders for each of these four levels need to be identified if medical group leaders are to construct a "map" of their evolving practices. Even though such a map may look complicated, it will reflect the reality of many medical groups in terms of actual or potential relationships.

Once the key stakeholders at each level of the web have been identified, leaders need to determine the goals and needs of these stakeholders and find out how the medical group can best meet these needs. The management of key stakeholders is not the cynical manipulation of others; rather, management determines their needs so the medical group can have a win-win relationship with each. However, meeting these key stakeholder goals and needs will pose challenges at each level of the web of relationships.

These challenges need to be identified and individual responsibility for meeting these challenges and managing each key stakeholder assigned. This may mean defining or redefining management roles. Once these roles have been defined, each key stakeholder at each level in the web is managed by one or more managers. These managers then need to build trust, build a relationship, and maintain or enhance the relationship with each of their key stakeholders. Small medical groups with limited managerial talent may have difficulty implementing the process just described. In this case, merger with another medical group or selling out to a practice management company may be the only alternative.

NAVIGATING THE STRATEGIC WEB

Choosing and prioritizing are clearly critical to managing mega-change (Sherer, 1995). The best approach to choosing and prioritizing is the process of strategic stakeholder relationship management. The generic process applies to all organizations and provides a systematic approach to what most healthcare executives do intuitively and nonsystematically. This process will be detailed in the following chapters. A key issue we will be examining throughout the book is the degree to which IDS/Ns add value. We will consider why they add value and for whom they add it. Even though a few integrated healthcare systems have a long history, the national movement toward IDS/Ns is new.

Based on interviews with leaders in their case study organizations, Coddington, Moore, and Fischer (1996) conclude that IDS/Ns *can* add value and improve competitive positioning by (1) improving the quality of care through reducing clinical variation, (2) emphasizing service by expanding conventional hours, short waiting time, and staff friendliness, (3) improving accessibility through convenient locations, (4) reducing unit costs through volume purchases, consolidation of facilities and services, downsizing of underused services, and spreading fixed costs over larger enrollments, (5) improving operating efficiency by reducing inappropriate or unnecessary care and using less-costly human resources, (6) strengthening customer ties by focusing on developing and sustaining long-term relationships between patients and physicians, and (7) enhancing product offerings to provide more choices of health-plan products to customers (employers and employees).

If these potential benefits are achieved, there will be value added for patients, the community, employers, employees, providers, managed care organizations, and physicians. Whether or not the potential benefits are achieved depends upon how well strategies, structures, and stakeholders are integrated and managed. Coddington, Moore, and Fischer (1996) conclude that even though IDS/Ns are achieving some benefits now, the opportunities for future gains are even more impressive. How medical groups can be managed to achieve these potential benefits is the focus of upcoming chapters.

Strategic management efforts, including strategic stakeholder management, can best be described as a proactive analysis and management framework. In other words, they can help identify key contingencies that are likely to lead to significant competitive threats and the risk of conflict, as well as opportunities for cooperation and synergy among key network stakeholders.

Few organizations have developed an integrated, articulated, strategic approach to competition, much less a similarly integrated approach for managing their key stakeholders. At best, for most organizations, executives' stakeholder management is underdeveloped and haphazard. At worst, they may display a total unawareness of, or involvement in, a systematic and effective stakeholder management approach. Healthcare leaders require a detailed, overall approach, along with specific tools and techniques, in order to compete effectively through facilitating the management of stakeholder relationships in a comparably strategic way linked to their overall competitive approach.

Navigating strategic and operational webs is a new concept. The navigation metaphor points to the direction-setting nature of strategic leadership, which includes paying attention to the challenges facing the organizational ship.

Navigating the web successfully means being effectively strategic in many areas, including (1) understanding your organization and determining its changing key stakeholders and environmental characteristics, (2) mapping your organizational and system operational webs, as well as your immediate and extended strategic webs, and determining what challenges each of these webs pose, (3) acting effectively to make entrepreneurial strategy or engineering strategy (or preferably both) real in positioning the organization competitively, and (4) making strategic choices in forming interorganizational relationships. In addition, successful navigation means assessing the stakeholders that affect your organization, formulating strategies to manage your supportive or nonsupportive relationships with those stakeholders, implementing those stakeholder management strategies, and, finally, reassessing everything just mentioned in a regular and self-critical, but not self-paralyzing, manner.

STEPS FOR NAVIGATING YOUR STRATEGIC WEB

Identifying key stakeholders within several webs is an important and often difficult challenge for medical group leaders. The following steps, supported by Toolkit 1, are suggested to aid in that process:

- Assess your group's web relationships and determine which are most important to your group's success.

    Determine which web or webs are most crucial to your group.

    Assess your group's ability to have an impact on each web level.

    Assess whether managerial responsibility has been assigned to each web or subcomponent within each web.

- Using Tool 1.1, identify the key internal and external stakeholders for your group. Do this for both now and three years from now. These twenty key stakeholders will be referred to throughout the book's toolkit applications.

    Have goals and needs been identified?

    Have strategies for managing each stakeholder been determined?

- Reexamine your choices of key stakeholders.

   Are they primarily from the organizational web? The competitive web?

   Does this change your outlook on who your key stakeholders are?

- Make changes if necessary to correctly identify your key stakeholders from all levels of the web.

- Using Tools 1.2 and 1.3, assess your stakeholders' overall power level and whether that power will increase, stay the same, or decrease.

- Identify your internal and external stakeholders' sources of power in relationships now and in three years, using Tool 1.4.

- Determine the core values of your internal and external stakeholders now and in three years. Use Tool 1.5.

- Summarize the five key issues facing the organization from the perspective of your key stakeholders. Use Tool 1.6.

TOOLKIT 1

Assessing Key Stakeholders

Tool 1.1. Portfolio of Key Internal and Key External Stakeholder Relationships.

Note: Each of the stakeholder relationships referred to in this part could be either *internal* or *external* to your organization. If they are *internal,* they are either part of your organization or are closely associated with you. If they are *external,* they are neither part of your organization nor are they closely associated with you. For some stakeholders, certain subgroups within each stakeholder group might be internal, and others might be external.

Instructions: List 5 key *internal* and 5 key *external* stakeholder relationships to your organization for *now* and *3 years from now.* Some current key stakeholder relationships may also be key 3 years from now. These 20 key stakeholders will be referred to in multiple toolkits. For example, if you list OB/GYN Physicians as internal stakeholder #3 now, that same stakeholder will represent internal stakeholder #3 throughout the toolkit. Each stakeholder, whether internal or external, will be identified 1–5 if key *now* and 6–10 if key *3 years from now.*

Internal Stakeholder Relationships

Now	3 Years from Now
1._____	6._____
2._____	7._____
3._____	8._____
4._____	9._____
5._____	10._____

External Stakeholder Relationships

Now	3 Years from Now
1._____	6._____
2._____	7._____
3._____	8._____
4._____	9._____
5._____	10._____

Tool 1.2. Key Internal Stakeholders and Their Power.

Instructions: Using your key stakeholders identified in Tool 1.1, circle the overall power level for your *internal* stakeholders *now* and *3 years from now.*

Your Key Internal Stakeholders Now (1–5)	Overall Power Level*	Stakeholder's Power
1 →	VG G M L VL	INC SAME DEC
2 →	VG G M L VL	INC SAME DEC
3 →	VG G M L VL	INC SAME DEC
4 →	VG G M L VL	INC SAME DEC
5 →	VG G M L VL	INC SAME DEC

Your Key Internal Stakeholders 3 Years from Now (6–10)	Overall Power Level	Stakeholder's Power
6 →	VG G M L VL	INC SAME DEC
7 →	VG G M L VL	INC SAME DEC
8 →	VG G M L VL	INC SAME DEC
9 →	VG G M L VL	INC SAME DEC
10 →	VG G M L VL	INC SAME DEC

*VG = Very Great; G = Great; M = Moderate; L = Little; VL = Very Little; INC = Increasing; SAME = No Change; DEC = Decreasing

Tool 1.3. Key External Stakeholders and Their Power.

Instructions: Using your key stakeholders in Tool 1.1, circle the overall power level for your *external* stakeholders *now* and *3 years from now.*

Your Key Stakeholders Now (1–5)	Overall Power Level*	Stakeholder's Power
1 →	VG G M L VL	INC SAME DEC
2 →	VG G M L VL	INC SAME DEC
3 →	VG G M L VL	INC SAME DEC
4 →	VG G M L VL	INC SAME DEC
5 →	VG G M L VL	INC SAME DEC

Your Key External Stakeholders 3 Years from Now (6–10)	Overall Power Level	Stakeholder's Power
6 →	VG G M L VL	INC SAME DEC
7 →	VG G M L VL	INC SAME DEC
8 →	VG G M L VL	INC SAME DEC
9 →	VG G M L VL	INC SAME DEC
10 →	VG G M L VL	INC SAME DEC

*VG = Very Great; G = Great; M = Moderate; L = Little; VL = Very Little; INC = Increasing; SAME = No Change; DEC = Decreasing

Tool 1.4. Sources of Key Organizational Stakeholders' Power.

The sources of a stakeholder's power are very important for an organization to assess. These sources of power may influence the potential for either cooperation with or threat to your organization.

Instructions: Identify your key stakeholders' sources of power in their relationships *now* and *3 years from now.* Using Tool 1.1 as a guide, use this Tool for both internal and external stakeholder relationships, for now and in the future.

Your Key Stakeholders
Internal or *External* (circle one)
Now or *3 Years from Now* (circle one)

**Stakeholder's Sources
of Power in Relationships**

#_____ →
1._____
2._____
3._____
4._____

#_____ →
1._____
2._____
3._____
4._____

#_____ →
1._____
2._____
3._____
4._____

#_____ →
1._____
2._____
3._____
4._____

#_____ →
1._____
2._____
3._____
4._____

Tool 1.5. Goals and Needs of Key Stakeholders.

Instructions: Using Tool 1.1 as a guide, list your key stakeholders' goals and needs for their organization.

Your Key Stakeholders
Internal or *External* (circle one)
Now or *3 Years from Now* (circle one)   **Stakeholder's Goals and Needs**

#_____ →   1._____

                              2._____

                              3._____

                              4._____

#_____ →   1._____

                              2._____

                              3._____

                              4._____

#_____ →   1._____

                              2._____

                              3._____

                              4._____

#_____ →   1._____

                              2._____

                              3._____

                              4._____

#_____ →   1._____

                              2._____

                              3._____

                              4._____

Tool 1.6. Organization Stakeholder Issue Matrix.

Instructions: Using Tool 1.1 as a guide, indicate the major issues facing your organization. Then indicate for each issue whether each stakeholder views the issue as "critically important," "somewhat important," or "not at all important." Rate the importance on a scale of 1–5, where 1 = critically important, 3 = somewhat important, and 5 = not at all important.

5 Key Issues Facing
Your Organization

Key Stakeholders

#_____ #_____ #_____ #_____ #_____

1._____

2._____

3._____

4._____

5._____

CHAPTER TWO

WHY IS YOUR
STRATEGIC WEB CHANGING?

Leaders of medical groups are facing environmental hyperturbulence and the stressful uncertainty of not knowing what the future holds. Even though most senior executives have spent their careers coping with the unknown, the pace of change has accelerated and uncertainty has increased. Healthcare executives in general and medical group executives in particular are struggling to find solutions to new problems and challenges. Even as optimal solutions to these new opportunities are being pursued, one thing is clear. The changes brought about by the uncertainty within the healthcare industry are sure to affect the way healthcare services will be delivered in the future.

Earlier in this decade, much attention was given in the media and among health care policy analysts to whether governmental health care reform would take place. In fact, it was already taking place at the institutional level; health care delivery and financing became integrated because of pressure in the health care marketplace. These market reforms were influenced, of course, by the threat of governmental reform, but the result has been a restructuring of the strategic web for health care organizations.

The full effects of reform—whether government-mandated or driven by private-sector initiatives such as managed care or powerful buyer groups demanding more health care for less money—are not fully known. However, the future of the health care industry has already been redirected by the development of increasingly complex, integrated health care delivery systems and networks that mirror restructuring in other industries such as banking, insurance, and transportation.

The strategic web of relationships in health care is being fundamentally restructured as a result of the accelerating move to organized delivery systems that aspire to be truly integrated. This rapid emergence of integrated delivery systems/networks (IDS/Ns) has changed the strategic web within which health care organizations find themselves. For the organizations in the web, the overwhelming shift is from independence to interdependence.

Given its importance to the health and well-being of individuals and to the economy, the health care industry will ultimately adapt to these changes. However, the emergence of IDS/Ns raises many questions for society as a whole and medical groups in particular. Can IDS/Ns be effective mechanisms for delivering high-quality, cost-effective care? If so, in what forms (vertical integration, virtual integration) will the mechanisms appear? Which will be most effective? Who will dominate these evolving systems, and what values will drive their decisions? How successfully will medical group practices adapt to these systems?

What strategies will be most successful and least successful in adapting to IDS/Ns and the emerging environment? Which medical group stakeholders will be increasing or decreasing in importance? What structural and relationship changes must occur? Which structural relationships will be most appropriate for medical groups, and under what conditions will they be appropriate? What must leaders know if they are to effectively move their organizations into this uncertain future?

In 1993, several health care associations and consulting firms conducted a national survey of 925 medical practice executives (Montague, 1994). The sample was representative of all sections of the United States—urban, suburban, and rural facilities. Also represented were single-specialty and multispecialty groups, as well as groups of all sizes. When respondents were asked what was the top issue the organization needed to address if they were to have continued success, the largest single response (42 percent) was *effective group leadership*. The response was even stronger in the West, in larger organizations, and in urban and suburban areas that have been most affected by managed care. Moreover, 68 percent of the respondents expect to be part of or to lead an IDS/N in the future. To accomplish this, most group practice executives need to modify their group's traditional mind-set and culture. About 39 percent said they were beginning to learn, and another 30 percent were prepared to learn.

In this chapter, we lay out the predictions of medical practice executives concerning the emerging health care environment and the changing key stakeholders present in the evolving context of health care organizations. We report on medical practice executives'(MPEs') perceptions of changes in their organizations' environment and identify the major leadership challenges that result from the integrating future, including the restructuring of network/strategic webs. Web restructuring has made navigating relationships and steering organizations toward strategic goals that much more uncertain. We will explain why your strategic web looks the way it does.

CHANGES IN THE EXTERNAL
ENVIRONMENT OF MEDICAL GROUPS

We surveyed group leaders concerning the external environment of their organizations in the past and in the future. Table 2.1 shows medical group executives' perceptions of their organization's external environments. They reported that they expect four factors to show continuity. First, the turbulent environment will continue to be turbulent; stability is unlikely over the next five years. Second, health care organizations will continue to be driven by both cost and quality considerations. There will not be a radical shift to one or the other. Third, the system will continue to be directed by both government and market. There is no strong tendency for it to be dominated by one or the other in the near future. Fourth, both physicians and nonphysicians will continue as managers.

However, several environmental factors are expected to see significant change. Fee-for-service medicine is expected to continue to decline as capitation becomes the dominant form of reimbursement. The system will also be more payor-driven and less provider-driven. Our respondents also predict a future with more collaboration and less competition between providers but with a more limited choice of providers for consumers.

Table 2.1. Perceptions of Continuity and Change.

Past	Future
Continuity	
Turbulent	**Turbulent**
Cost- *and* quality-driven ⟶	Cost- *and* quality-driven
Market- *and* government-directed ⟶	Market- *and* government-directed
Physicians *and* nonphysicians ⟶ as managers	Physicians *and* nonphysicians as managers
Change	
Fee-for-service ⟶	Capitation
Provider-driven ⟶	Payor-driven
Competitive ⟶	Collaborative
Wide choice of providers ⟶	Limited choice of providers
Clinically driven ⟶	Managerially driven
Physicians as entrepreneurs ⟶	Physicians as employees
Provider organizations ⟶ as free-standing entities	Provider organizations as members of fully integrated delivery system

Our respondents expect a more managerially driven and less clinically driven system. Physicians will be employed by organizations and will be less entrepreneurial. Finally, our respondents expect provider organizations to be members of fully integrated systems and not to be free-standing practices.

We also looked at how leaders of different types of medical groups view their external environments. Those in larger organizations, as well as those who have higher managed care penetration, tended to view their past environment as more turbulent, capitated, and integrated, and as having a greater role for physicians as managers. Academic practices were similar to those in larger practices except that they perceived more emphasis on quality and fee-for-service. There was much more agreement about the future than the present, as the views of respondents from various subgroups of organizations converged. However, there was still a tendency for medical group executives from academic practices, smaller organizations, and those with less managed care experience to perceive less capitation and more fee-for-service, as well as less integration in the future. Whether or not these perceptions of the future are on-target is unknown. However, it seems clear that the future impact of capitation, payor interference, patient choice limitations, and structural integration will vary from place to place and practice to practice.

In addition to our medical group executive respondents, many other commentators have noted the external environmental factors that will be affecting medical groups in the future. Larkin (1993) notes that healthcare is experiencing an industrial revolution in which solo practices are banding together into groups, groups are merging to form larger groups, and larger groups are looking for a variety of nonphysician partners. Most medical groups are merging, affiliating, or considering mergers or affiliations with other medical groups, a hospital, or an insurance company or managed care organization. We are seeing an industrial revolution in which a cottage industry of solo practices or small group practices is disappearing rapidly.

This consolidation in the medical group industry is market-driven (Larkin, 1993). Companies that embrace continuous quality improvement are especially likely to push for healthcare provided by a single, integrated organization. However, all corporate executives prefer dealing with a single provider base that consistently controls the cost and quality of services rather than many separate medical groups that cannot.

As practices grow and integrate with others, it is more likely that physicians will be employees or independent contractors (Larkin, 1993). Fewer physicians will be entrepreneurs or owners; physician autonomy will decline. Physicians will see goals set for how many patients they must see and for how much income they must generate. Specific protocols for referrals and procedures will also be the rule.

The growth of capitation for a full range of health services means more risk for medical groups (Larkin, 1993). Competing for managed care contracts requires larger investments in sophisticated equipment that could fail to generate enough revenue to cover costs. Capitation also puts groups directly at risk for controlling expenses. Unless the group is very large, a few catastrophic cases could mean bankruptcy. To help control those risks, medical groups are looking for business partners with experience in technology assessment, management contracting, insurance contracting, and capital financing.

Hospitals and insurance companies are the two traditional business partners. However, because many physicians and medical group executives are concerned about partnering with potential rivals in their own market, they are also turning to for-profit national practice management companies such as Nashville-based PhyCor or Birmingham-based MedPartners. These arrangements bring professional management to medical groups. The trade-off may be a lack of physician control; also, patients' best interests might be compromised by investors' desire for profit.

The physician practice management (PPM) industry is a potent revolutionary force (Bianco and Schine, 1997). It strengthens doctors' hands in negotiating terms with HMOs, PPOs, and other providers. As a result, the percentage of physicians who are employees has risen from 24 percent in 1983 to 44 percent in 1994 (Bianco and Schine, 1997). Most of these are workers for medical groups owned by PPM companies.

Most of the medical groups that sign PPM contracts do so because they lack the capital, the business know-how, or the sheer nerve to go it alone in the world of managed care. The PPM corporation then buys the assets of the group, and physicians continue as employees of their own professional corporation; they have authority over medical policy and physician personnel matters. The PPM company also reduces overhead, revises staffing patterns to emphasize primary care, and invests in new computer systems.

A recent *BusinessWeek* article (McNamee, 1997) noted that in 1997, the easy savings from managed care have already been achieved. With their drive for market share behind them, managed care companies will be focusing on enhancing their profits through higher premiums. Physicians, medical groups, and hospitals are banding together to resist insurers' demands for discounts. To make up for cuts in Medicare and Medicaid, providers will seek higher prices from corporate customers. Proposed legislation would mandate benefits and provide patients with weapons to fight managed care restrictions. This could potentially increase healthcare costs.

In this current, stormy environment there are many visions of how physicians, hospitals, medical groups, insurers, and health systems might relate to each other. However, there is no single best structure or strategy. Robert Katana, executive director of Presbyterian Healthcare Associates Corporation, a physician group practice that is part of an IDS/N in Charlotte, North Carolina, notes, "In this environment anything can make sense. But what may make sense now and in the future may be different" (Tokarski, 1995, p. 40).

CHANGES IN STAKEHOLDER RELATIONSHIPS

The concept of stakeholders has received much more attention from the public and the press in recent years than it did in the 1980s. In October of 1995, the *Times-Mirror Center for the Press and the People* questioned a cross-section of Americans about whose interests they thought corporations actually had been putting first and whose interests the same corporations *should* put first (Phillips, 1996). The results were stunning. Eighty percent thought corporations put stockholders and top executives first, but virtually the same percentage thought they should put other stakeholders (employees, customers, and communities) first.

Another survey conducted by Louis Harris and Associates for *BusinessWeek* in February of 1996 found that only 5 percent of 1,004 adults believe that U.S. corporations should have only one purpose—to make the most profit for their shareholders—and the pursuit of that goal will be best for Americans in the long run ("Harris Poll," 1996). Alternatively, 95 percent agreed that U.S. corporations should have more than one purpose. Corporations also owe something to their workers and the communities in which they operate; they should sometimes sacrifice a profit for the sake of making things better for their workers and communities. This survey found that only 12 percent of respondents felt that the wave of mergers and acquisitions sweeping the country (akin to some of the current and anticipated restructuring in healthcare) was good for the country.

As a result of such public attitudes, the winds of political change are blowing. States such as Ohio, Indiana, and Pennsylvania have put stakeholder rights into their merger and takeover statutes (Phillips, 1996). Senators Thomas Daschle (Democrat from South Dakota) and Jeff Bingaman (Democrat from New Mexico) are proposing a new kind of federally chartered corporation. The proposed federal tax laws could be used to give lower tax rates to corporations that meet stakeholder criteria as opposed to merely enriching shareholders. Former U.S. Labor Secretary, Robert Reich, recently wrote in a *New York Times* op-ed piece, "The corporation is, after all, a creation of law. If we want corporations to take more responsibility, we will have to alter their mix of advantages and disadvantages to provide the proper incentive" (Kuttner, 1996, p. 22).

The idea of stakeholder capitalism is becoming the signature proposal of the British Labor Party leader Tony Blair, who is the new prime minister (Phillips, 1996). Moreover, a number of major British corporations, including Cadbury, Schweppes, and Guiness, have publicly stated that successful companies in the future will focus less exclusively on shareholders and increase their emphasis on stakeholder relations.

Recently, a leader in the U.S. healthcare industry has called for a shift from an exclusive short-term focus on survival and growth of the organization (a market-based approach) to developing a multipurpose delivery system with a community-based focus (Chapman, 1993). This type of focus requires leadership that (1) exploits change for the good of the organization and the community, (2) serves as an educator, communicator, and comforter for divergent stakeholders, and (3) reestablishes a greater balance between short-term goals and long-term vision.

Past Stakeholders

Our executive group leaders expect their key stakeholders to shift between the past (the time of the survey in 1995) and the future (2000). Key stakeholders are those who are most important to the medical group because they directly or indirectly control reimbursement, information, approvals, or other resources valued by the organization, or they are in a position to impose costs. In other words, they have a high potential for threat, cooperation, or both.

In the past, three key stakeholders were identified by over 50 percent of our respondents: patients, physicians as individual caregivers, and managed care organizations. Patients were key because they presumably are the reason the medical practices exist. Providing good service to patients meets the needs of patients and ensures repeat business. The physicians are key stakeholders because their skills are needed to provide services to patients. Managed care organizations provide reimbursement for services for an increasing percentage of patients.

Other key stakeholders identified by 25 to 50 percent of our respondents include employers, governments, other medical practices, system hospitals, independent hospitals, and IDS/Ns. Employers are important to some medical groups because they influence the terms and conditions of reimbursements as they attempt to control their own health benefit costs. Governments are important because of their powers to regulate and their reimbursement for health services rendered to eligible patients under programs such as Medicare and Medicaid. The others are important because they may be sources of referrals or referral sites.

Future Stakeholders

In the future, some key stakeholders will remain stable; others will change. The stable key stakeholders are the patients and the managed care organizations, which were key stakeholders identified by more than 50 percent of respondents in both years. Although patients are predicted to decline slightly in importance, managed care organizations are predicted to increase in importance. They will remain as the top two stakeholders in the future.

However, employers and integrated delivery systems are the two new key stakeholders who have emerged from the second tier to join patients and managed care organizations as future key stakeholders. Employers are becoming key stakeholders for medical group practices because they are more actively managing their employee health benefits as individual employers or through employee coalitions (Appleby, 1995b). Integrated delivery systems (which showed the greatest percentage increase) are becoming increasingly important in many parts of the country, as the industry attempts to provide a seamless system of horizontally and vertically integrated health services on a capitated basis. Our respondents are predicting IDS/Ns will control an increasing share of the market for medical group services in the future.

Physicians, as individual caregivers, and independent hospitals will decline in importance, according to our study. This is the corollary of the expected increase in the predominance of IDS/Ns. Other medical groups are also expected to decline in importance, while governments maintain—but do not increase—their degree of importance. Other medical groups may be relatively less important in the future because (unlike patients and MCOs) they do not control significant revenues for the focal medical group.

DIFFERENCES AMONG ORGANIZATIONS

Many differences among medical practices may affect what their world is like or how their leaders see that world. We examine differences based primarily on three key variables: (1) the size of the organization, (2) whether it is an academic medical group practice or not, and (3) what managed care penetration exists in its specific market. Data on several other potential differences were also collected but are not presented because they were highly correlated with one of these three variables.

To look at the impact of the differing sizes of the organizations in the sample, we divided them into three categories: (1) small—those with less than ten full-time equivalent physicians, (2) medium—those with between ten and fifty full-time equivalent physicians, and (3) large—those with over fifty full-time equivalent physicians. These sizes may be deceptive because they do not include, although they imply, the much larger number of other employees in administrative, clinical, and support roles in each medical group. The actual employee size of the organization will be larger than the full-time equivalent physician size, which is the common benchmark for medical group size (as is the number of beds for hospitals).

To look at the impact of differing managed care penetration experienced among the organizations in the sample, we divided them into two categories: (1) those with less than 25 percent managed care in their practice and (2) those with 25 percent or more.

Several other differences that could be important are incorporated in the categories we will be using. For example, almost all small medical groups are single-specialty, and almost all large groups are multispecialty, as are academic practices. Small groups were also less likely than were larger practices to have

a current, written strategic plan that has been updated in the last twelve to eighteen months or to have physician executive leaders in nonacademic practices.
Consequently, large size is also a proxy for multispecialty, a current, written
strategic plan, and physician leaders. Academic practice is also a proxy for
higher education levels of medical group executives.

We also compared subgroups to determine how different types of organizations perceived their stakeholders in the past and how they will perceive them
in the future. The most important conclusion was that there was a high degree
of consensus among all medical practices based on organizational size, academic
versus nonacademic group practice, and the extent of managed care penetration.

For the future, larger medical groups were more likely to identify employers
and patients as their key stakeholders than were smaller medical groups. At the
same time, they were less likely to identify managed care organizations and other
healthcare professionals (except physicians) as key stakeholders. Respondents
associated with academic medical practices were much more likely than their
nonacademic counterparts to identify medical school group practices and independent hospitals as key stakeholders in the future. They were also less likely to
identify other medical practices, other healthcare professionals, and employers
as key stakeholders in the future. Those medical groups with high managed care
penetration in their practice were more likely to identify patients and physicians
as individual caregivers and key stakeholders but less likely to see independent
hospitals and medical school group practices as key stakeholders.

The implications of these comparisons become clear if one focuses on those
stakeholders likely to become more predominant in the future. As a result of the
evolution of medical groups over time, those that are larger, multispecialty, and
more integrated are likely to increase in importance in the future ("The Rise of
Group Practice,"1995; Delmar, 1995). Executives from these types of practices
are more likely than their colleagues to identify physicians and other health professionals as key stakeholders. Such data increase the significance of the shifts
in key stakeholders noted earlier in this chapter. The IDS/Ns and the patients
are key stakeholders for all respondents but are more important to those likely
to dominate the future of medical group practice.

One of the most ominous implications of our work is the relative decline in
the importance of internal stakeholder relationships predicted by our executive
respondents. Internal stakeholders are those who function outside the boundaries of the organization (Blair and Fottler, 1990). Physicians as individual caregivers (primarily internal stakeholders) decline from being key stakeholders for
73 percent of the respondents in the past to only 46 percent in the future. Other
healthcare professionals (typically internal stakeholders) begin as marginal stakeholders selected by a mere 12 percent as key stakeholders in the past. They then
decline to only 9 percent in the future. Moreover, the types of medical groups
that are likely to dominate in the future (large, multispecialty, and integrated)

are even less likely than their colleagues to identify those stakeholders as one of their key stakeholder relationships.

These results are disturbing but not surprising, given the current environmental pressures to reorganize, restructure, collaborate, capitate, and become cost-effective. Most of these pressures create incentives for the organization to attempt to manage external stakeholder relationships. However, a failure to view the internal stakeholders as key stakeholder relationships may mean they are ignored as the organization struggles to align itself with the external environment. The result for many medical groups might be a restructured organization that is part of an IDS/N, with many capitated contracts to provide specific services to defined populations at a relatively low reimbursement. This situation could be associated with understaffing, long waits for appointments and services, low staff morale, high turnover, high levels of staff stress and burnout, and patient dissatisfaction.

As medical groups attempt to manage their key stakeholder relationships and become part of integrating systems in the future, they have one major advantage: public support. A recent Louis Harris and Associates poll of 1,005 adults found that healthcare is a top concern (Louis Harris and Associates, 1997). Although 83 percent believe their doctors (or medical groups) do a good job for them, they take a dim view of large organizations overseeing the healthcare system (health insurance and managed care organizations), which they believe sometimes block necessary care. In this poll, only 55 percent of health insurers and 51 percent of managed care companies were perceived to be doing a good job.

Other polls show similar results. One poll of Connecticut residents conducted by the Center for Research and Public Policy in New Haven shows that 57 percent agreed "that we are moving from quality medical care to adequate medical care under managed care" ("Managed Care: Connecticut Residents Divided on Benefits," 1997). Nearly 37 percent believe it has hurt the quality of medical care. About 45 percent said they would support state legislation to regulate managed care plans. A large majority complained that managed care saves costs by not paying bills and creating difficulty for patients when navigating the managed care system. Another poll of 1,000 Texans showed that 49 percent of those enrolled in managed care had perceived problems such as getting appointments, high physician turnover, and delays in care ("Texas Poll: Shows Satisfaction with Managed Care Plans," 1997).

LEADERSHIP IMPLICATIONS

The changing healthcare environment creates both threats and opportunities for the typical healthcare organization. In particular, the external environment will undoubtedly be more capitated, payor-driven, and integrated, and patient choice will be more limited in the future. The major leadership challenges in this emerging environment are whether to become part of an IDS/N and how to align strategy, structure, and a diverse and ever-changing group of key stakeholders (inside or outside an IDS/N). In the future, most medical groups will need to establish and manage relationships (at a minimum) with IDS/Ns, managed care organizations, hospitals, patients, and employers. This can be done by providing cost-effective, high-quality services (efficiency and effectiveness) and then developing the database to demonstrate and market these services to the external stakeholders.

These findings represent general environmental trends and emerging key stakeholders for most medical groups—and probably for most healthcare organizations (Blair and others, 1995). For some organizations, the key stakeholders identified earlier may be less important, whereas other stakeholders may be of greater significance. This reflects the different environments for various subgroups of medical groups. For example, academic practices operate in a different environment than do nonacademic medical groups and may have some different key stakeholders. Each organization's executives will have to develop a stakeholder map for their organization and then focus time, money, and other resources on the key stakeholders.

The pace of change in the healthcare marketplace is unrelenting. That will not change in the next five years. Speed in the marketplace is important for survival, and executives are likely to consider many change initiatives. For example, medical group executives must adopt entrepreneurial or engineering (efficiency) strategies and tactics (or both).

How can organizations respond to the change and uncertainty described in this chapter? Responding effectively means acting strategically and efficiently. As valuable as continuous quality improvement, patient education, improved patient scheduling, or electronic billing can be operationally, thinking strategically about what will happen and why—and then making informed decisions about how to strategically position one's practice in the market—may be more important (Blair and Boal, 1991; Porter, 1980; Shortell, Morrison, and Friedman, 1990).

Strategic action also confronts the increasingly difficult questions of which IDS/N or partner to become aligned with, or whether to align with any other organization. It might be best to remain independent. Strategic thinking and action on these types of issues, as well as the effectiveness of operational implementation, will be crucial to the success—possibly the survival—of the medical group.

Whether or not the environmental and key stakeholder predictions in this chapter come true, when most members of any group believe something and are prepared to act on what they believe, those beliefs often become a self-fulfilling prophesy (Merton, 1957). Thus, the widespread perceptions of integration as the required treatment for uncertainty about the future can lead to integration being prescribed and then becoming reality. What the results of that would be are unclear. (Blair, Fottler, Paolino, and Rotarius, 1995).

In light of rapid environmental and stakeholder changes, medical group leaders need to develop a philosophy regarding change. Their philosophy may well determine their success and the success of their organizations over the next few decades. As Thomas W. Chapman, president and CEO of the Greater Southeast Healthcare System has noted:

> Leaders have several options to choose from as the countdown toward reform winds down. We can *ignore* change and risk being swept away by the surging tide of new developments. We can *tolerate* change and make only those organizational adjustments that allow us to get by. Or we can *embrace* change as an opportunity to restore values, strengthen our organizations, and repair a dysfunctional healthcare system. Those organizations that are most viable in the next century will look back to the 1990s and point to executives who demonstrated a knack for anticipating and exploiting change [Chapman, 1993, p. 11].

We hope this book will contribute to our readers' knack for anticipating, recognizing, and exploiting change.

STEPS FOR ASSESSING THE ENVIRONMENT FOR YOUR MEDICAL GROUP

To assess your group's environmental situation, we recommend the following steps, which are supported by Toolkit 2:

- Analyze the external environment of your group and determine its implications for your organization. Using Tool 2.1, assess the environmental characteristics that most appropriately describe your organization's external environment.

- Compare and contrast your group's external environmental characteristics with those of the medical groups given in the text. How are they different? How are they the same?

- Assess how individual environmental characteristics have affected key stakeholder relationships. Have those characteristics created new relationships, altered former relationships, or had no effect? Using Tools 2.2 through Tool 2.5, circle the appropriate letter(s) to indicate how that particular characteristic has affected the key stakeholder relationships from Tool 1.1. Use a similar format for any additional environmental characteristics that apply.

- Review Steps 2–1 through 2–3 and determine how the complexity and uncertainty of your strategic web is related to changes in the external environment.

TOOLKIT 2

Assessing Change

Tool 2.1. Assessing Your Group's Environment.

Instructions: Assess your group's external environment by circling the response that most appropriately characterizes your organization's environment both *now* and *3 years from now.*

1.	**Stable**								**Turbulent**
	Now	1	2	3	4	5	6	7	
	In 3 years	1	2	3	4	5	6	7	
2.	**Competitive**								**Collaborative**
	Now	1	2	3	4	5	6	7	
	In 3 years	1	2	3	4	5	6	7	
3.	**Clinically driven**								**Managerially driven**
	Now	1	2	3	4	5	6	7	
	In 3 years	1	2	3	4	5	6	7	
4.	**Cost-driven**								**Quality-driven**
	Now	1	2	3	4	5	6	7	
	In 3 years	1	2	3	4	5	6	7	
5.	**Provider-driven**								**Payor-driven**
	Now	1	2	3	4	5	6	7	
	In 3 years	1	2	3	4	5	6	7	
6.	**Market-directed**								**Government-directed**
	Now	1	2	3	4	5	6	7	
	In 3 years	1	2	3	4	5	6	7	
7.	**Capitation**								**Fee-for-service**
	Now	1	2	3	4	5	6	7	
	In 3 years	1	2	3	4	5	6	7	
8.	**Provider organizations as free-standing entities**								**Provider organizations as members of fully integrated delivery systems/networks**
	Now	1	2	3	4	5	6	7	
	In 3 years	1	2	3	4	5	6	7	
9.	**Wide patient choice of providers**								**Limited patient choice of providers**
	Now	1	2	3	4	5	6	7	
	In 3 years	1	2	3	4	5	6	7	
10.	**Physicians as employees**								**Physicians as entrepreneurs**
	Now	1	2	3	4	5	6	7	
	In 3 years	1	2	3	4	5	6	7	
11.	**Physicians as managers**								**Nonphysicians as managers**
	Now	1	2	3	4	5	6	7	
	In 3 years	1	2	3	4	5	6	7	

Tool 2.2. Impact of Environmental Stability or Turbulence on Stakeholder Relationships.

Instructions: From the key stakeholders identified in *Tool 1.1,* indicate, by circling the appropriate letter(s), how each relationship has been (or will be) affected by the indicated organizational characteristic assessed in *Tool 2.1.* Each stakeholder relationship could have been (or will be) newly developed, made more positive, made more negative, or unaffected by the specified environmental characteristic.

How has each stakeholder relationship been affected by the *stability* or *turbulence* in the external environment?

Your Key *Internal* Stakeholders Now (1–5)				Your Key *Internal* Stakeholders 3 Years from Now (6–10)			
Newly Developed	More Positive	More Negative	Unaffected	Newly Developed	More Positive	More Negative	Unaffected
1 → ND	+	–	U	6 → ND	+	–	U
2 → ND	+	–	U	7 → ND	+	–	U
3 → ND	+	–	U	8 → ND	+	–	U
4 → ND	+	–	U	9 → ND	+	–	U
5 → ND	+	–	U	10 → ND	+	–	U

Your Key *External* Stakeholders Now (1–5)				Your Key *External* Stakeholders 3 Years from Now (6–10)			
Newly Developed	More Positive	More Negative	Unaffected	Newly Developed	More Positive	More Negative	Unaffected
1 → ND	+	–	U	6 → ND	+	–	U
2 → ND	+	–	U	7 → ND	+	–	U
3 → ND	+	–	U	8 → ND	+	–	U
4 → ND	+	–	U	9 → ND	+	–	U
5 → ND	+	–	U	10 → ND	+	–	U

Tool 2.3. Impact of Capitation Versus Fee-for-Service.

Instructions: From the key stakeholders identified in *Tool 1.1,* indicate, by circling the appropriate letter(s), how each relationship has been (or will be) affected by the indicated organizational characteristic assessed in *Tool 2.1.* Each stakeholder relationship could have been (or will be) newly developed, made more positive, made more negative, or unaffected by the specified environmental characteristic.

How has each stakeholder relationship been affected by the *capitation* or *fee-for-service* change in the external environment?

	Your Key *Internal* Stakeholders Now (1–5)					Your Key *Internal* Stakeholders 3 Years from Now (6–10)			
	Newly Developed	More Positive	More Negative	Unaffected		Newly Developed	More Positive	More Negative	Unaffected
1 →	ND	+	–	U	6 →	ND	+	–	U
2 →	ND	+	–	U	7 →	ND	+	–	U
3 →	ND	+	–	U	8 →	ND	+	–	U
4 →	ND	+	–	U	9 →	ND	+	–	U
5 →	ND	+	–	U	10 →	ND	+	–	U

	Your Key *External* Stakeholders Now (1–5)					Your Key *External* Stakeholders 3 Years from Now (6–10)			
	Newly Developed	More Positive	More Negative	Unaffected		Newly Developed	More Positive	More Negative	Unaffected
1 →	ND	+	–	U	6 →	ND	+	–	U
2 →	ND	+	–	U	7 →	ND	+	–	U
3 →	ND	+	–	U	8 →	ND	+	–	U
4 →	ND	+	–	U	9 →	ND	+	–	U
5 →	ND	+	–	U	10 →	ND	+	–	U

Tool 2.4. Impact of Being Free-Standing Entities Versus Part of Fully Integrated IDS/Ns.

Instructions: From the key stakeholders identified in *Tool 1.1*, indicate, by circling the appropriate letter(s), how each relationship has been (or will be) affected by the indicated organizational characteristic assessed in *Tool 2.1*. Each stakeholder relationship could have been (or will be) newly developed, made more positive, made more negative, or unaffected by the specified environmental characteristic.

How has each stakeholder relationship been affected by the *provider organizations as free-standing entities* or *provider organizations as members of fully integrated delivery systems/networks* change in the external environment?

Your Key *Internal* Stakeholders Now (1–5)				Your Key *Internal* Stakeholders 3 Years from Now (6–10)			
Newly Developed	More Positive	More Negative	Unaffected	Newly Developed	More Positive	More Negative	Unaffected
1 → ND	+	–	U	6 → ND	+	–	U
2 → ND	+	–	U	7 → ND	+	–	U
3 → ND	+	–	U	8 → ND	+	–	U
4 → ND	+	–	U	9 → ND	+	–	U
5 → ND	+	–	U	10 → ND	+	–	U

Your Key *External* Stakeholders Now (1–5)				Your Key *External* Stakeholders 3 Years from Now (6–10)			
Newly Developed	More Positive	More Negative	Unaffected	Newly Developed	More Positive	More Negative	Unaffected
1 → ND	+	–	U	6 → ND	+	–	U
2 → ND	+	–	U	7 → ND	+	–	U
3 → ND	+	–	U	8 → ND	+	–	U
4 → ND	+	–	U	9 → ND	+	–	U
5 → ND	+	–	U	10 → ND	+	–	U

Tool 2.5. Impact of Wide Patient Choice of Providers Versus Limited Patient Choice.

Instructions: From the key stakeholders identified in *Tool 1.1,* indicate, by circling the appropriate letter(s), how each relationship has been (or will be) affected by the indicated organizational characteristic assessed in *Tool 2.1.* Each stakeholder relationship could have been (or will be) newly developed, made more positive, made more negative, or unaffected by the specified environmental characteristic.

How has each stakeholder relationship been affected by the *wide patient choice of providers* or *limited patient choice of providers* change in the external environment?

	Your Key *Internal* Stakeholders Now (1–5)					Your Key *Internal* Stakeholders 3 Years from Now (6–10)			
	Newly Developed	More Positive	More Negative	Unaffected		Newly Developed	More Positive	More Negative	Unaffected
1 →	ND	+	–	U	6 →	ND	+	–	U
2 →	ND	+	–	U	7 →	ND	+	–	U
3 →	ND	+	–	U	8 →	ND	+	–	U
4 →	ND	+	–	U	9 →	ND	+	–	U
5 →	ND	+	–	U	10 →	ND	+	–	U

	Your Key *External* Stakeholders Now (1–5)					Your Key *External* Stakeholders 3 Years from Now (6–10)			
	Newly Developed	More Positive	More Negative	Unaffected		Newly Developed	More Positive	More Negative	Unaffected
1 →	ND	+	–	U	6 →	ND	+	–	U
2 →	ND	+	–	U	7 →	ND	+	–	U
3 →	ND	+	–	U	8 →	ND	+	–	U
4 →	ND	+	–	U	9 →	ND	+	–	U
5 →	ND	+	–	U	10 →	ND	+	–	U

CHAPTER THREE

BEYOND THE STRATEGIC OSTRICH

In the first two chapters, we discussed the changing environment, the stakeholders, and the strategic and organizational webs of healthcare organizations. We introduced the concept of the strategic web and its components, as well as the strategic navigation perspective. To navigate strategically, the organization must make good choices about two different but interrelated sets of issues: (1) strategic management issues such as gaining and sustaining competitive advantage or, at a minimum, strategic parity and (2) the management of relationships with key stakeholders in an explicit and strategic way.

In the present chapter, we look at strategic management issues and examine what medical groups were doing strategically in the past and what they will do in the future. We identify four strategic types of medical groups in terms of their fundamental strategic priorities (orientations) and the relative prevalence of each in the past and the future. This four-fold model of strategic types combines both entrepreneurial and "engineering" (our term) strategic priorities. The types are the Strategic Navigator, the Strategic Engineer, the Strategic Entrepreneur, and the Strategic Ostrich. We then assess the degree of fit between stated strategic priorities and actual tactics.

More specifically, this chapter will

- Examine the perceptions of medical group executives concerning their past and future organizational goals.
- Report their perceptions of their current performance relative to local competitors.

- Analyze their past and future strategic priorities.
- Determine the prevalence of four strategic types, based on strategic priorities for both the past and future.
- Analyze their past and future tactical actions.
- Evaluate the degree of fit between medical groups' strategic priorities and tactical actions in the past and the future.

Our results should be of interest to medical group leaders as they ponder their own strategic orientation, tactics, and stakeholder management strategies, given the nature of their own organizations and local markets. We encourage them to provide their own answers to the questions posed here by using Toolkit 3, which appears at the end of the chapter.

ORGANIZATIONAL GOALS AND RELATIVE PERFORMANCE

Table 3.1 shows our respondents' perceptions concerning the relative importance of various organizational goals in the past and the future. Obviously, the strategic orientation of a healthcare organization is determined in part by the goals its leaders seek and the way these goals change over time. The three most important goals in the past for our respondent medical group organizations have been to maintain or increase profitability, to maintain or improve clinical quality, and to maintain or increase market share.

In the future, the relative importance of clinical quality will increase, and the importance of market share will remain constant. However, profitability will become

Table 3.1. The Relative Importance of Various Organizational Goals.

	Percent Indicating Each Goal Is One of Top Three		
Organizational Goals	Past	Future	Change
1. Maintain or Increase Profitability	54	37	−17
2. Maintain or Increase Clinical Quality	53	62	+9
3. Maintain or Increase Market Share	50	50	—
4. Maintain or Increase Cost-Effectiveness	45	53	+8
5. Maintain or Increase Service Orientation	41	41	—
6. Ensure Organizational Survival	39	33	−6
7. Fulfill Key Stakeholders' Needs	24	31	+7

much less important. The goal of maintaining or increasing cost-effectiveness increases in the future so that it becomes one of the top three goals, along with clinical quality and market share. The implication is that healthcare executives know they will need to provide service that is both cost-effective and of high clinical quality in the future if they hope to be competitive and maintain (or increase) their market share. An exclusive focus on profitability would also appear to be misplaced in the future. Each medical group executive should assess his or her organization's mission and goals to guide its strategies and tactics.

STRATEGIC PRIORITIES

Strategic orientation is a term that is based on the strategic priorities of a given organization. We use the term *priorities* rather than *orientation* to describe overall patterns of strategic action rather than specific actions. The best-known work on strategic priorities is that of Miles and Snow (1978); the authors outline four strategic types—the Analyzer, the Prospector, the Defender, and the Reactor. The Prospector is proactive in seeking out market opportunities; the Defender focuses on defending its existing markets; the Analyzer does some of each; and the Reactor has no coherent strategy. By contrast, our organizations appear to fall into four categories: the Strategic Navigator, the Strategic Entrepreneur, the Strategic Engineer, and the Strategic Ostrich. The Strategic Entrepreneur is similar to the Prospector, with an emphasis on entrepreneurial priorities; the Strategic Engineer focuses on efficiency; the Strategic Navigator focuses on both efficiency and entrepreneurship; and the Strategic Ostrich emphasizes neither efficiency nor entrepreneurship and is similar to Miles and Snow's Reactor.

Each of our strategic types' priorities has a needed—but not automatic—counterpart in terms of the strategic actions and tactics used. We examine whether this fit between what executives report their strategy to be and the tactics they follow actually exists, whether that fit makes a difference, and whether that fit will increase or decrease in the future.

Table 3.2 shows two major strategic orientations (entrepreneurial priorities and engineering priorities), their components, and the degree to which our respondents felt a statement was or was not descriptive of their own organizations. An *entrepreneurial* strategic orientation is one that focuses on growth and the provision of new services to existing or new market opportunities. Alternatively, the *engineering* orientation focuses on efficiency, control systems, planning, and low-risk approaches to market opportunity. These two dimensions are drawn from Miles and Snow (1978) and focus on two of the key strategic problems that they indicate face all organizations: entrepreneurial and engineering problems.

Table 3.2. Strategic Priorities.

	Percent That Agree/Strongly Agree		
Entrepreneurial Priorities	Past	Future	Change
1. We are willing to sacrifice short-term profitability for long-term goals.	57	74	+17
2. Whenever there is ambiguity in government regulations, we will move proactively to try to take the lead.	46	62	+16
3. In making strategic decisions, we constantly seek to introduce new services or new products.	46	58	+12
4. In making strategic decisions, we tend to focus on investments that have a high risk and high return.	22	31	+9
5. We search for big opportunities, and favor large, bold decisions despite the uncertainty of their outcomes.	18	26	+8
Engineering Priorities	Past	Future	Change
1. We seek opportunities that have been shown to be promising.	75	82	+7
2. In analyzing situations, we evaluate possible consequences thoroughly and obtain alternatives.	68	85	+17
3. We constantly modify our operating systems and technology to achieve efficiency.	62	91	+29
4. In making strategic decisions, we emphasize planning techniques and information systems.	55	85	+30
5. We emphasize the use of control systems for monitoring performance.	45	80	+35

For the past and the future, the engineering orientation was more prevalent. Both orientations are expected to increase in the future, but the engineering orientation will increase more. In the future, all of the engineering-oriented statements elicit a higher degree of agreement than any of the entrepreneurial-oriented statements. Our respondents are clearly conservative in their strategic orientations, focusing more on cost containment and getting the organization and its systems to work efficiently than on market expansion.

The major engineering priorities for the future include modifying operating systems and technology to achieve efficiency and using planning techniques and information systems. Receiving the lowest ranking for the future are the entrepreneurial-oriented priorities to search for big opportunities and large, bold decisions and focusing on investments with a high risk and high return. It appears that most respondents expect to follow a conservative, engineering-oriented strategic orientation in the future.

We divided our respondents into "high" and "low" categories, based on the level of their "priority on strategic engineering" and "priority on strategic entrepreneurship." (A "high" on either scale required a mean score of 4.0 or above. Any mean score below 4.0 for either scale is defined as "low.")

STRATEGIC TYPES

In our classification, shown in Figure 3.1, four different combinations of dichotomous versions of the two scales means that each organization can be assigned to one of four types: the Strategic Navigator organization rates high on both entrepreneurial and engineering priorities. The Strategic Engineer is high on engineering priorities but low on entrepreneurial ones. The Strategic Entrepreneur is high on entrepreneurial priorities but low on engineering priorities. And the Strategic Ostrich organization is low on both.

In the past, the Ostrich organization was dominant (54 percent). The Engineer was second with 28 percent, followed by the Navigator (12 percent) and the Entrepreneur (6 percent). The distribution shifts significantly among the four categories in the future. First, the Engineer becomes the dominant strategic type (53 percent), followed by the Navigator (31 percent) and the Ostrich (14 percent). The Entrepreneur organization will continue to be the least prevalent strategic type at a mere 2 percent.

Our four strategic types are both similar to and different from the four strategic types identified by Miles and Snow (1978). Their Prospector is similar to our Strategic Entrepreneur, and their Defender is similar to our Strategic Engineer. However, our Strategic Navigator and Strategic Ostrich have no counterparts in their typology. Our Strategic Navigator combines entrepreneurial priorities and engineering priorities. Miles and Snow (1978) do not consider such a possibil-

Figure 3.1. Strategic Navigation Types—Priorities in Navigating Strategic Decisions.

Priority on Strategic Engineering

	High	Low
High	**Strategic Navigator** **Past:* 12% ***Future:* 31%	**Strategic Entrepreneur** *Past:* 6% *Future:* 2%
Low	**Strategic Engineer** *Past:* 28% *Future:* 53%	**Strategic Ostrich** *Past:* 54% *Future:* 14%

(Row label: Priority on Strategic Entrepreneursip)

*Percent of organizations fitting each type in the past

**Percent of organizations expected to fit each type in the future

ity. Their Analyzer does some of each but at different times and does not simultaneously pursue both as a coherent strategy. Their Reactor is different from our Strategic Ostrich because the former reacts in different ways to changes in the external environment and has an inherent strategy. Our Reactors have no strategy at all. For this reason, we label them Ostriches. Our typology seems to better fit our survey data and to have some intuitive logic for healthcare in general and for the medical group industry in particular.

Both stability and change were present in the strategic priorities (orientation) in our responding organizations. Those who were already Strategic Navigators or Strategic Engineers were likely to persist in their original orientation into the future. Those who were either Strategic Entrepreneurs or Strategic Ostriches in the past expect to move to one of the other categories. Apparently, our respondents believe that being a Navigator (high in both entrepreneurial orientation and engineering orientation) or an Engineer (high in engineering orientation alone) will be more effective than either the pure Entrepreneur or Ostrich orientations in the future.

The implications for medical practice executives seem clear. Based upon what they themselves believe (as opposed to the views of outside "experts"), they need to adopt a strategic orientation in the future if they expect to survive. Moreover, that orientation needs to either exclusively focus on an engineering orientation in order to be cost-competitive or to incorporate both an engineering orientation and an entrepreneurial orientation. This means emphasizing planning systems, information systems, control systems, and efficient operating systems while seeking out promising new services to better serve existing or new markets.

An example of an organization that is attempting to become successful through both engineering priorities and entrepreneurial priorities is the Mount Sinai Health System in New York (Montague, 1996). This system is in the process of developing a cost-effective, regional network of providers (Montague, 1996). They are hoping this system will provide enough money to train the next generation of physicians to work in ambulatory care settings, community-based facilities, and other primary care sites.

To accomplish these tasks, they developed three goals: (1) achieve success in the marketplace, (2) develop training opportunities for residents, and (3) conduct outcomes- and quality-of-care research to help them remodel their system. They are also establishing a new department to track the quality of care provided by every clinical employee in the system. Physicians themselves will help design the guidelines they will use in the future. The ultimate goal is to have MCOs seek them out to provide care because they have documented cost-effective care with the greatest clinical effectiveness.

Obviously, medical practices could follow similar strategies as those pursued by a hospital-based system. They could develop local or regional networks, simultaneously pursue efficiency and new markets, and document the quality and cost-effectiveness of their services.

WHITHER THE STRATEGIC OSTRICH?

The major expected change in the future is for the number of Ostrich organizations to decline. About half who were Strategic Ostriches in the past expect to pursue strategies and tactics to be classified as Strategic Engineers in the future. Another quarter of them expect to become Navigators. Medical group leaders apparently believe they will need to develop coherent strategies and tactics that either emphasize engineering priorities and actions alone (the Engineer organization) or emphasize a combination of engineering tactics and actions and entrepreneurial priorities and actions (the Navigator organization). Few expect that an exclusive focus on entrepreneurial priorities and actions without high levels of engineering priorities and actions (the Entrepreneur organization) will be successful.

The Ostrich organization is of particular interest here because of its prevalence among medical groups and its lack of coherent strategy. An organization's strategy is the result of a series of activities and managerial decisions that coalesce into a pattern and logic. The key word is *pattern*. Strategy is present when a sequence of top managerial decisions exhibits a consistency and pattern over time (Mintzberg, 1978). An Ostrich organization that exhibits no pattern in decisions is strategy-less.

If an organization has a strategy (Navigator, Engineer, or Entrepreneur), it may be a good strategy that leads to sustainable competitive advantage, or it may be a bad strategy that leads to failure. Likewise, an organization with no coherent strategy (Ostrich) may be more or less successful (Chrisman, Hofer, and Boulton, 1988).

The absence of a strategy may occur in the life cycle of an organization. Young organizations will not have a history of decisions that have evolved into a coherent pattern. Moreover, any organization undergoing a transition could be temporarily without a strategy. Organizations in transition may be successful as long as the transition is not too lengthy.

Inkpen and Choudhury (1995) note that the temporary absence of strategy might be a virtue. Organizations facing a changing and increasingly competitive environment (like healthcare) must be flexible and adaptive. The deliberate building in of strategy absence *may* promote flexibility in an organization. Some have suggested that organizations in changing environments need "tents" instead of "palaces" because tents place greater emphasis on flexibility, immediacy, and initiative than on authority, clarity, and decisiveness (Hedberg, Nystrom, and Starbuck, 1976). A palace, like an entrenched strategy, is stable and may be unresponsive to change.

Entrenched strategies may act like blinders and block out a firm's peripheral vision. When a strategy becomes embedded in the mind of the strategist, change can be impeded (Mintzberg, 1990). Alternatively, having no initial strategic orientation or tactics allows flexibility (a potential advantage), but this advantage can only be attained if a strategic orientation and reinforcing tactics are then developed and implemented.

Thus, the Ostrich might be seen as symptomatic of failure on the part of management. A struggling medical group with no strategy may have no legitimate rationale for decision making and will lack guidance regarding the capabilities it needs to protect, enhance, or add in order to compete successfully (Nelson, 1991). Alternatively, the Ostrich might reflect a constructive and positive phenomenon that contributes to the effectiveness of a medical group. The absence of strategy can have a liberating effect on management and possibly stimulate the innovation and creativity needed to generate winning ideas and services. It is possible for medical groups to implement strategy absence (Ostrich) positively, so as to foster an atmosphere of strategic flexibility. However, they must then develop a strategy and implement reinforcing tactics to implement that strategy if they are to be competitive.

The Strategic Ostrich can be a symptom of either mismanagement or a lack of management. Inherent in any successful medical practice is a goal-driven management guided by explicit value and vision, by written strategies, goals, and objectives, and by explicit commitment from physician partners. But physicians often have neither the interest nor the inclination for the management aspects of the practice. They are often pressed for time and tend to devote discretionary work time to clinical issues. Rarely are group goals and perspectives clearly discussed among physician partners. Such goal setting is a necessary prerequisite to successful strategic planning.

Similarly, medical practices rarely have a written mission statement or agreed-upon strategic plan. Consequently, physician partners and their executive directors may have very different views of the competitive position of their shared practice and not even be aware of their differences. The result is a medical practice that is like an unguided missile. Shared goals are a prerequisite to achievement of Strategic Navigator status because the likely result is higher-quality care, lower costs, and improved market penetration.

The Ostrich approach to strategy may be either unintentional or deliberate. An unintentional Ostrich strategy could occur in either a munificent or a hostile environment. In 1997, most medical groups in urban areas exist in hostile environments with extremely high levels of competition and managed care; alternatively, some still exist in munificent environments with low levels of competition and managed care (in some states and rural areas). In a munificent environment, an Ostrich medical group is not necessarily on the road to failure. These medical groups can stumble along without a strategy because the environment provides an abundance of critical resources.

However, as the managed care environment becomes more hostile and competitive, resources become scarce (Inkpen and Choudhury, 1995). A likely outcome of an unintentional strategy absence in this environment is organizational failure.

In the case of a deliberate Ostrich strategy, positive outcomes might be expected in munificent environments when a young medical group is in the process of developing an emerging strategy, or a mature medical group is experimenting to see what works. In a hostile environment, young medical groups in transition and mature medical groups undergoing forced transitions may be without a strategy (Ostriches) for a while. However, the lack of strategy is not sustainable in the long run in this environment.

PRIORITIES VERSUS ACTIONS

The long-term goals and objectives and the strategic orientation of healthcare organizations are important to understand because they tell us where medical groups want to go and how they expect to get there. However, what they *do* rather than what they *plan* explains their past and future success or failure.

As Karl Weick (1987, p. 223) has noted:

Followers are often lost and even the leader is not sure where to go. All the leader knows is that the plan on the map he has in front of him is not sufficient by itself to get them out. . . . The generic process involved is that meaning is produced because the leader treats a vague map or plan as if it had some meaning even though he knows full well that the real meaning will come only when people respond to the map and do something.

In other words, tactical actions may be more important than strategic priorities or orientation. Weick (1987, p. 225) goes on to note that strong presumptions (a strong strategic orientation) lead to strong actions that impose considerable order. Weaker presumptions lead to more hesitant actions, which means that leaders will be most influenced by present circumstances or that they can create only a weak order. One might interpret this (in our context) to mean that Strategic Ostriches (who have no strong strategic priorities) are less likely than other organizations to impose order and to take the strong actions necessary to survive in a rapidly changing environment. In the face of massive uncertainty, beliefs of some sort are necessary to evoke some action, which can then begin to give meaning to a medical group. Goals that are sought vigorously are more likely to be achieved.

The lesson is that strong beliefs that single out and intensify consistent action can bring events into existence (Snyder, 1984). Both the motivation toward a particular strategic orientation *and* tactical actions to implement that orientation are required for successful execution of that strategy. Organizations having no clear strategic priorities will likely fail, but so too will those having strong strategic priorities that are not reinforced by related tactical actions.

Figure 3.2 illustrates a range of possible relationships between strategic priorities and tactical actions based on the previous work of Mintzberg (1988) and Weick (1987). In the real world, these situations range from the simple to the convoluted.

- The simplest situation is represented by the top line, where the intended strategy is implemented through congruent tactical actions so that the intended strategy and the implemented strategy are identical.

- In the second case (indicated by the downward vertical arrow), the strategic priorities are *not* implemented by tactical actions. Even though the original strategic priorities continue, the tactical actions reflect an alternative strategy that emerges. The result is that an unintended strategy is implemented.

- In the third case (represented by the bottom line), there are no coherent strategic priorities. However, recognizable patterns of strategic actions may emerge. In this case, there is an improvised strategy, even though there were no coherent strategic priorities.

Figure 3.2. Making Strategy Real.

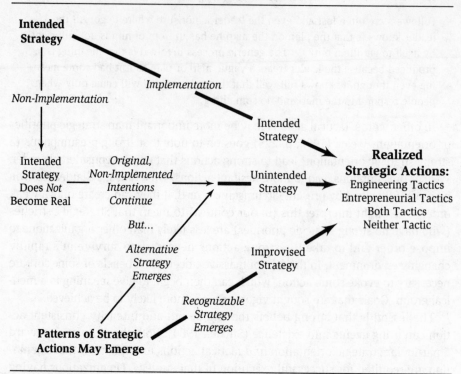

Synthesis and extension of a model by Mintzberg (1978), with additional perspectives from Weick (1987). *Intended strategy* means the intended strategy becomes real through strategic actions that implement it. *Unintended strategy* means the intended strategy is *not* implemented, but an alternative strategy emerges. *Improvised strategy* means without clear strategic intentions, emergent strategies are improvised.

- Finally, a situation could exist in which no coherent strategic priorities *and* no recognizable patterns of strategic actions exist. Here, there is no strategy.

In other words, the strategic orientation or priorities of a medical group may or may not predict its actual strategic actions or tactics. To have a complete picture of the medical group from a strategic viewpoint, we need to know *both* strategic priorities and tactical actions.

The reasons why a strategy is necessary to organizational performance and why a "failure to choose" implicit in the Strategic Ostrich approach is deficient has been articulated by Porter (1996, p. 77):

Strategy renders choices about what not to do as important as choices about what to do. Indeed, setting limits is another function of leadership. Deciding which target group of customers, varieties, and needs the company should serve is fundamental in developing a strategy. So is deciding not to serve other customers or needs and not to offer certain features or services. Thus, strategy requires constant discipline and clear communication. Indeed, one of the most important functions of an explicit, communicated strategy is to guide employees in making choices that arise because of trade-offs in their individual activities and in day-to-day decisions.

Porter (1996) goes on to note that the challenge of developing or reestablishing a clear strategy is often primarily organizational and depends on leadership. With so many forces at work against making choices and trade-offs in organizations, a clear intellectual framework to guide strategy is a necessary counterweight. Moreover, strong leaders willing to make choices are essential.

THE IMPORTANCE OF STRATEGIC MANAGEMENT SKILLS

Porter (1991) has argued that the issue of why organizations succeed or fail is the central question in strategic management. A strategy enables management to ensure the consistency of individual actions and choices. The absence of consistency implies an absence of strategy. The task of strategy is to maintain a dynamic balance between an organization's strengths and weaknesses and environmental opportunities and threats. Again, the lack of balance may mean strategy absence.

Indeed, a survey of 291 healthcare CEOs of top hospitals and healthcare systems in 1993 shows that they believed that strategic management and leadership will be the key to success in the next century (Green, 1993). The respondents felt that an effective strategy will be more important than ever in the future. Most believed that many hospitals faltered in the 1980s because healthcare leaders were inflexible and unable to anticipate and meet the need for alternative health services and products. The respondents anticipated the increasing importance of providing ambulatory care (in competition with medical groups), increasing revenue from managed care plans, restructuring their boards, reducing CEO turnover, and rationing their health services. Yet, most felt they have insufficient management depth to cope with these challenges. Management depth is even more of a problem in the typical medical group.

A major challenge facing medical practices as they attempt to be Strategic Navigators (or Web Navigators, as will be discussed in Chapters Five and Six) is the dearth of appropriate management skills (Shortell and others, 1996). Most physicians who lead (or follow) in medical practices were not trained as managers or as organizational team players. Nonphysician group practice managers often lack the education and the level of experience necessary to develop and implement Strategic Navigator strategies and tactics.

The management skills developed by insurers and hospitals under the old system were often not the skills required to lead medical practices. Even organizing primary care solo or small group physician practices into contractual networks required different skills than those insurers or hospital managers had previously acquired in the hospital or insurance sectors. Organizing and managing primary care physicians appears to be the most important and most difficult task facing newly emerging health systems (Miller, 1996). It is difficult to motivate primary care physicians appropriately, particularly when these physicians feel they are being dominated by hospital or insurer leadership and agendas.

We expect that medical groups who pursue a coherent strategy (Navigator, Engineer, or Entrepreneur) will perform better than those who do not (Ostrich). It is unclear which of the first three strategies will be most successful; success will vary, depending on the environment. We will examine the issue of organizational performance and the degree to which it is affected by strategic type, size, academic practice, and the penetration of managed care in the local market in the next chapter. Moreover, we expect performance to vary with the particular strategy pursued. These issues and a process for determining particular strategies and tactics for a given group are provided in Chapter Four.

LEADERSHIP IMPLICATIONS

In this chapter, we examined the strategic priorities reported by executives about their own medical groups. We then introduced four strategic types: Navigator, Engineer, Entrepreneur, and Ostrich and looked at findings related to these different strategies (or nonstrategy in the case of the Ostrich). Four primary leadership implications emerge from the analyses in this chapter. First, medical practice executives need to determine their organization's strengths and weaknesses relative to market demands, as well as their organization's relative position in the marketplace and in the eyes of key stakeholders. Predictions regarding each should be made prior to developing a new strategy. They also need to develop a shared vision and values, as well as a mission statement, prior to developing a strategic plan. Second, medical practice executives need to improve both their clinical quality and their cost-effectiveness to respond to environmental pressures in the future. Strategies to improve both should be implemented and monitored. Documentation of these data will also be required. Third, some strategy is better than no strategy. Strategic Ostriches are less likely to impose order and take strong actions necessary to survive in a hostile and rapidly changing environment. Fourth, strategic priorities must be reinforced by matching tactical actions if the potential success of the original priorities is to be achieved.

STEPS FOR ASSESSING OVERALL GOALS
AND STRATEGIC PRIORITIES

To assess your group's goals and strategic type, we recommend the following steps:

- Formulate new or identify current broad-based goals that your group wishes to actively pursue now and in the next three years. Using Tool 3.1, check the desired goals, thus indicating your group's primary concerns.

- Refer to Tool 3.1. Compare differences in your desired goals to those of the respondents for both now and in the future. Assess the implications of any differences.

  Should your focus be on alternate goals?

  Do your stakeholder web relationships alter with different goals?

- Identify the decision process in your organization now and in three years. Indicate your group's entrepreneurial and engineering priorities using Tools 3.2 and 3.3.

- Assess whether your group is primarily a Strategic Navigator, Strategic Engineer, Strategic Entrepreneur, or Strategic Ostrich. How did you predict your organization would be in three years?

- Compare your priorities with those reported in the text.

- Chart out your Strategic Navigation Types on Tool 3.4 to graphically show types for both now and three years from now. Do you predict movements similar to those described in the text?

- What are the implications of this movement from one type to another (is your type altered)? Assess how this change will affect each level of web relationships.

TOOLKIT 3

Setting Your Strategic Navigation Priorities

Tool 3.1. Your Group's Overall Goals.

Instructions: Check the desired goals for your group for both *now* and *3 years from now.* Check no more than three. This will indicate your group's primary goals.

Now	3 Years from Now	
☐	☐	Maintain/Improve Clinical Quality
☐	☐	Maintain/Improve Service Orientation
☐	☐	Maintain/Increase Market Share
☐	☐	Maintain/Increase Profitability
☐	☐	Maintain/Increase Cost-Effectiveness
☐	☐	Ensure Organizational Survival
☐	☐	Fulfillment of Key Stakeholders' Needs
☐	☐	Other (describe): _____

Tool 3.2. Your Entrepreneurial Priorities.

Instructions: What is the strategic decision process in your organization now? What will it be 3 years from now? In the boxes to the left, check all statements that accurately describe your organization now or as it will be in the future.

Now	3 Years from Now	
☐	☐	We are willing to sacrifice short-term profitability for long-term goals.
☐	☐	Whenever there is ambiguity in government regulation, we will move proactively to try to take a lead.
☐	☐	In making strategic decisions, we constantly seek to introduce new services or new products.
☐	☐	In making strategic decisions, we tend to focus on investments that have a high risk and high return.
☐	☐	We search for big opportunities and favor large, bold decisions despite the uncertainty of their outcomes.

Tool 3.3. Your Engineering Priorities.

Instructions: What is the strategic decision process in your organization now? What will it be 3 years from now? In the boxes to the left, check all statements that accurately describe your organization now or as it will be in the future.

Now	3 Years from Now	
☐	☐	We seek opportunities that have been shown to be promising.
☐	☐	In analyzing situations, we evaluate possible consequences thoroughly and obtain alternatives.
☐	☐	We constantly modify our operating systems and technology to achieve efficiency.
☐	☐	In making strategic decisions, we emphasize planning techniques and information systems.
☐	☐	We emphasize the use of control systems for monitoring performance.

Tool 3.4. Your Strategic Navigation Type.

Instructions: Add up your organization's current entrepreneurial priorities in Tool 3.2. The score should be between 0–5; plot this number to show your overall entrepreneurial priorities *now*. Do the same for your *in 3 years* checklists. Plot your engineering priorities for *now* and *in 3 years* from Tool 3.3.

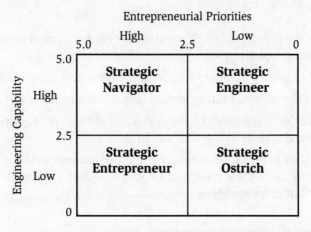

CHAPTER FOUR

DOES STRATEGIC NAVIGATION MAKE A DIFFERENCE?

This chapter builds on the previous chapter by relating our four strategic navigation types to various dimensions of organizational performance. For example, do certain strategic types exhibit higher levels of performance along a number of dimensions than do others?

More specifically, this chapter will

- Look at the prevalence of different tactics along the entrepreneurial and engineering dimensions.

- Present examples of tactics that combine these two dimensions.

- Analyze the past and future tactical actions of medical groups.

- Evaluate the degree of fit between medical groups' strategic priorities and tactical actions in the past and in the future.

- Report their perceptions of their current performance relative to local competitors and show how performance is related to strategic priorities, tactics, and other variables.

THE PREVALENCE OF DIFFERENT TACTICS

Tactics are the specific actions an organization takes to implement its strategic plan. A factor analysis of our data on the tactics used by our respondents indicates that the twelve tactics we studied loaded on two dimensions (factors).

This means there were two distinct underlying factors into which the twelve items could be categorized. The first was an entrepreneurial dimension, which is focused on better serving existing or new *external markets*. The second is the engineering dimension, which focuses on improving *internal operations* through quality and efficiency improvements.

The specific entrepreneurial or engineering tactics that medical group executives have used or expect to use in the future are given in Table 4.1. Among the entrepreneurial tactics, the most prevalent in the past were to (1) expand or diversify the types of products and services for the market being served, (2) invest in expensive technologies, facilities, and services, and (3) integrate with local markets horizontally (merge with similar organizations). In the future, local market *vertical* integration along the continuum of care will be the most prevalent tactic, followed by local market horizontal integration and diversification. The major *increases* will be local market vertical integration and national horizontal integration by contract.

Examining the engineering tactics, we note that the most prevalent tactics in the past were for organizations to (1) differentiate based on the services orientation of employees and systems, (2) empower employees, and (3) tighten controls on physician use of resources. In the future, the most prevalent engineering tactics are expected to be to (1) tighten controls on physician use of resources, (2) differentiate based on *both* technical *and* service quality, and (3) initiate or expand TQM and CQI processes. The greatest *increases* are expected to be differentiation based on technical quality and tightened controls on physician use of resources.

This information indicates an expected increase in entrepreneurial *and* engineering tactics. Our respondents believe they will have to provide high-quality, cost-effective care, link with others through horizontal and vertical integration, and exploit new markets. Elsewhere in our data, they also indicated that they would rely more on IDS/Ns and MCOs in implementing those tactics in the future. At the same time, physicians and patients will be much less important in implementing entrepreneurial and engineering tactics in the future than they have been in the past.

A reasonable conclusion from these data is that most medical groups do *not* match their strategic priorities with congruent tactical actions. Moreover, they do not expect to implement tactics that are congruent with their strategic priorities in the future. The exception is the Strategic Ostrich, which tends to act like an Ostrich tactically as well, in both the past and future. In sum, medical groups either intend to be Strategic Ostriches and act consistently with that orientation, or they intend to pursue a different strategy. They are likely to end up implementing an unintended strategy by using the tactics of a Strategic Ostrich. This provides additional evidence that we need to consider both strategic priorities and tactical actions when examining organizational strategy.

Table 4.1. Entrepreneurial and Engineering Tactics.

	Percent of Respondents		
Entrepreneurial Tactics	Past	Future	Change
1. Expand or diversify the types of products and services for the market served.	59	61	+2
2. Invest in selective expensive technologies, facilities, and services.	57	51	−6
3. Expansion through local market horizontal integration (merge with similar organizations).	55	65	+10
4. Expand through local market vertical integration along the continuum of care.	49	66	+17
5. Shift domain (substitute new markets on new stakeholders for old).	28	41	+13
6. Expansion through national horizontal integration by contractual relationship with similar organizations in other markets.	23	44	+21
Engineering Tactics	Past	Future	Change
1. Differentiate ourselves based on the service orientation of our employees and systems.	63	68	+5
2. Empower employees/encourage self-directed work teams.	57	57	—
3. Tighten controls on physician use of resources.	56	75	+19
4. Initiate or expand TQM or CQI processes.	54	64	+10
5. Differentiate ourselves based on the technical quality of our services.	47	67	+20
6. Utilize the results of cost-benefit studies to consolidate provision of duplicative services.	43	59	+16

Following up strategic priorities with specific tactical actions tailored to the needs of key stakeholders identified in Chapter Two is particularly useful in better serving patients. A key element in the success and survival of medical practices is making sure they meet the needs of patients in order to retain existing patients and attract new patients (Borchardt, 1994). The patients' needs must be put first as tactics are implemented. Retaining patients who do not believe they are receiving quality care will be difficult. A disenchanted patient can also cost the medical practice by generating fewer patient-to-patient referrals.

Our earlier discussion noted the importance of any organization determining their sources of competitive advantage by identifying their distinctive competencies (Porter, 1996). The medical practice must also question what distinguishes it from the competitor down the street. Establishing a patient-focused and patient-centered philosophy is an excellent step toward distinguishing a medical practice from its competitors.

The medical group must also function and provide services cost-effectively. The practice that demonstrates an ability to provide quality care at reduced cost is poised for success (Kaufman, 1995). CQI programs provide one approach to improving patient satisfaction while reducing the costs associated with providing this care (DeNelsky, 1994). CQI programs emphasize the need for the organization to continually change by using scientific methods. First, the processes by which a particular system or event occurred are evaluated. Then, strategies are developed and tested to improve the system or event. The approach works in a continuous cycle that takes a significant amount of time, resources, and sponsorship to implement.

CQI programs can be implemented to improve the quality of patient care, and CQI methods can be applied to management aspects of an organization as well. For example, the process by which the billing and collecting occur in an organization may need improvement. Applying CQI methods to different processes within those areas may lead to positive outcomes. The goal is to provide cost-effective, high-quality patient care.

Why are the majority of medical practices aspiring to be Strategic Engineers (an exclusive focus on engineering strategies) or Strategic Navigators (focusing on both engineering and entrepreneurship) in the future? Our respondents recognize that the successful medical group of the future will be able to demonstrate both quality and efficiency. Efficiency currently is taking the predominant role. Efficient delivery of quality care will continue to be the key to survival under managed care.

With the increasing formation of "select" panels of providers that are based on utilization history, the medical group should demonstrate cost-efficient care if it wants to be involved in new service offerings. If it can demonstrate efficiency, it is better positioned to demand higher compensation per unit, leading to managed care contracts with little or no discounting.

Medical groups should first define efficient care in a measurable way, and providers should be evaluated against these standards. Some medical groups attempt to define efficiency by comparing utilization or claim costs (office visits per member or claim costs per member) within physician specialties or departments (pediatricians, interns, and so on). Although these measures may be useful in identifying outlier performers relative to other providers, demographic and case intensity adjustments should also be considered. Efficiency could better be measured by comparing actual treatment against predefined treatment guidelines. These guidelines should be consistent with the medical group's beliefs, philosophy, and strategy and be developed with input from the affected physicians.

Because they are already controlled and often managed by physicians, medical groups are often better able to generate clinically based savings while maintaining the quality that managed care and other purchasers are demanding (Montague, Nordhaus-Bike, and Sandrick, 1996). The Dean Medical Center, a 350-physician group in Madison, Wisconsin, began evaluating their own performance and eliminating unnecessary tests and procedures by comparing themselves to others in high managed care states like California. As a result, they drastically cut lengths of hospital stay for many common procedures. They also standardized procedures, equipment, and supplies used in many common procedures, which meant that larger, less-costly purchases could be made from one or two vendors instead of seven or eight.

The Fallon Clinic in Worcester, Massachusetts, also seeks savings based on available data (Montague and others, 1996). However, after purchasing a local hospital, they cut down on many tests and exams that had previously been repeated in outpatient, surgery, and other departments. Using this more coordinated, seamless approach, Fallon's doctors have saved more than $100 per patient without sacrificing quality by doing the tests once instead of several times. Fallon's physicians have also moved some former inpatient procedures into outpatient settings.

DETERMINANTS OF ORGANIZATIONAL PERFORMANCE

We asked our respondents to indicate their organization's performance relative to competitors in their local markets. The seven dimensions of performance we examined were clinical quality, service orientation, profitability, cost-effectiveness, market share, organizational survival, and ability to meet stakeholder needs.

The Success of the Strategic Navigator

The most consistent finding across all seven of the dimensions of organizational performance is that in the past, the Strategic Navigator performed best and the Ostrich performed worst. A significantly higher percentage of Navigators had a competitive advantage in all seven of the dimensions, as compared to Ostriches. The other two strategic types (Engineer and Entrepreneur) were in the middle in performance between the Navigator and the Ostrich. For both the cost-effectiveness and profitability dimensions, the Navigator and the Engineer each had significantly higher percentages with a competitive advantage, as compared to Entrepreneurs and Ostriches.

In the future, the Ostrich *expected* to do as well as the other strategic types along most dimensions of performance. The exceptions were clinical quality and organizational survival, where the Navigators continued to expect to do better than the other strategic types.

The fact is that Navigators seem to perform best across most dimensions of performance, and complete Ostriches perform worst. What is surprising is the consistency and strength of the relationship. It appears that success requires a medical group to be both entrepreneurial-oriented and engineering-oriented. In addition, an Engineer who is primarily operations-oriented might also be successful in terms of cost-effectiveness and profitability.

What causes Strategic Navigators to assess their past and future competitive position in their local markets along a number of dimensions more positively than the other strategic types do? We asked our respondents and found that the Strategic Navigator was more likely to have engaged in the following entrepreneurial tactics in the past:

- Invest assets in a particular niche in the market.
- Modify services in markets served.
- Engage in horizontal integration at the local level.
- Engage in national horizontal integration through contracts.
- Shift their domain of activity in response to regulation.

The following integrating tactics were also more prevalent among Strategic Navigators:

- Develop electronic interfaces and pool data within their system or network.
- Develop performance standards within their network.
- Integrate finance and delivery of care.

Engineering tactics that were more prevalent included

- Using cost-benefit studies to consolidate duplicative services.
- Tightening physician utilization controls.
- Differentiating based on technical quality.
- Initiating or expanding TQM or CQI activities.

For the future, there is some convergence of expected tactics between Navigators and Ostriches. However, Navigators are still more likely than Ostriches to expect to modify services, engage in local market horizontal integration, shift domain, and initiate or expand TQM or CQI activities. It appears that Ostriches expect to imitate Navigators in their integrating tactics and engineering tactics but not in their entrepreneurial tactics.

Examples of Strategic Navigation

An example of an organization attempting to be both entrepreneurial- and engineering-oriented (a Strategic Navigator) is Blue Shield of Massachusetts. This organization has recently unveiled ATM-like interactive, multimedia computers that will provide information on wellness, local primary care physicians, prescription drugs, and other health-related topics (Appleby, 1995a, b). The computers are housed in kiosks; they offer consumers twenty-four-hour interactive access to a virtual encyclopedia of information and target customers accustomed to using technology to tap into information. Currently, four kiosks are in operation: one at its Boston headquarters, another at a shopping mall, and two at large employers' offices designed to serve employee plan members.

The system is coincidentally called the Health Navigator and is designed to get information to consumers wherever and whenever they need it. The PC-based system is essentially a high-tech customer service center. It uses attractive graphics, along with digital video, sound, and animation, to communicate with customers. An interactive video host guides users through available options, enabling them to request information via a touch-screen monitor. Each kiosk is equipped with a laser printer so users can leave with the information they need in writing. By selecting a "members only" option and swiping their identification card, Blue Cross-Blue Shield of Massachusetts can also obtain a print-out of their member profile, switch to a new primary care physician, learn what hospitals a physician is affiliated with, and make appointments.

The new technology is eventually expected to lower administrative costs, as customer use increases and demands on customer service representatives decline. In addition, it provides a method for simultaneously managing two of the key stakeholders of medical groups identified in Chapter Two: patients and employers. Obviously, patients are managed by providing alternative mechanisms for generating information. Employers may see it as a natural addition to their human resources and benefits management office by providing their employees with consistent, round-the-clock access to current health and wellness information.

From the perspective of a medical practice executive, a similar approach could be used to simultaneously achieve both cost-efficiency and opportunities for new markets (that is, to be a Strategic Navigator). The network of group practices or the IDS/N could provide consumers with twenty-four-hour access to information via the Internet in key locations in the local community and at several employer locations. The goals would be to reduce demands on administrative personnel and to market the services of the network or system to new members.

The Kaiser Foundation Health Plan provides another example of an organization that has developed both an entrepreneurial and an engineering focus. For health plans trying to raise their enrollments, two strategic truths stand out (Lumsdon, 1995). The first is that people want a choice of doctors and hospitals. The second is that doctors listen to and learn from other doctors. The entrepreneurial approach for Kaiser was that it allows subscribers to choose from a new network of 2,000 "community" doctors in Charlotte, Raleigh, Durham, and Chapel Hill, North Carolina, or they can stick with doctors who work in clinics run by Kaiser. Such a move represents a major departure for plans such as Kaiser's, which have traditionally restricted patients to doctors employed by their own medical groups.

The change follows recent polls confirming that healthcare consumers wish to choose their own doctors and want more information, such as report cards, to help them identify cost-effective, quality providers (Lumsdon, 1995). As a result of these consumer preferences, Kaiser signed contracts with three groups of independent physicians in North Carolina and is pursuing others. Other Kaiser plans in other states have taken similar steps. Its Ohio plan recently announced a three-tiered option allowing subsidiaries to choose from doctors working for Kaiser's medical group, doctors in a "preferred provider" community network, or doctors outside its network. In the Ohio example, deductibles increase based on the option the subscriber chooses.

In North Carolina, Kaiser employs the second strategic truth in teaching community physicians Kaiser's way to manage care (Lumsdon, 1995)—the engineering focus discussed earlier. First, they fortify the computer systems that track and analyze everything from the quality of care to administrative details. The second step involves working with doctors in its network to ensure that they follow Kaiser's protocols for patient care. Toward this end, Kaiser has teamed up physicians in its medical group with community physicians so the latter can learn how to apply guidelines to patients in the hospital and other settings. Physicians would much prefer to learn from colleagues than to do so under the threat of economic coercion—possibly from a nameless nurse over the telephone.

The implications of the Kaiser example for medical practice executives should be obvious. It is not necessary for physicians to become employees of managed care plans or physician practice management companies in order to survive economically. They can join together in networks to negotiate contracts with employers and MCOs, providing they can offer and document high-quality, cost-effective care.

Other Determinants of Success

We also looked at the effect of academic practice, medical group size, and the percentage of managed care in the local market on our performance dimensions. The strongest and most consistent finding was that academic medical groups rated more poorly than nonacademic medical groups along most performance dimensions. Among those performance dimensions were service orientation, market share, profitability, cost-effectiveness, organizational survival, and meeting stakeholder needs. The only exception was the dimension of clinical quality, where the academic medical groups performed slightly better than the nonacademic medical groups (although the differences were not statistically significant).

Medical group size did not predict clinical quality, cost-effectiveness, profitability, or ability to meet stakeholder needs. However, size did predict service orientation, market share, and organizational survival. Larger medical groups performed better than smaller medical groups in terms of market share and organizational survival. However, they performed worse in terms of service orientation.

Finally, we examined the relationship between managed care penetration in the local market and the medical group's performance along our seven dimensions. We found no significant differences in medical group performance in markets with high managed care penetration (25 percent or more) as opposed to markets with low managed care penetration (less than 25 percent penetration). The result is not surprising because we did not measure the absolute level of medical group performance; rather, we measured the respondents' perceptions of their performance across the seven dimensions relative to local competitors. Presumably, a market with high penetration of managed care could negatively affect the absolute profitability of all medical groups without affecting their performance relative to one another.

Why do academic medical practices appear to be less competitive than their nonacademic counterparts? One major stumbling block is the difficulty of developing large, clinically efficient primary care practices side by side with traditional academic practice (Golembesky, Malcolm, and Levin, 1994). Integrating efficient primary care into the academic milieu has historically been of little value or interest to faculty physicians because their mission and incentives are fundamentally different. Academic specialists gain prestige and advancement by demonstrating subspecialized, leading-edge expertise.

In most academic medical centers, the specialty departments control most of the "disposable" income through their practice plan. Each has its own research and clinical priorities and heavily influences or controls executive decision making. Moreover, a medical practice that supports research and teaching of students is more time consuming, less productive, and more costly than the services that managed care payors are willing to fund. Faculty tend to look at what it takes to be a managed care physician as a diversion of resources and a threat to their way of doing business. Repositioning for managed care success doesn't become a priority until there is a crisis.

In an academic medical center, investment priorities, management systems, standards, and incentives are not uniform because they are largely prerogatives of departments. They are rigorously defended in support of divergent, academically driven clinical, research, and teaching agendas. Even partially aligning incentives, standards, and financing to build an essentially nonacademic, centrally directed physician system represents a major change that is difficult to implement.

Moreover, primary care practitioners have tended to be viewed as second-class citizens. Academic faculty often respond negatively to what they view as the assembly-line nature of capitated medicine, clinical protocols, and "cookbook medicine." Conversely, capitated primary care physicians feel they provide excellent role models for real-world practice. For all these reasons, academic medical practices are ill-suited to today's increasingly capitated, cost-conscious environment.

One model for how these problems might be addressed is the joint venture between the University of Chicago Medical Center and Meyer Medical, a thirty-seven-physician primary care group with roughly fifty thousand covered lives (Golembesky and others, 1994). With managed care increasing in the Chicago market, the faculty first agreed to expand their own general medical clinics. The medical center then began to acquire primary care practices in the community. Next, the center formed a management services organization to manage the primary care network that was being assembled. The faculty has expanded the tenure and promotion criteria to be able to offer faculty status to more community physicians as a recruiting tool. The medical center also launched a campaign to reduce its costs, install an accurate cost-accounting and tracking system for managed care patients, and develop the financial and actuarial tools for enlightened negotiations with payors. Specialty and packaged price contracts were particularly attractive to payors.

The Meyer/UCMC joint venture emerged as a means of allowing both parties to achieve the common goal of eventually controlling a major block of managed care enrollees. The goal of the joint venture is to eventually have two hundred physicians, four-hundred thousand enrollees, and 20 percent of the South Chicago managed care market. The joint venture created a management services organization (MSO) as a 50–50 partnership to contract with plans and employers and to subcapitate the Meyer Group and others for primary care services. The MSO will negotiate capitation and other arrangements with the UCMC and community hospitals for inpatient care. Other hospitals will be brought into the network if they are needed to improve access, efficiency, or convenience. The medical center will provide start-up capital, which will be used to establish new clinic sites.

This example represents one approach to strategically merging an academic medical center and its associated medical practices in the current environment. It establishes a new, jointly owned entity in which both parties have a clearly defined interest. It does not attempt to integrate an established, clinically oriented culture into the academic tradition. This also provides a good example of a Strategic Navigator approach because it is both entrepreneurial in developing new markets and engineering-focused in attempting to measure and contain costs. One element of the system (Meyer) is heavily focused on meeting the needs of patients.

The issue of group size also deserves comment. As noted earlier, larger practices perform better than smaller practices in terms of market share and organizational survival. Because large groups tend to be multispecialty, they can offer a wide range of services and are therefore more likely to receive managed care contracts. They are also better able to handle the level of risk they must assume under a capitated plan (Wallen, 1993). Their larger resource base also allows them to buy sophisticated information systems, hire managed care expertise, have market bargaining power, achieve economies of scale, provide one-stop shopping, and develop managerial expertise. They can afford to hire experts in billing, coding, contract negotiation, contract administration, financial analysis, and information systems.

Small medical practices that are highly personal and allow maximum interaction with patients may be best in a perfect world. Indeed, they performed better than their larger counterparts in terms of their service orientation. However, they cannot be competitive in the future. First, the level of expertise required to manage the external environment and the associated emerging key stakeholders is not affordable to the small practice. Third-party insurance, complex personnel regulations, the need to be open at odd hours, and a general need for more sophisticated management won't pass away for doctors any more than they did for mom-and-pop grocery stores.

Second, medical technology is moving against small practice as well. Good practices increasingly need specialized expertise. The days of computerized diagnostic and therapeutic guidelines are fast approaching. Expensive medical equipment is increasingly becoming important for proper patient care. These managerial and clinical features are best afforded by larger organizations.

Association with larger groups may be the only answer. The exact organizational structure for "large groups" can range from a loose alliance to an outright merger. It may not matter as long as there are incentives to provide high-quality, cost-effective care. In the past, independent practice association (IPAs) and other loosely organized groups have not been able to attain these goals because members were not at financial risk for overuse and poor quality. This could change if the leadership of a network of group practices is strong enough.

CHALLENGES AND CHOICES

A major strategic choice for medical groups is to determine which organizations they should align with and how they can provide high-quality, cost-effective care with an opportunity to be a dominant market player. First, they could become the indispensable provider of choice in the market, focusing on building a high-quality, low-cost delivery system and contracting with an array of insurance companies and HMOs (McManis, Pavia, Ackerman, and Connelly, 1996). Ultimately, providers who choose not to assume risk under a capitated plan will be at the mercy of insurers and MCOs that will continue to seek discounts in fees to protect their own margins. Being a provider of choice for all but the largest, multispecialty practices usually means aligning with a network of other group practices. This means some loss of autonomy, but the benefits typically outweigh the costs in a managed care environment.

A second option is to join a network developed by an insurer. Health insurers are now building their own physician group practices (DelaFuente, 1994). For physicians entering these new relationships, health insurers bring capital, information system resources, managed care expertise, and marketing know-how. Conversely, health insurers gain long-term provider relationships and more control over how dollars are spent by physicians.

Among the more active participants pursuing physicians and organizing medical groups and provider networks are Aetna Health Plans, Prudential Health Care System, and MetLife Healthcare (DelaFuente, 1994). The idea is to first build a primary care network. Then, its leverage is used to align hospitals and physician specialists needed for seamless delivery in the future. By acquiring medical practices, insurers expand their role to include care delivery and financing. When they build or buy their own primary care group practices, they also gain some tangible competitive advantages.

For example, Prudential estimates its costs are 5–15 percent lower in the sixteen cities where the company operates its own clinics. Prudential's strategy is to garner control of a particular market's primary care base in order to have the leverage necessary to negotiate the best deals with local hospitals and specialty physicians. Costs are controlled by physicians, who are enticed with salary bonuses based on efficiencies such as providing quality care and eliminating unnecessary tests and medical procedures.

The fact is that a medical group could choose to go it alone. However, it will have a higher probability of market success if it partners with a network of other medical groups in the area or sells out to an insurer (like Prudential) or to a physician practice management company like MedPartners. The important criteria in choosing a partner is the ability of the potential partner to allow the practice to be a skilled Strategic Navigator that can simultaneously provide cost-effective, high-quality care to existing customers while being entrepreneurial in exploiting new markets.

The potential partner should have a track record of working well with physicians; the partner should share the original group's values and be trustworthy if an affiliation, merger, or acquisition is planned. The new organization should acknowledge an expertise that is valuable for the long term and not just for market power. Given that the type of partnership arrangement will require giving up some degree of autonomy, the benefits should outweigh the costs.

LEADERSHIP IMPLICATIONS

In this chapter, we examined the impact of strategic navigation types and other variables that describe medical practices (size, academic or nonacademic, and so forth) on various dimensions of strategic tactics and organizational performance. We also provided examples of how healthcare organizations are using the tactics of the Strategic Navigator to enhance their performance. The following are leadership implications of the analyses in this chapter:

- Medical practice executives should strive to become Strategic Navigators by emphasizing both engineering and entrepreneurial tactics.

- Because most medical groups do not match their tactics to intentions, more attention needs to be given to developing and implementing reinforcing tactics once the strategic intentions have been determined.

- Medical groups should be using TQM, CQI, or other managerial techniques to measure, control, and improve physician use of resources, the technical quality of services, and the service orientation toward patients. These types of data and improvement in outcomes will be increasingly demanded by MCOs and IDS/Ns.

- Academic medical practices have particularly difficult challenges in a high managed care environment due to their academic cultures. Alignment with primary care group practices in the community provide one model for future success.

- Larger medical groups need to give more attention to the issue of service orientation; smaller medical groups need to be more concerned with market share and long-term organizational survival.

- As cost-effectiveness is the performance dimension with the poorest current performance, major attention needs to be given to innovative engineering approaches that will generate cost savings.

- Although managed care penetration in the local market may affect the absolute level of organizational performance (perhaps negatively for some dimensions), it does not appear to affect the performance of a medical group relative to its local competitors.

- Managerial expertise to simultaneously manage both internal operations and external relationships is a challenge for all healthcare organizations, particularly for smaller medical practices.

- Medical practices need to hire managerial expertise to manage internal operations (the engineering focus) as well as external relationships (the entrepreneurial focus), or else they should contract for these services.

- Medical practices need to choose strategically positioned partners (other medical practices, insurance companies, practice management companies) who can bring resources (capital, management, market power) not possessed by the medical practice.

- Medical practices should move incrementally to develop a strategy, align their tactics with the strategy, reengineer their systems to enhance customer value, and change their culture to be more comparable with market realities.

- Physicians themselves should be involved in developing new clinical protocols, methods of measuring cost-effective care, methods of measuring clinical outcomes, and methods of measuring service quality.

- Physicians and others providing clinical services to patients should then be evaluated against these standards as well as external benchmarks.

- The use of technology by a network of medical practices can greatly enhance service and provision of information to patients, potential patients, and other key stakeholders.

STEPS FOR DETERMINING
YOUR STRATEGIC NAVIGATION TYPE

We suggest the following steps, supported by Toolkit 4, to determine your strategic navigation type and facilitate your movement toward becoming a Strategic Navigator:

- Identify your organization's tactics for both now and three years from now. Indicate which strategy-based tactics are being used (or will be used) by checking the appropriate boxes in Tool 4.1 (entrepreneurial tactics) and Tool 4.2 (engineering tactics).

- Compare your strategic tactics with those reported in the text.
- Assess whether your group's tactics align with the priorities of a Strategic Navigator, Engineer, Entrepreneur, or Ostrich.

   How will your group change in three years?

   Do your tactics align with the strategic type you identified in Toolkit 3?

- Using Tool 4.3, compare your performance vis-à-vis your local competitors to those reported in the text. How will that change in the future? Assess the implications of any differences.
- Compare your group's performance to your assessed strategic type by referring to Tool 4.3 and Tool 3.7. Do your assessments correspond to those reported in the text? How might your goals be altered to increase your group's performance?
- Develop and list several examples of approaches that combine entrepreneurial and engineering tactics to be used by your group.
- Determine the feasibility of each tactic just identified. Make adjustments to account for financial, personal, or physical limitations. Develop and implement specific tactics that fit those approaches.
- Make applicable adjustments if specific challenges exist due to your group being

   An academic practice

   A larger or smaller group

   At various levels of managed care penetration

TOOLKIT 4

Acting to Navigate Strategically

Tool 4.1. Your Entrepreneurial Tactics.

What are your organization's tactics now? What will they be 3 years from now?

Instructions: In the boxes to the left, check all strategy-based tactics that you are using now or will be using in the future.

Now   **In 3 Years**

☐   ☐   Expand or diversify the types of products/services for the market served.

☐   ☐   Invest in selective expensive technologies, facilities, and services.

☐   ☐   Expand through local market horizontal integration (merge with similar organizations).

☐   ☐   Expand through local market vertical integration along the continuum of care.

☐   ☐   Shift domain (substitute new markets and new stakeholders for old).

☐   ☐   Expand through national horizontal integration through contractual relationships with similar organizations in other markets.

Tool 4.2. Your Engineering Tactics.

What are your organization's tactics now? What will they be 3 years from now?

Instructions: In the boxes to the left, check all strategy-based tactics that you are using now or will be using in the future.

Now   **In 3 Years**

☐   ☐   Differentiate ourselves based on the service orientation of our employees and systems.

☐   ☐   Empower employees and encourage self-directed work teams.

☐   ☐   Tighten controls on physician utilization of resources.

☐   ☐   Initiate or expand TQM or CQI processes.

☐   ☐   Differentiate ourselves based on technical quality of our services/products (HEDIS measures, and so forth).

☐   ☐   Use the results of cost/benefit studies to consolidate provision of duplicative services.

Tool 4.3. Assessing Your Group's Overall Current and Future Performance.

Instructions: Circle the ranking for each goal that best describes your group's performance *compared to your local competitors.* Look ahead 3 years; how do you expect to be performing compared to your competitors? What does your expected performance mean for the specific tactics you are pursuing?

		Much Worse ↓		Same ↓		Much Better ↓
Clinical Quality	Now	MW	W	S	B	MB
	Future	MW	W	S	B	MB
Service Orientation	Now	MW	W	S	B	MB
	Future	MW	W	S	B	MB
Market Share	Now	MW	W	S	B	MB
	Future	MW	W	S	B	MB
Profitability	Now	MW	W	S	B	MB
	Future	MW	W	S	B	MB
Cost-Effectiveness	Now	MW	W	S	B	MB
	Future	MW	W	S	B	MB
Organizational	Now	MW	W	S	B	MB
Survival	Future	MW	W	S	B	MB
Fulfillment of Key	Now	MW	W	S	B	MB
Stakeholders' Needs	Future	MW	W	S	B	MB
Other: _____	Now	MW	W	S	B	MB
	Future	MW	W	S	B	MB

Tool 4.4. Planning Tool for Implementing Key Needed Tactics.

Instructions: Complete this exhibit *for each of the tactics* your group plans to implement.

Tactic: _____

Your Group's Strategic Type (based on your strategic priorities plotted in Tool 3.4). Check the most appropriate *now* and *in 3 years.*

Now	In 3 Years	
____	____	Strategic Entrepreneur
____	____	Strategic Engineer
____	____	Strategic Ostrich
____	____	Strategic Navigator

Tool 4.4. Planning Tool for Implementing Key Needed Tactics, cont'd.

1. What actions do you recommend for your group in meeting this challenge? Be specific!

   Immediately?
   Over the next 3 years?

2. In what ways do your recommended actions support your group's overall strategic intentions and other tactical actions?

   Immediately?
   Over the next 3 years?

3. What is your specific plan for implementing each of the proposed actions?

   Immediately?
   Over the next 3 years?

4. What are the most significant factors that could undermine the implementation process, and how can they be dealt with?

   Immediately?
   Over the next 3 years?

5. What resources will be required for implementation, and are they available?

   Immediately?
   Over the next 3 years?

6. How cost-effective are your recommendations? If they are not cost-effective, what alternative actions can you take?

   Immediately?
   Over the next 3 years?

7. Which physician and/or administrative managers will have the lead role in implementing these particular actions?

   Immediately?
   Over the next 3 years?

8. Do the responsible managers have the necessary abilities and authority to effectively implement these actions? What will you do to improve their abilities and ensure their authority?

   Immediately?
   Over the next 3 years?

9. What other group or system managers or other personnel—as internal stakeholders—should be involved in the implementation process?

   Immediately?
   Over the next 3 years?

10. If the implementation process does not work as planned, what contingency approach will you go to next? Why will it work if this process did not?

    Immediately?
    Over the next 3 years?

CHAPTER FIVE

IN SEARCH OF
THE WEB NAVIGATOR

The previous U.S. healthcare industry that was made up of individual, free-standing providers has become a complex web of systems, alliances, and networks. The provision of care has been evolving from individual units to multiprovider units to integrated multiprovider systems that address the continuum of healthcare needs at a local or regional level.

One characteristic of these new, loosely integrated networks and more tightly integrated systems is that leaders of medical groups—whether inside or outside the systems/networks—must manage relationships with a growing number of active, powerful, and sometimes competing stakeholders. Thus, the increasingly complex set of relationships we examined in Chapter Two magnifies the need for managers to engage in effective *and* strategic management of institutions with key stakeholders.

In this chapter, we will focus on

- Presentation of the four basic types of medical groups as navigators of their strategic webs. We will discuss the Web Navigator, the Web Optimist, the Web Pessimist, and the Web Ostrich organizations—classifications we developed based on our respondents' priorities for enhancing cooperation or reducing threat in their web relationships.

- Assessment of relationships on the issues of relative power, control over key resources, and supportive and nonsupportive coalition formation.

- Diagnosis of relationships in terms of their potential for threat and for cooperation.

WEB NAVIGATION

Few organizations have developed and articulated highly integrated, strategic approaches for managing their key organizational relationships. At best, most organizations approach relationship assessment and management in incomplete, underdeveloped, and haphazard ways. At worst, they display a total lack of awareness of, and involvement in, a systematic and effective management of relationships with key stakeholders. Medical group leaders—whether physician executives or administrative executives—should use a detailed, overall approach, along with specific tools and techniques, to facilitate managing relationships. The strategic approach to relationship management gives these leaders a way to identify all the players, their roles, and the nature of their stake in a medical group practice.

As we discussed in Chapter One, stakeholders are any individuals, groups, or organizations that have a stake in the decisions and actions of an organization and that attempt to influence those decisions and actions; stakeholders can exert a direct or an indirect influence on every healthcare management issue. The exact nature of the relationships with these key stakeholders must be recognized and evaluated for their potential to threaten the organization and its competitive goals or to cooperate with it in achieving those goals.

There are six stages in the process of managing relationships with key stakeholders in all four levels of the strategic web: (1) relationship identification, (2) relationship assessment, (3) relationship diagnosis and classification, (4) relationship priorities formulation, (5) relationship tactics implementation, and (6) the evaluation of relationship management effectiveness.

In Chapters One and Two, we discussed the identification of a particular group's key relationships as part of determining the nature of the multiple webs that make up an overall strategic web. To be complete, this identification stage includes not only determining which relationships are to be considered key to the organization but also the *relative* priorities placed by each stakeholder in those relationships on important values such as cost, quality, and access to medical services.

Once all the relationships have been identified, it becomes obvious that organizations do not face just one or a few relationships. Rather, executives must learn to manage a portfolio of relationships. It is vital that the leaders of medical group organizations see their strategic webs as relationship portfolios. It is even more important that they sort out the strategic and operational implications of those portfolios.

No longer can managers be concerned with just the obvious relationships that fall within their own responsibilities. Instead, they must be aware of all the other relationships that are influenced by their one-on-one episodes of dealing with specific stakeholders. Further, the challenge facing medical group administrative and physician executives is the creation of consistency and effectiveness in all of these individual relationship "navigation" episodes.

The theoretical basis of the "Facing the Uncertain Future" and "Strategy in Action" studies is the conceptual framework of relationship diagnosis and generic relationship management developed by Blair and Whitehead (1988) and elaborated by Blair and Fottler (1990). Earlier contributions in this area were made by Mason and Mitroff (1981) and Freeman (1984). This theoretical framework was developed on the basis of qualitative interviews with practicing healthcare executives. It has also shown its utility outside the healthcare industry in understanding airlines' relationships with their key stakeholders (Savage, Nix, Whitehead, and Blair, 1991).

In managing relationships, leaders are involved in a continuous process of internal and external scanning when making strategic decisions. They go beyond the traditional issues in strategic management such as the likely actions of competitors or the attractiveness of different markets. They also look for those internal and external stakeholders who are likely to influence the organization's decisions. Managers make two critical assessments about these relationships: (1) their potential to threaten the organization and (2) their potential to cooperate with it (Blair and Whitehead, 1988; Blair and Fottler, 1990).

WHAT IS IMPORTANT TO YOUR ORGANIZATION?

How does your group approach the navigation of its strategic web relationships? What are you concerned about when considering your portfolio of relationships? Are you most concerned about seeking opportunities by enhancing the level of cooperation in your relationship with a particular key stakeholder? Or are you most worried about the need to reduce potential or actual threat in that relationship? Are you equally concerned about both—or about neither?

Web Navigation Priorities of Medical Groups

Next, we modify and apply our own stakeholder management approach to effectively navigating the changing strategic web. Instead of focusing only on the stakeholder or the stakeholder relationships, as we have in the past, we first look at the fundamental way an organization approaches navigating the range of web relationships with key stakeholders.

For executives, this means taking a hard look at how they think about relationships. Do they primarily focus on opportunities (potential for cooperation) or on threat (potential for threat) when they see the web of relationships that is emerging?

This is parallel to the way we examined medical groups' patterns of strategic priorities in Chapter Three. There we examined such patterns as indicative of a strategic navigation type. Here we will look at comparable patterns in navigating the portfolio of web relationships in terms of organizational priorities in web navigation.

According our data, those medical groups with a high priority on "reducing the level of actual or potential threat" in relationships were dominant.

Of the same medical groups, those with a high priority on "enhancing the level of actual or potential cooperation" were prevalent for both the past and the future. *Both* priorities are expected to increase in the future, although the cooperation enhancement priority will increase to a greater degree. Our respondents clearly reflect the overall "collaboration bias" in the healthcare industry, focusing more on potential opportunities in relationships than on the potentially threatening aspects of those relationships such as growing dependence on a particular relationship. Threats are not being ignored, however. In particular, the large change in both threat and cooperation priorities for IDS/Ns and MCOs reflects a recognition among many medical groups of the fact that such relationships will be a mixed blessing in the future.

WHAT TYPE OF MEDICAL GROUP DO YOU LEAD?

Specifically, we identify four types of organizations based on two priorities in managing effective relationships with key stakeholders in the strategic web: the *cooperation-enhancing* priority and the *threat-reducing* priority. Later in this chapter, we will look at the variety of web relationships themselves and the kind of tactics that are most effective with each.

We divided our respondents into "high" and "low" categories, based on the average level of their threat-reducing priorities and their cooperation-enhancing priorities across all six stakeholder relationships. Figure 5.1 shows the resulting four cells of the web navigation priorities of our responding organizations.

Four different combinations of dichotomous versions of the two scales allow the assignment of each organization to one of four types: the Web Navigator organization (high on both threat-reducing and cooperation-enhancing priorities); the Web Pessimist (high on threat-reducing but low on cooperation-enhancing priorities); the Web Optimist (high on cooperation-enhancing but low on threat-reducing priorities); and the Web Ostrich organization (low on both).

Web Navigator Medical Groups

Web Navigator organizations have a high priority both on reducing stakeholder threat and on enhancing cooperation in web relationships. Does this mean they are unwilling to recognize that there are both "good guys" and "bad guys" in the world? No, it does not. It reflects the most sophisticated view of the emerging world of web relationships: most relationships will contain opportunities as well as threats.

Figure 5.1. Web Navigation Types—Priorities in Navigating Web Relationships.

Priority on Reducing Stakeholder
Threat in Web Relationships

		High	Low
Priority on Enhancing Stakeholder Cooperation in Web Relationships	High	**Web Navigator** *Past:* 12% **Future:* 30%	**Web Optimist** *Past:* 16% *Future:* 32%
	Low	**Web Pessimist** *Past:* 9% *Future:* 8%	**Web Ostrich** *Past:* 64% *Future:* 31%

*Percent of organizations fitting each type in the past

**Percent of organizations expected to fit each type in the future

Later in this chapter, we will talk about the most difficult but increasingly common type of web relationship—that with a mixed-blessing stakeholder. Such a relationship may be necessary because of the stakeholder's control over key resources your organization needs, yet that same resource control can be threatening to you because your access can be withdrawn.

The managed care organization is the classic example. As managed care becomes more prevalent—especially with emerging state managed care programs for Medicaid and increasing risk contracting for Medicare—the potential for cooperation and for threat in the relationship with a major market-share, managed care organization increases.

Web Optimists

Web Optimist medical groups focus on the potential for cooperation. Even though they know they might not always be dealing with good guys, they are optimistic about what they can do together, with little regard for the dark side of the relationship. They believe that almost every relationship can be made into a win-win situation for both parties.

These organizations certainly do not miss opportunities that others might, but they can put their medical groups at risk. They might, for example, ignore or downplay the implications of a growing dependence on one managed care organization. They might want to collaborate successfully with that organization to capture market share in the most precious of all strategic resources—covered lives. But growing dependence could leave them highly vulnerable.

Web Pessimists

Web Pessimists see relationships primarily in terms of their potential for threat. They know they might not always be dealing with bad guys, but they are basically pessimistic about what they can do together. As the mirror image of a Web Optimist, they have little regard for the positive side of the relationship. They believe that most relationships are risk-laden.

Leaders of these medical groups certainly do not put their organizations at risk through ignoring or downplaying the implications, for example, of growing dependence. However, they may be reluctant to explore key opportunities for what can, in fact, be win-win relationships. They are at risk primarily in producing negative, self-fulfilling prophecies. That is, because they distrust the motives or trustworthiness of others, they either do not seek to form useful strategic relationships, or they put excessively burdensome restrictions and contractual guarantees on potential partners—who then choose to work with some other group instead.

Web Ostriches

As with the Strategic Ostrich discussed in Chapter Three, the Web Ostrich probably is an unintended Ostrich. These leaders appear unwilling or unable to think systematically about the threat and cooperation potentials inherent in the web relationships surrounding them and, therefore, cannot establish a pattern of priorities to reduce those threats or to enhance cooperative potential in the relationships.

Facing the Uncertain Future Medical Groups

Figure 5.1 indicates changes in each of the four cells in the past and in the future. In the past, the Web Ostrich was the dominant web navigation orientation, representing 64 percent of the organizations. The Web Optimist was the second most prevalent web orientation in the past with 16 percent. The least prevalent strategic orientations in the past were the Web Navigator (12 percent) and the Web Pessimist (9 percent).

However, our respondents expect some significant shift in the future. First, the Web Ostrich type is expected to decline from 64 to 31 percent. Second, the Web Optimist and (to a lesser degree) the Web Navigator are the major beneficiaries of the shift out of the Web Ostrich category. The Web Optimist increases from 16 to 32 percent of the groups, whereas the Web Navigator increases from 12 to 30 percent. Third, the Web Pessimist orientation remains essentially the same (from 9 to 8 percent). As a result of these shifts, the Web Optimist, the Web Ostrich, and the Web Navigator orientations will be fundamentally the same, with a small number of medical groups having only pessimistic perspectives on web relationships.

Whither the Web Ostrich?

As with Strategic Ostrich organizations, we also looked at changes expected within the medical groups we surveyed in the "Facing the Uncertain Future" study. The major expected change in the future is for the number of Ostrich organizations to decline. Nineteen of the 65 percent who were Web Ostriches in the past expect to pursue web navigation priorities, which would cause them to be classified as Web Optimists in the future. Another 12 percent of them expect to become Web Navigators. However, 29 percent expect to remain Web Ostriches.

ANOTHER LOOK AT THE BOTTOM LINE IN WEB RELATIONSHIPS

The two dimensions of potential for threat or for cooperation are the effective bottom line in web relationships. These two classifications measure relationship supportiveness or lack thereof and incorporate information from many power and coalition factors. Hostility or threat often appears as a key variable when looking at organization-environment-strategy relationships. Managed care organizations (MCOs), for example, are often explicitly identified as a stakeholder group that applies (or could apply) extensive pressure on medical groups, thereby affecting the groups' effective strategic management (Whitehead and others, 1989; Blair and Boal, 1991; Blair, Fottler, Paolino, and Rotarius, 1995). Looking at the current or anticipated threat inherent in the relationship with a particular stakeholder or group of stakeholders is similar to developing a worst-case scenario in that it may protect managers from unpleasant surprises or unanticipated consequences.

Stakeholder power and its relevance for any particular issue confronting the organization's managers is a major determinant of the relationship's potential for threat. Power is primarily a function of the dependence of the organization on the relationship. Generally, the more dependent the organization, the more powerful the stakeholder.

For example, the power of primary care physicians lies in specialists' dependence on them for patient referrals. The growing power of MCOs has further increased primary care physicians' potential for threat to specialists. We will say more about the nature of power later in this chapter.

We are arguing that medical group managers need to anticipate and evaluate actual or potential threats in relationships with various stakeholders and, in some cases, evaluate threats that face their supportive relationships. These threats may be focused on the stakeholder's attempt to obtain items (that may or may not be provided) such as financial resources, participation in decision making, and certain organizational policies. Alternatively, these threats may focus on undermining the fundamental viability of the organization.

Of the responding medical groups in our study, the changes in percentages of those medical groups that see a high potential of each stakeholder relationship "to threaten your organization" are as follows:

- *MCOs:* change from 40 percent in the past to 60 percent in the future
- *Competitors:* no change—39 percent in the past and 39 percent in the future
- *Physicians:* from 34 percent to 27 percent
- *Hospitals:* from 32 percent to 30 percent
- *IDS/Ns:* from 31 percent to 61 percent
- *Patients:* from 25 percent to 26 percent

Clearly, the potential for threat in relationships is not being ignored. In particular, the large change in threat potentials for IDS/Ns and MCOs reflects a recognition among many medical groups of the growing importance and risky nature of such relationships in the future.

Because strategic analyses usually emphasize the types and magnitude of threats that relationships pose for the organization, the second dimension of cooperation in the organization's relationship with its stakeholders is easily ignored. We feel that this dimension should be equally emphasized as executives attempt relationship diagnosis. This more clearly directs attention to potential relationship management strategies that go beyond the merely defensive or offensive in confronting stakeholder pressures. Diagnosing this dimension suggests the potential for using more cooperative strategies in stakeholder relationships.

An example of competitors joining together against a common enemy is occurring as solo and small group practices merge to reduce the bargaining power of MCOs. MCOs have been able to demand price concessions from physicians in markets where independent physicians compete for market share. With the growing consolidation of physicians and MCOs, as well as the formation of IDS/Ns, the MCO may be left with only one dominant organization to negotiate with and may be in a weaker position because it cannot as easily threaten to send its patient-members elsewhere.

However, stakeholder management does not end for medical group executives planning to implement this relationship. Although the antitrust division of the U.S. Justice Department is carefully monitoring these types of mergers, there is an increasing awareness by both the public and regulators that in order to meet the three criteria of cost, quality, and access, mergers like this may be necessary. Healthcare executives need to anticipate the likely reaction of regulators—who represent the voice of the public—regarding prospective mergers (Fottler and Malvey, 1995).

Medical groups today find cooperative potential particularly relevant because it may allow them to join forces by creating networks and other systems with new stakeholders to better manage their respective environments. We look at the cooperative potential of a relationship in the same way we look at potential threat. We formulate a best-case scenario and, in so doing, may discover new possibilities that would otherwise be ignored.

The stakeholder's dependence on the organization and the organization's relevance for any particular issue facing the stakeholder determines the relationship's cooperative potential. Generally, the more dependent the stakeholder is on the organization, the higher the potential for cooperation. Often, however, the organization and the stakeholder may be interdependent. For example, in a medium-size town with a limited number of physician groups and one major tertiary care hospital, the hospital and the physicians are usually dependent on each other. Physicians from the community's major medical group may feel threatened by the hospital when leaders try to restrict investments in new, hospital-based technology that physicians need. Declining reimbursement revenues could precipitate such a move. At the same time, physicians may have cooperation from that same hospital leadership, who try to keep patients in their own community rather than send them to another, better-equipped hospital in a larger city.

The changes in those medical groups that see a high potential of each stakeholder relationship "to cooperate with your organization" are as follows:

- *Physicians:* change from 70 percent in the past to 84 percent in the future
- *Hospitals:* from 52 percent to 67 percent
- *Patients:* from 52 percent to 64 percent
- *MCOs:* from 46 percent to 74 percent
- *IDS/Ns:* from 43 percent to 76 percent
- *Competitors:* from 15 percent to 33 percent

For both the past and the future, the perception of potential for cooperation in relationships was more prevalent than the perception of threat. *Both* threat and cooperation are expected to increase in the future, although the cooperation-enhancement priority will increase across all stakeholders and threat, primarily among MCOs and IDS/Ns. The growth of mergers and acquisitions, as well as informal and formal strategic alliances, is consistent with this, but so is the changing nature of the relationships among providers (including competitors) and with patients.

LEADERSHIP IMPLICATIONS

This new face of healthcare will require that leaders learn to manage new players and relationships. Every healthcare leader will be surrounded by a growing number of active, powerful, and sometimes competing stakeholders (individuals, groups, or organizations) who have a stake in the decisions and actions of an organization and who attempt to influence those decisions and actions. These stakeholders exert an influence on every healthcare management issue and must be recognized and evaluated for their potential to support or threaten the organization and its competitive goals. By following a systematic program of web navigation, the healthcare leader will be able to accurately assess, diagnose, and strategically manage the many diverse relationships that will emerge in the future.

The relationship assessment presented here leads to several implications for medical group executives. These implications indicate the importance of relationship assessment techniques and imply that significant effort (including human and monetary resources) must be spent on relationship assessment. Accurate measures of the medical groups' reliance on resources from various stakeholders should be developed and periodically evaluated. Due to the turbulence in the healthcare market, key relationships must be continually assessed for their potential to threaten or cooperate with the medical group. These ongoing assessments should help physician administrative executives to seek fruitful coalitions and avoid or reduce threatening dependencies.

Medical group leaders need to do more than merely identify stakeholders or react to stakeholder demands. They must proactively develop or enhance their organization's capacity for strategic relationship management. This means they need to anticipate the goals of their key stakeholders and then offer appropriate inducements in exchange for essential contributions. Even with effective strategic relationship management activities, many challenges exist. The turbulence will continue within the U.S. healthcare industry. Government reforms, especially at the state level, will continue to be proffered (Savage and Purtell, 1995). Employer coalitions will gain in strength and will demand concessions from providers and administrators. MCOs and IDS/Ns will become stronger forces. Healthcare organizations taking an active lead in assessing their stakeholders will be winners.

Perhaps the most important findings from our study are that (1) the relationships that make up integrated systems or networks and their component organizations are increasing in potential for threat to medical groups, but (2) medical group executives are not taking steps to protect against this threat. Instead, the priorities of medical groups are becoming more oriented toward enhancing cooperation. Organizations may be focusing too much on enhancing cooperation, leaving themselves open to the threats posed by IDS/Ns and their components. Although now they may be too defensive, in the future they may be too open.

Medical group executives are continuing to develop their skills in identifying, assessing, and diagnosing their key relationships. They also must continue to formulate and successfully implement strategies that effectively manage their groups' important, but often unclear, relationships with these key stakeholders.

Physician executives and administrative executives face this new era of strategic stakeholder management together. Both should be involved in determining the parameters of the new programs, especially those controlling key medical group resources. As the boundaries for resource management are determined using such tools as critical pathways, control may be lost if the one perspective is not taken into account. It is not in the best interest of the medical group to ignore any key viewpoint during organizational restructuring, contract negotiation, or the myriad of other issues discussed in this article. The physician opinion, for example, is too valuable to be heard only after a new system is put in place.

Although physician executives and administrative executives share many of the responsibilities for dealing with and managing numerous issues, physicians and nonphysicians will likely have different areas of focus. For example, physician executives must prepare for changes affecting *both* the clinical and business aspects of their organizations. This means physician executives must extend and assert their role of medical expert beyond the examining room and into the strategic and organizational structures of their practices.

Administrative and physician executives may act to reduce threat from their relationships. Some existing medical organizations can do just that. For example, academic medical centers often have the most potential to meet organizational threat. They are likely to be some of the largest and most diverse group practices in a particular community or region. In addition, academic medical centers seem to have natural beginnings of vertically integrated systems that have their own or affiliated hospitals. These relationships may, by their very existence, reduce the potential for threat from the already-affiliated stakeholders.

The increasingly important issue of coalition formation and the concept that coalitions tend to increase the potential for cooperation from relationships seem to have been in practice for some time now in the healthcare industry. Entrepreneurial physicians and medical group executives began building coalitions and vertically integrating with other organizations many years ago, presumably in anticipation of today's complex healthcare delivery realities.

Even though many of these collaborative endeavors were effectively blocked by legislative efforts and legal challenges, the skills used and the insights gained by these entrepreneurial spirits during the creation of joint ventures and other partnering arrangements can be fine-tuned now in order to prepare for the emerging, integrated organizational forms. The more active medical group executives are today, the less threatening these newly emerging IDS/Ns will be to them.

The changing relative power of stakeholders indicates a power shift toward IDS/Ns and MCOs. This is indicated by purchasing power changes. As large employers begin to view healthcare services as a commodity rather than an individual service, the power of the individual provider diminishes. Medical groups often lack the economy of scale or the scope of service to provide comprehensive contracts to these purchasers. Therefore, in order to combat this power shift away from providers and toward purchasers (employers), medical groups and other healthcare provider organizations will have to form various alliances and coalitions to effectively negotiate with large purchasers of medical services.

Strategic and operational actions consistent with our findings are as follows:

- Developing a vision of how executives would like to relate to key relationships in the future, the nature of their contractual relationships, and who within their organizations will be able to bring about the desired state of affairs
- Contracting with specialists, if necessary, to hire representatives to deal with the two key stakeholders (IDS/Ns and MCOs)
- Developing evaluation and analysis skills to understand contracts and cooperative agreements in order to protect organizations from financial risk
- Developing tools and techniques to assess which resources are vital and which resources have substitutes available
- Reducing the medical group's dependence on stakeholders who will control key resources but who will likely threaten rather than cooperate with the medical group

The overall managerial implications of these findings are that healthcare executives need to identify their own key relationships in the emerging integrated systems of which they will be a part. Then they need to allocate time, effort, and economic resources to diagnosing the relationships, as we have done in this chapter.

STEPS FOR SETTING WEB NAVIGATION PRIORITIES

The steps we recommend for effective web relationship navigation include the following and are supported by Toolkit 5:

- Critically examine your own organization's web navigation priorities and classify your pattern as one of four types of medical groups—in terms of your priorities to either enhance cooperation in relationships or to reduce threat or to do both. Use Tools 5.1, 5.2, and 5.3. Then consider whether your organization is a

Web Navigator medical group

Web Optimist medical group

Web Pessimist medical group

Web Ostrich medical group

- Locate these relationships within the strategic web your organization needs to navigate strategically. Review Tool 1.1.

- Assess each relationship in terms of control over key resources, using Tool 5.4.

- Assess each relationship in terms of the two major *coalition* factors: supportive coalition formation and nonsupportive coalition formation, using Tools 5.5 and 5.6.

- Diagnose each relationship in terms of potential for threat and potential for cooperation, using Tools 5.7 and 5.8.

- Ensure that the diagnosis for each relationship is relevant for the specific issue facing your medical group. Review Tool 1.6.

TOOLKIT 5

Determining Your Strategic Navigation Priorities

Tool 5.1. Your Priority on Reducing Stakeholder Threat in Web Relationships.

Instructions: Indicate whether your organization puts a high priority on reducing threat in its relationships *now.* What will its priority be *3 years from now?*

Our organization puts a high priority on reducing the level of actual or potential *threat* from:

	Now	3 Years from Now
Physicians	☐	☐
Patients	☐	☐
Hospitals	☐	☐
Competitors	☐	☐
MCOs	☐	☐
IDS/Ns	☐	☐
Total checks	Now___	3 Years from Now___

Tool 5.2. Your Priority on Enhancing Stakeholder Cooperation in Web Relationships.

Instructions: Indicate whether your organization puts a high priority on enhancing cooperation in its relationships *now.* What will its priority be *3 years from now?*

Our organization puts a high priority on enhancing the level of actual or potential *cooperation* from:

	Now	3 Years from Now
Physicians	☐	☐
Patients	☐	☐
Hospitals	☐	☐
Competitors	☐	☐
MCOs	☐	☐
IDS/Ns	☐	☐
Total checks	Now___	3 Years from Now___

Tool 5.3. Your Web Navigation Type.

Instructions: Add up your organization's current stakeholder priorities for reducing threat in Tools 5.1 and 5.2. The score should be between 0–6. Plot this number to show your overall threat-reducing priorities *now.* Do the same for your *in 3 years* checklists.

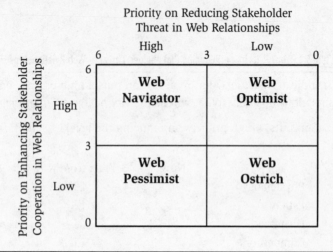

Priority on Reducing Stakeholder
Threat in Web Relationships

	High	Low
High	Web Navigator	Web Optimist
Low	Web Pessimist	Web Ostrich

Priority on Enhancing Stakeholder Cooperation in Web Relationships

Tool 5.4. Assessing Control Over Your Key Resources.

Instructions: Using the key stakeholders you have listed in Tool 1.1, check the appropriate box to indicate how your organization assesses your *internal* and *external* web relationships *now* and *3 years from now* in relation to the question below.

To what extent does each stakeholder control key resources?

Your Key *Internal* Stakeholders
Now (1–5)

Stakeholders	Very Little	Very Great
1 →	☐	☐
2 →	☐	☐
3 →	☐	☐
4 →	☐	☐
5 →	☐	☐

Your Key *Internal* Stakeholders
3 Years from Now (6–10)

Stakeholders	Very Little	Very Great
6 →	☐	☐
7 →	☐	☐
8 →	☐	☐
9 →	☐	☐
10 →	☐	☐

Your Key *External* Stakeholders
Now (1–5)

Stakeholders	Very Little	Very Great
1 →	☐	☐
2 →	☐	☐
3 →	☐	☐
4 →	☐	☐
5 →	☐	☐

Your Key *External* Stakeholders
3 Years from Now (6–10)

Stakeholders	Very Little	Very Great
6 →	☐	☐
7 →	☐	☐
8 →	☐	☐
9 →	☐	☐
10 →	☐	☐

Tool 5.5. Assessing Positive Coalitions of Your Organization.

Instructions: Using the key stakeholders you have listed in Tool 1.1, check the appropriate box to indicate how your organization assesses your *internal* and *external* web relationships *now* and *3 years from now* in relation to the question below.

How likely is each stakeholder to form a coalition with your organization?

Your Key *Internal* Stakeholders Now (1–5)			Your Key *Internal* Stakeholders 3 Years from Now (6–10)		
Stakeholders	Very Unlikely	Very Likely	Stakeholders	Very Unlikely	Very Likely
1 →	☐	☐	6 →	☐	☐
2 →	☐	☐	7 →	☐	☐
3 →	☐	☐	8 →	☐	☐
4 →	☐	☐	9 →	☐	☐
5 →	☐	☐	10 →	☐	☐

Your Key *External* Stakeholders Now (1–5)			Your Key *External* Stakeholders 3 Years from Now (6–10)		
Stakeholders	Very Unlikely	Very Likely	Stakeholders	Very Unlikely	Very Likely
1 →	☐	☐	6 →	☐	☐
2 →	☐	☐	7 →	☐	☐
3 →	☐	☐	8 →	☐	☐
4 →	☐	☐	9 →	☐	☐
5 →	☐	☐	10 →	☐	☐

Tool 5.6. Assessing Negative Coalitions of Your Organization.

Instructions: Using the key stakeholders you have listed in Tool 1.1, check the appropriate box to indicate how your organization assesses your *internal* and *external* web relationships *now* and *3 years from now* in relation to the question below.

How likely is each stakeholder to join a coalition excluding your organization?

Your Key *Internal* Stakeholders Now (1–5)			Your Key *Internal* Stakeholders 3 Years from Now (6–10)		
Stakeholders	Very Unlikely	Very Likely	Stakeholders	Very Unlikely	Very Likely
1 →	☐	☐	6 →	☐	☐
2 →	☐	☐	7 →	☐	☐
3 →	☐	☐	8 →	☐	☐
4 →	☐	☐	9 →	☐	☐
5 →	☐	☐	10 →	☐	☐

Your Key *External* Stakeholders Now (1–5)			Your Key *External* Stakeholders 3 Years from Now (6–10)		
Stakeholders	Very Unlikely	Very Likely	Stakeholders	Very Unlikely	Very Likely
1 →	☐	☐	6 →	☐	☐
2 →	☐	☐	7 →	☐	☐
3 →	☐	☐	8 →	☐	☐
4 →	☐	☐	9 →	☐	☐
5 →	☐	☐	10 →	☐	☐

Tool 5.7. Assessing Potential Threat to Your Organization.

Instructions: Based on the impact of power and coalition factors you have listed in Tools 5.4 through 5.7, use Tool 5.1 to help you diagnose the web relationship bottom line in terms of threat. Using the key stakeholders you have listed in Tool 1.1, check the appropriate box to indicate how your organization assesses your *internal* and *external* web relationships *now* and *3 years from now* in relation to the question below.

What is the potential of each stakeholder to threaten your organization?

Your Key *Internal* Stakeholders Now (1–5)			Your Key *Internal* Stakeholders *3 Years from Now* (6–10)		
Stakeholders	Very Little	Very Great	Stakeholders	Very Little	Very Great
1 →	☐	☐	6 →	☐	☐
2 →	☐	☐	7 →	☐	☐
3 →	☐	☐	8 →	☐	☐
4 →	☐	☐	9 →	☐	☐
5 →	☐	☐	10 →	☐	☐

Your Key *External* Stakeholders Now (1–5)			Your Key *External* Stakeholders *3 Years from Now* (6–10)		
Stakeholders	Very Little	Very Great	Stakeholders	Very Little	Very Great
1 →	☐	☐	6 →	☐	☐
2 →	☐	☐	7 →	☐	☐
3 →	☐	☐	8 →	☐	☐
4 →	☐	☐	9 →	☐	☐
5 →	☐	☐	10 →	☐	☐

Tool 5.8. Assessing Potential Cooperation with Your Organization.

Instructions: Based on the impact of power and coalition factors you have listed in Tools 5.4 through 5.7, use Tool 5.1 to help you diagnose the web relationship bottom line in terms of cooperation. Using the key stakeholders you have listed in Tool 1.1, check the appropriate box to indicate how your organization assesses your *internal* and *external* web relationships *now* and *3 years from now* in relation to the question below.

What is the potential of each stakeholder to cooperate with your organization?

Your Key *Internal* Stakeholders Now (1–5)			Your Key *Internal* Stakeholders *3 Years from Now* (6–10)		
Stakeholders	Very Little	Very Great	Stakeholders	Very Little	Very Great
1 →	☐	☐	6 →	☐	☐
2 →	☐	☐	7 →	☐	☐
3 →	☐	☐	8 →	☐	☐
4 →	☐	☐	9 →	☐	☐
5 →	☐	☐	10 →	☐	☐

Your Key *External* Stakeholders Now (1–5)			Your Key *External* Stakeholders *3 Years from Now* (6–10)		
Stakeholders	Very Little	Very Great	Stakeholders	Very Little	Very Great
1 →	☐	☐	6 →	☐	☐
2 →	☐	☐	7 →	☐	☐
3 →	☐	☐	8 →	☐	☐
4 →	☐	☐	9 →	☐	☐
5 →	☐	☐	10 →	☐	☐

TACTICS FOR NAVIGATING
WEB RELATIONSHIPS

Today, the need for understanding how to manage relationships in a systematic and strategic manner is even more crucial because the nature of those relationships is changing. All medical groups face similar challenges and strategic issues as their leaders navigate their way around the obstacles to building a supportive strategic web in the emerging environment. Once group leaders have classified a web relationship, as described in Chapter Five, that relationship has to be managed—which is the subject of Chapter Six.

To a great extent, the key relationships an organization needs are becoming more threatening and uncertain. In this chapter, we examine in some detail medical groups' relationships with six major stakeholder groups: physicians, patients, hospitals, competitors, managed care organizations, and IDS/Ns.

Effective web navigation requires managing relationships with key stakeholders explicitly and strategically within the increasingly complex set of interrelated webs for medical groups. Specifically, we will focus on the following:

- Classification of both *internal* and *external* web relationships into four types: *mixed-blessing, supportive, nonsupportive,* and *marginal* relationships

- Development of four generic web navigation tactics that have optimal fits with corresponding web relationships: *collaborate cautiously* in the mixed-blessing relationship, *involve trustingly* in the supportive relationship, *defend proactively* in the nonsupportive relationship, and *monitor efficiently* in the marginal relationship

TYPES OF WEB RELATIONSHIPS

The Mixed-Blessing Relationship

The mixed-blessing relationship plays a key role in creating web navigation challenges. With mixed-blessing relationships, the medical group executive faces a situation in which the relationship is high on both types of potential discussed in the previous chapter: threat and cooperation. Normally, relationships of the mixed-blessing type would include referral source physicians not part of the group, managed care organizations, insured patients, midlevel practitioners such as physicians' assistants and nurse practitioners, and physician groups with complementary but not competing services.

Hospitals are increasingly a mixed-blessing relationship for the medical group. Although hospitals can and do much that benefits medical groups, hospitals also can threaten because of their control over acquiring new technologies and providing clinical services and staff needed by group physicians. Also, hospital-driven CQI processes may make the management of patient care (involving patients and their families, other key stakeholders) more cost-effective for the hospital but more difficult, time consuming, and expensive for physicians. Such CQI efforts may include significant pressure for reducing the length of hospital stay through the use of clinical benchmarking or critical pathways. These monitoring mechanisms may constrain physician choice and flexibility, decrease the effective use of physicians' time, and eventually serve as the basis for "decredentialing."

Some special interest groups are also a mixed blessing. For example, substance abuse programs directed by psychiatrists are influenced by such groups as Alcoholics Anonymous (AA). These groups may have a significant stake in the clinical program and its therapeutic approach. Such groups can either enhance referrals to the program or can undermine it, thereby greatly affecting a program's clinical and financial viability.

Relationships with MCOs are increasingly, at best, mixed blessings, especially in contrast with indemnity insurance companies that were, for the most part, a near prototype of the next type to be discussed—the supportive relationship. Now, they often appear as a still less attractive type—the nonsupportive relationship.

The Supportive Relationship

The ideal relationship is one that supports the organization's goals and actions. Executives wish all their relationships were of this type. Such a relationship is low on potential threat but high on potential for cooperation. Usually, for a well-managed medical group, its board, managers, staff employees, physician members, and the local community will be of this type. In many large groups with multispecialty clinics, a common administrative support structure with shared staff typify the concept of the supportive relationship (although centralized support staff can, at times, be clearly a mixed blessing).

The Nonsupportive Relationship

Relationships of this type are the most distressing for a medical group and its managers. They are high on potential for threat but low on potential for cooperation. Typical nonsupportive relationships for medical groups include competing medical groups; competing hospital-based ambulatory centers; less expensive alternative sources of similar "medical services" such as chiropractors, podiatrists, and optometrists (which are increasingly acceptable and desirable to MCOs); employee unions; the federal government and other governmental regulatory agencies; indigent patients; and employer healthcare coalitions.

Interestingly, an MCO, even though it may be in a nonsupportive relationship to a medical group, is one of the two necessary organizations required for a medical group to form a fully integrated healthcare delivery system (the other being a hospital). This type of mixed situation presents the major strategic issue facing today's medical group executives: how to effectively manage nonsupportive relationships so that in the future those same relationships will be less threatening and more cooperative. We will return to this issue later in this chapter.

The Marginal Relationship

Marginal relationships are high on neither threat nor cooperative potential. Although they potentially have a stake in the medical group and its decisions, they are generally not relevant for most issues. For a typical medical group, marginal relationships of this kind may include the local media, volunteer groups in the community, county or state taxpayers, and professional associations for employees. However, certain issues such as cost containment or access to care could activate one or more of these relationships, such as the media, causing their potential for either threat or cooperation to increase.

Issue-Specific Relationship Diagnosis

Not everyone will agree with the set of relationships we have used as examples for each type. There is good reason to be uncomfortable with such global classifications. For one thing, the most important issues facing medical groups and their managers at any given time change constantly. Of all the possible relationships for a medical group, the ones that will be relevant to its managers depends on the competitive strategies being pursued as well as the particular issue involved. If the issue is cost containment, the relationships will be different than if the issue is access to healthcare.

The same issue specificity appears if the issue is whether the medical group should be merged into a fully integrated delivery system being built by the group's primary admitting hospital or whether a new clinic should be built as a cooperative venture between a specific hospital and a particular specialty group within the medical group. The *diagnosis* of the relevant relationships in terms of the four relationship types will probably be different for each of these four issues as well.

Moreover, whatever the diagnosis of a particular relationship on a specific issue, managers should *explicitly* classify relationships to surface inadvertent managerial biases. For example, if a manager identifies all relationships for any particular issue as nonsupportive, then the manager should critically examine his or her assessment of those relationships.

Also, if a particular relationship is always thought of as the same in terms of threat and cooperation, the manager may be missing opportunities for capitalizing on the *potential* for cooperation but may also be running the risk of being blind-sided by underestimating the *potential* for threat on a specific issue.

For a thorough, step-by-step guide to identifying, assessing, and diagnosing relationships, see Blair and Fottler (1990). There we present toolkits that facilitate the important steps in the strategic relationship management process.

TACTICS FOR NAVIGATING KEY WEB RELATIONSHIPS

The four diagnostic types of relationships suggest four generic tactics for managing different combinations of the levels of potential for threat and potential for cooperation. Each of these tactics can be either proactive or reactive. Because medical group executives continually manage a wide variety of relationships (in terms of their potential for cooperation and threat), they may use a combination of web navigation tactics at any one time.

Collaborate Cautiously in the Mixed-Blessing Relationship

The mixed-blessing relationship, high on both dimensions of potential threat and potential cooperation, may best be managed through cautious collaboration. The ultimate goal of this tactic is to turn mixed-blessing relationships into supportive relationships. In implementing this tactic, medical group executives seek to enhance the potential for cooperation while protecting the group from the potential threat.

For example, a proposed strategic alliance between a medical group and a hospital represents a collaborative relationship. If this alliance takes the form of the medical group shelving plans to build a center that competes with hospital-based surgery, and the hospital builds a free-standing surgical center that meets the needs of the medical group physicians, such a collaboration would effectively enhance the hospital's cooperation with the medical group while reducing competitive threat. The hospital could contribute its name and capital resources; the medical group could send their patients to the free-standing surgical center. Both the hospital and the medical group would benefit, and the medical group will not have been damaged by the hospital becoming a competitor. Both threat-reduction and cooperation-enhancement priorities will have been met.

Another example involves interorganizational collaboration within an integrating system. Even in the same system, the managed care organization's HMO still may represent a mixed-blessing relationship to the system's medical group(s), especially in contrast to discounted fee-for-service plans that might be seen as relatively supportive relationships. If the system medical group and the system HMO together developed and implemented an activity-based cost-accounting system for physician practices to effectively contain their costs, such collaboration would benefit both. The medical group's goals of retaining capitation dollars for their cost-cutting efforts and the HMO's goals of being able to be price-competitive without hurting the system's own physician providers would be possible with such collaboration.

These kinds of collaborative tactics indicate the caution that must be undertaken when using this relationship. This caution is warranted because of the inherent instability of mixed-blessing relationships vis-à-vis the medical group. An effective collaborative relationship with them may well determine the long-term stakeholder-medical group relationship. In other words, if this type of relationship is not properly managed through the use of a collaborative relationship, the "diagnostic instability" of these types of relationships could lead to a mixed-blessing relationship becoming a nonsupportive relationship. Likewise, a well-managed collaborative relationship may result in changing a mixed-blessing relationship into a supportive relationship.

Of the responding medical groups in our study, the changes in medical groups reporting that "their organizations spend great time and other resources to *collaborate* with each of the following stakeholders in joint problem solving or other joint activities" are as follows:

- *Physicians:* from 76 percent in the past to 85 percent in the future
- *Hospitals:* from 49 percent to 52 percent
- *MCOs:* from 22 percent to 65 percent
- *Patients:* from 19 percent to 46 percent
- *IDS/Ns:* from 16 percent to 68 percent
- *Competitors:* from 6 percent to 14 percent

Clearly, our responding medical groups indicate a widespread use of collaboration tactics to manage current physician and hospital relationships. The relationships with MCOs, patients, and IDS/Ns are expected to increasingly be managed through collaboration as well. In particular, the extremely large increase in the projected use of collaboration tactics for IDS/Ns and MCOs reflects a recognition among many medical groups of the growing importance of such relationships in the future.

Involve Trustingly in the Supportive Relationship

By involving those stakeholders who have supportive relationships, medical group executives can capitalize on cooperative potential. Because these relationships pose a low threat potential, they may be ignored and, therefore, their cooperative potential may be ignored as well. It is important to distinguish between collaborating with a stakeholder and involving a stakeholder. Because collaboration and win-win strategies are often discussed and, indeed, prescribed as the basic solution in the healthcare management literature, the collaborative relationship is often confused with the involvement relationship.

Involvement differs from *collaboration* in two ways: (1) involvement further activates or enhances the supportive capability of an already supportive relationship, and (2) collaboration includes an element of caution due to the high potential for threat inherent in mixed-blessing relationships. With the involvement relationship, the emphasis is not on reducing threat; threat potential is low. Instead, this relationship attempts to capitalize on the already existing potential for cooperation by converting even more of the *potential* into *actual* cooperation. Collaboration, however, involves much more of a give and take by the medical group and the stakeholder. Collaboration may require the medical group to give up or expend certain key resources or change important policies to gain stakeholder support either by lowering threat or by increasing cooperation.

As mentioned earlier, collaboration tactics should contain an element of caution that is not needed in involvement strategies. Collaboration may even have a defensive element to protect the organization against potential threat. For example, *collaboration* is more likely to involve formal, highly specified contracts that are not necessary with fully supportive stakeholders who can be *involved* with a higher level of trust (and lack of risk) on the part of the organization.

Managers can operationalize the involvement relationship through empowering employees by using participative management techniques, decentralizing authority to clinical managers, and engaging in other tactics to increase the decision-making participation of these supportive stakeholders. For example, senior management may invite laboratory clinic managers to participate in the analysis and planning for eliminating redundant programs. The laboratory clinic managers who participate in the decision-making process will more likely become committed to achieving such an organizational objective than if they had not been involved in establishing it. A key requirement for the success of this type of relationship is the ability of the managers to enlarge their vision regarding ways to further involve supportive relationships. This results in better cooperation.

Many medical groups are now involving their supportive employees and in-house volunteer stakeholders by training them to manage mixed-blessing relationships such as those with funded patients and patients' families. They are doing this through "guest" or "customer" relations programs designed to more effectively manage one or more of their potentially threatening relationships (for example, funded patients) by increasing the cooperative potential of a key internal relationship (for example, employees).

Another use of the involvement relationship is explicitly strategic. It systematically links human resource management systems and practices to overall strategic management. The approach is called strategic human resource management (SHRM) and has only recently been introduced into the field of health-care management (Fottler, Phillips, Blair, and Duran, 1990; Fottler, Hernandez, and Joiner, 1994). It is consistent with our strategic relationship management approach because SHRM increases involvement of a generally supportive internal stakeholder (employees) in furthering the strategic goals of the medical group through effective, strategic linking of human resource management. The medical group can then determine what employee behaviors are desirable in managing various external key relationships and can manage human resources by selection, training, compensation, and so forth to produce these behaviors.

Having looked at both collaborative and involving strategies, it is important not to misdiagnose a mixed-blessing relationship as a supportive relationship. For example, medical group executives need to be aware of hospital perceptions when entering into alliances with hospitals. Hospitals are generally considered to be mixed-blessing relationships from a physician perspective. They may wish to control a relationship rather than view their affiliated medical groups as full partners.

Medical group executives, however, may mismanage a mixed-blessing hospital (which still has a high potential for threat) by using involvement strategies (which assume a low potential for threat) to manage their relationship with the hospital. This can strain the physician-hospital relationship. We will discuss the broader issue of diagnosis and relationship fit, or lack of fit, later in this chapter.

Assume a hospital buys a physician group practice, thereby making all the physicians employees of the hospital. The physicians may view themselves as partners in the venture and expect to be involved in strategic decision making at the highest levels. However, when the hospital executives try to exert typical hierarchical authority and typical involvement strategies over the newly acquired physicians, the physicians will most likely rebel. This example is a classic case in which medical group executives misdiagnose a hospital as a nonthreatening, supportive relationship when, in fact, the hospital is a powerful, mixed-blessing stakeholder.

In our study, the changes in medical groups reporting that "their organizations spend great time and other resources to *involve* each of the following stakeholders in their decision making" are as follows:

- *Physicians:* from 81 percent in the past to 87 percent in the future
- *Hospitals:* from 29 percent to 43 percent
- *IDS/Ns:* from 18 percent to 71 percent
- *MCOs:* from 17 percent to 61 percent
- *Patients:* from 15 percent to 46 percent
- *Competitors:* from 3 percent to 11 percent

As with collaboration, our respondents indicate a widespread use of involvement tactics to manage current physician and hospital relationships. The relationships with MCOs, patients, and IDS/Ns are expected to increasingly be managed through involvement as well. In particular, the extremely large increase in the projected use of involvement tactics for IDS/Ns and MCOs reflects a recognition among increasing medical groups of the integrating strategic web in their futures.

Defend Proactively in the Nonsupportive Relationship

Relationships that pose high threat but whose potential for cooperation is low are best managed using a defensive tactic. Relations with the federal government and indigent patients are good examples. In Kotter's (1979) framework on external dependence, the defensive relationship tries to reduce the dependence that forms the basis for stakeholders' interest in the organization. In our terms, a defensive relationship involves preventing the stakeholder from imposing costs—or other disincentives—on the medical group.

However, medical group executives should *not* attempt to totally eliminate their dependence on nonsupportive relationships. Such efforts are either doomed to failure or may result in a negative image for the medical group. For example, trying to sever all ties with the federal government is counterproductive if a physician group hopes to serve older patients. Another example is when a physician group denies access to all indigent patients. This will almost surely be viewed negatively by the public, the media, and the local government. It could have negative repercussions in terms of adverse publicity, an unwillingness of other providers to make referrals to the physician group, and a loss of some insured patients. Further, if the local government is a large local employer, it could exclude the physician group from the provider network available to its employees.

Let us consider an example of this defensive relationship in action, using the federal government's regulatory agencies as the stakeholder. Given the regulations physicians face, their most appropriate tactic is to explore ways of complying with the demands imposed by the federal government at the least possible cost. Hence, medical group executives might do the following: modify the services they offer based on activity-based cost accounting; out-source not-so-profitable tasks such as simple lab tests; or invest in more effective management information systems. These are all part of using a defensive relationship to manage a nonsupportive, demanding, third-party payor or regulator.

The best defensive management of nonsupportive relationships is to shift the medical group's dependencies (where possible) from nonsupportive to mixed-blessing or supportive relationships. For example, if government reimbursement is restricted, the medical group can attract more private-pay patients. Another defensive relationship is for the medical group to acquire physician practices in strategic locations and, at the same time, to link (for common managed care contract negotiations) with other medical practices in the area through a closed, independent practice association.

Both of these strategic acts form types of horizontal integration among physician providers. This approach allows the medical group and its partners to negotiate contracts to provide particular medical services over a wide geographical area. Being able to provide medical service to employees who reside throughout an SMSA or regional area also provides more leverage in negotiating contracts directly with a coalition of employers.

The changes in medical groups reporting that "their organization spends great time and other resources to *defend* itself against potentially threatening actions from each of the following stakeholders" are as follows:

- *Competitors:* from 32 percent in the past to 43 percent in the future
- *MCOs:* from 20 percent to 43 percent
- *Physicians:* from 19 percent to 26 percent
- *Hospitals:* from 19 percent to 26 percent
- *Patients:* from 15 percent to 22 percent
- *IDS/Ns:* from 13 percent to 42 percent

Unlike with collaboration and involvement tactics, our respondents indicate a much less widespread use of defending tactics to manage current web relationships. As one would expect, they are used often in relationships with competitors. However, in the future, relationships with MCOs and IDS/Ns are expected to increasingly be managed through defending tactics as well. In particular, the modest increase in the projected use of defending tactics for IDS/Ns and MCOs, as well as for competitors, may reflect medical groups' perceptions of "taking sides" in their future, more fully integrating strategic web.

Monitor Efficiently in the Marginal Relationship

Monitoring is the relationship management technique to use to manage marginal relationships whose potential for both threat and cooperation is low. The underlying philosophy for managing marginal relationships is proactively maintaining the status quo while ensuring that the use of such resources as finances and management time is kept to a minimum.

The general thrust of this approach is to let sleeping dogs lie but watch them in case they wake up. The medical group executive looks for and is aware of sensitive issues that could activate these groups into becoming threats. This monitoring activity is necessary because if a marginal stakeholder "wakes up," the medical group executive must be proactive in directing the stakeholder's activities.

Typically, these groups have only a marginal stake in the activities of the medical group, affecting operations indirectly through advocating a moral or ethical standpoint. Special interest groups are often seen as marginal stakeholders. They can be passive for some time and suddenly become activated by a trigger episode.

Threats from interest groups can come in many forms. For example, if two hospitals of different religious affiliations merge, the respective cultures may not agree on such controversial issues as fertility and abortion. As a result, a medical group that was only affiliated with the premerger hospital that did not perform fertility and abortion procedures may suddenly find itself affiliated with other physician groups performing such procedures. This entry into such an unexpected trigger episode can result in the medical group suddenly being targeted by a previously marginal stakeholder (an anti-abortion special interest group). As this example illustrates, if an issue is of enough importance to a marginal stakeholder, that relationship can become activated, resulting in the medical group requiring a different management relationship (such as collaborate, involve, or defend).

Often, patient families represent marginal stakeholders. Leaving this key marginal relationship unmonitored ignores the possibility of the development of a supportive relationship that can make a decisive difference in facilitating the course of patient care. Conversely, dissatisfied patient families that go unnoticed can wreak havoc on a medical group. Assigning specific responsibility for monitoring this relationship to a member of the patient care team can avert disaster for the medical group's management.

Marginal stakeholders are—in general—minimally satisfied. What it takes to keep a particular marginal stakeholder minimally satisfied may increase over time, thus necessitating greater involvement of managerial time and other medical group resources. Managers must monitor such expenditures of inducements and disinducements to determine whether they have become excessive or whether they are perhaps inadequate because the marginal stakeholder has become a key stakeholder (either in general or on a particular issue).

An Overarching Relationship Management Tactic

In addition to using the four tactics specifically tailored for relationships that have been placed in one of the four diagnostic categories, medical group executives may also employ an overarching tactic, that is, to move the relationship from a less favorable category to a more favorable one. The relationship can then be managed using the generic relationship most appropriate for that "new" diagnostic category.

For example, let us assume the medical group's relationship with the news media is marginal. Rather than implement an aggressive, expensive program of external relations with the media, the group could give the marketing director the explicit responsibility of paying attention to local issues that could spill over to the group.

If successful, this efficient monitoring would prevent news media relations from becoming threatening—that is, becoming a nonsupportive relationship. Allowing the relationship to be managed through an efficient monitoring tactic should prevent threat. If the medical group is willing to invest more time, energy, skill, and money in the effort, the media relationship might even be moved to a high enough degree to become supportive.

In another example, if a medical group is contemplating a strategic alliance with a mixed-blessing stakeholder (such as a hospital), we see an opportunity for the group. The medical group could effectively manage the hospital with a collaborative relationship such as referring inpatient care to the hospital in exchange for the hospital building a surgical center for the group of physicians. In this case, the medical group may also have successfully turned a mixed-blessing relationship into a less threatening, supportive relationship.

In our discussion of the collaborative relationship, we talk about moving from collaborative to supportive tactics. However, it is important to recognize that even if mixed-blessing relationships are collaboratively managed, they may or may not become supportive relationships. Every player in this new era of healthcare delivery is not voluntarily becoming involved and integrated. As such, stakeholders do not always react as the relationship suggests. Additionally, if long-term strategic goals are pursued without appropriate management tactics to implement the relationship, relationship management will not work effectively. For example, physician groups, hospitals, and MCOs together can create structural integration (strategic integration) fairly easily. However, if social-cultural integration (tactical integration) is not achieved, then the new structure may not work. Achieving such tactical integration is a much more significant challenge than achieving structural integration.

Of course, stakeholders will not just sit still and be managed. Stakeholders who are powerful and threatening are as likely to try to manage medical groups as groups are to manage hospitals. Many medical groups and their stakeholders continuously engage in management and countermanagement strategies. To negotiate these relationships effectively, medical group executives should continuously identify stakeholders and match their diagnosis with appropriate strategies. In other words, we suggest periodically repeating the prior steps to ensure that key assumptions still apply.

Web Navigation Proactivity or Reactivity?

As a summary measure, we asked our respondents to characterize their organization's web management strategies in the past and for the future. A 7-point scale was provided, with one end of the scale indicating a reactive posture and the other a proactive posture. The reactive posture was "We modify our organization's activities, goals, values, and norms to be compatible with those of current and changing stakeholder needs." The proactive posture was "We influence the stakeholder's activities, goals, values, and norms to make them compatible with those of the organization."

Only 20 and 21 percent of the medical group respondents in the past and future, respectively, identified their organization with the reactive posture (1 and 2 on the 7-point scale). Just 14 percent proactively managed their relationships in the past, but 34 percent expect to do so in the future. In sum, our respondents expect to be more proactive in managing their relationships in the future. Navigators were more proactive than Ostriches, and the other independent predictor variables do not seem to matter.

THE PROBLEMATIC FIT OF DIAGNOSIS AND TACTIC

For each of the four categories of relationships, we asserted that there is an optimal tactical choice—one that provides the optimal fit between diagnosis and tactic. In this section, we will look at the problematic fit of diagnosis and tactic.

"Suboptimal" fits can (and do) occur for a variety of reasons (Blair and others, 1996). Three ways to end up with suboptimal diagnosis-relationship fits are:

- A medical group initially misdiagnoses a relationship and then uses the relationship that would have been appropriate had the diagnosis been correct (for example, misdiagnosing a marginal relationship as supportive and then using an involving tactic instead of the appropriate monitoring relationship).

- The stakeholder purposefully misleads the organization so the relationship is misdiagnosed (for example, a stakeholder in a nonsupportive relationship acts as though it is supportive, which leads the organization to use a high-trust, involving tactic instead of the appropriate proactive, defending tactic).

- The organization's management has developed as a strategic strength one particular type of relationship management tactic. Therefore, they manage all types of relationships the same way.

For example, if a medical group desires to have their stakeholders view their organization as a good guy, leaders may use a *trustingly involving* tactic regardless of the diagnosis of the relationship, including its potential threat. Or if executives believe all relationships should be (or can be) win-win, they may use a collaboration tactic with all relationships.

In addition, if the organization's management is overly cautious, very risk-averse, and quite distrusting of everyone, they may rely only on the defending tactic. Finally, if the organization believes in the wait-and-see approach and, therefore, is reluctant to commit any resources to relationship management initially, the organization will likely use the monitoring relationship in all their dealings with any stakeholder.

Types of Diagnosis-Tactic Fits

We are arguing that the four basic types of fit have different implications for medical groups:

• Situations with optimal fit between relationship diagnosis and tactic are when the organization is effectively using its resources (including management time and attention) to navigate key relationships based on their appropriate levels of either potential for cooperation or threat or both. An example of an optimal fit is trustingly involving stakeholders when the relationship is supportive.

• Situations with suboptimal fit between relationship diagnosis and relationship result in missing opportunities; the organization is too distrusting (and defensive) in its relationships when, in fact, they may be high in cooperative potential. An example of this kind of suboptimal fit is collaborating in a cautious manner because of concerns over potential threat when the relationship is actually supportive so that some or all of the potential cooperation may not actually be realized.

• Situations with suboptimal fit between relationship diagnosis and relationship result in the organization being at risk; the organization is too trusting in its relationships when, in fact, they may be high in threat. An example of this kind of suboptimal fit is collaborating in a cautious manner in hopes of creating enhanced cooperation when, in fact, the relationship is nonsupportive. That would mean the level of information that must be shared in any kind of collaboration exposes the medical group to the actual threatening nature of the relationship without any real possibility of cooperation being enhanced.

• Situations with suboptimal fit between relationship diagnosis and relationship result in the organization focusing its attention and resources on low-potential relationships; the organization is wasting resources by focusing on relationships low in either potential for cooperation or threat. An example of this kind of suboptimal fit is defending proactively because of concerns over potential threat from a "squeaky wheel" stakeholder when the relationship is actually marginal so that resources are wasted without any real threat being stopped. Of course, this could even backfire if a powerful medical group is seen as over-whelming a less powerful (and not a key) stakeholder.

The Nature of Suboptimal Fits

If the medical group defends proactively in a mixed-blessing relationship, the organization misses opportunities. Why is this? If the stakeholder were another medical group of approximately the same size, offering the same medical services but only partially overlapping in traditional market area, it is reasonable to see that group as a mixed-blessing stakeholder. By seeing their counterpart organization as a mixed blessing, they are saying that the organization is *both* high in potential for cooperation and potential for threat.

Further, by choosing and implementing a defending tactic, the organization's executives are saying that their priorities are to reduce threat but are *not* also to increase cooperation (which is done through a collaborative relationship). Should the organization focus on that relationship? Yes, it has high potential because it can both threaten and cooperate. Are the organization's allocation of resources appropriate? No, there are inadequate resources devoted to enhancing cooperation, although there are enough (or maybe even too many) to prevent or reduce threat.

Thus, the organization's relationship is suboptimal because the organization's priority is only on reduction of threat when the relationship is high in potential for threat yet also has high potential for cooperation.

In this example, the organization should be examining the potential of collaborative research, such as a joint venture or strategic alliance with the other group. Indeed, a merger might well position them far more effectively to deal with another key stakeholder they both share—managed care organizations intent on even deeper discounts or seeking to limit its physician panels and focus on closed-panel, capitated health plans rather than open-panel, preferred provider plans.

By defending against the other medical group, the resources the organization is devoting to enhancing cooperation are inadequate, and the resources focused on reducing threat are potentially wasted because they do not allow for the potential for cooperation with the stakeholder. The relationship focuses on setting up constraints on cooperation and is thus potentially counterproductive.

DOES WEB NAVIGATION REALLY MATTER?

We examined perceptions of organizational effectiveness in managing various relationships as compared to their local competitors. Most respondents felt they did a better job in managing their own physicians and patients than in managing external stakeholders like hospitals, competitors, MCOs, and IDS/Ns.

Medical groups that are nonacademic, navigator, fully integrated, and proactive in managing their relationships do a better job of managing their relationships in general. Again, the size variable is ambiguous. Small practices do a better job of managing patients, but larger practices do a better job of managing physicians, hospitals, managed care organizations, and IDS/Ns. Medical groups in fully integrated systems do a better job of managing physicians, hospitals, and IDS/Ns as compared to medical groups that are not part of an IDS/N.

WHAT DO HIGH PERFORMERS IN NAVIGATING STAKEHOLDER RELATIONSHIPS DO?

Here we report a somewhat different extension of threat and cooperation assessments. We used relative medical group performance in effectively managing the stakeholder relationships as a basis for predicting their organizations' views of relationship assessment. This is similar to the best practices approach used by many consulting firms.

Medical groups that manage their relationships better differ from those who manage them the same or worse in terms of how they diagnose and manage these relationships. Medical group executives who perceive that they manage their relationships well tend to view the relationships as supportive or mixed-blessing. Alternatively, those who perceived they managed their relationships more poorly (same or worse) tended to assess the same relationships as nonsupportive or marginal.

Those who manage their relationships better tend to manage them with involvement and collaborative strategies, whereas those who manage the same relationships more poorly tend to defend against them and monitor them. It appears that medical group executives who assess their relationships more proactively and positively and those who involve and collaborate with them are more likely to feel they manage their relationships better than competitors. Alternatively, those who view them as marginal or nonsupportive and those who monitor and defend against them tend to feel they manage relationships the same or worse than competitors. Generally speaking, fully integrated medical groups view most of their relationships more positively (as more supportive) than do their nonintegrated counterparts.

The pattern is very clear. The leaders of the organizations in our sample connect their performance in managing relationships to their assessments of those relationships' threat and cooperation. High-performing organizations see higher potentials for cooperation and lower potentials for threat.

This confidence probably reflects more relationship management experience and more sophisticated management systems to do so—for example, more highly developed information technology and utilization review programs to manage MCO relationships. Or their confidence is very dangerous and could lead to suboptimal fits that put their medical groups at risk. It should be noted that the positive relationship between practice leaders' positive perceptions of other organizations having a high potential for cooperation and that practice's performance may reflect more than the power of positive thinking. It may be that these practices also manage these relationships in a more sophisticated way than others do.

LEADERSHIP IMPLICATIONS

Many of the barriers to development of fully integrated healthcare delivery systems identified by Shortell and his colleagues (1993) stem from a failure to accurately identify, assess, and appropriately manage relationships that are key to the success of the effort. Too much time, effort, and money is being spent on managing relationships that are marginal in terms of the development of integrated delivery systems.

At the same time, new opportunities are lost due to a failure to identify opportunities and relationships that are key to their implementation. Our study indicates that the reciprocal can be true for medical groups themselves—looking at integrated systems or networks such as those studied by Shortell and others (1993) as their stakeholders.

Until recently, there has been a gap between the literatures of strategic and operational management. Strategic plans do not typically drive the day-to-day activities of most managers and other organizational participants. The most important reason is a failure to consider implementation issues that require the management of key relationships.

Our study indicates that IDS/Ns and MCOs are expected to shift from being marginal to being mixed-blessing relationships, while physicians will become even more supportive in the future. A number of predictors of organizational performance, ability to manage key relationships, and other skills and abilities were examined. The data indicate that performance, in general, is better for nonacademic and Navigator medical groups and worse for academic and Ostrich medical groups. In managing key relationships the better medical groups again were nonacademic and navigators. However, they also tended to be fully integrated, proactive in managing their relationships, and larger. Better management of relationships was associated with a more positive assessment of relationships (viewing them as supportive) and attempting to involve and collaborate with them. Finally, medical groups that are large, nonacademic, and Navigators tend to have greater skills and abilities than do their counterparts.

Relationship management integrates in a systematic way what managers have often dealt with separately: strategic management, marketing, patient relations, human resources management, media and public relations, and social responsibility issues. To manage relationships, medical group executives are involved in a continuous process of internal and external scanning. They go beyond the traditional issues of strategic management such as the attractiveness of different markets and the likely actions of competitors.

Executives develop and implement not only the popular collaborative tactics to manage their external relationships but also involving, defending, and monitoring tactics. They likewise assess their internal stakeholders (nurses, technicians, administrative staff, and so on) and work toward preparing them to support the organizational changes that will be necessary to accommodate a more collaborative business environment.

The common theme is that, in the future, medical groups expect to be faced with an environment in which collaboration with stakeholders and the emergence of new organizational structures that include these stakeholders will be the norm. This means that effective strategic relationship assessment and management are critical to the success and viability of medical groups as they prepare for their organizations' roles in the future delivery of healthcare services.

STEPS FOR NAVIGATING
MULTIPLE TYPES OF WEB RELATIONSHIPS

The steps we recommend for tactically navigating multiple types of web relationships include the following, supported by Toolkit 6:

- Using Tools 6.1 and 6.2, classify each relationship as
    Mixed-blessing
    Supportive
    Nonsupportive
    Marginal
- Set organizational priorities, using Tools 6.3 and 6.4, as to what is important in navigating *this* web relationship:
    Reducing threat
    Enhancing cooperation
    Both
    Neither

- Use generic relationship navigation tactics that fit the nature of the relationship (use Tools 6.5 and 6.6).

  Collaborate cautiously in the mixed-blessing relationship.

  Involve trustingly in the supportive relationship.

  Defend proactively in the nonsupportive relationship.

  Monitor efficiently in the marginal relationship.

- Implement these generic tactics by developing specific actions and programs for each tactic and relationship combination (use Tools 6.7, 6.8, and 6.9).

- Determine which employees, as internal stakeholders, should be involved in the implementation process.

- Evaluate the success of the web navigation process and implement changes as needed. In particular, be sensitive to suboptimal fits between existing diagnoses of relationships and the tactics to navigate that relationship. Use Tools 6.10 and 6.11 to assess the fit of your group.

TOOLKIT 6

Navigating Web Relationships

Tool 6.1. Assessing Internal Relationships.

Instructions: Using the stakeholders listed in Tool 1.1, check the appropriate box to indicate how your organization assesses your *internal* relationships *now* or will assess them *3 years from now* in relation to the question below.

Overall, how would you describe each of the following stakeholders when they are "internal"?

Your Key *Internal* Stakeholders
Now (1–5)

Stakeholders	Marginal	Nonsupportive	Mixed-Blessing	Supportive
1 →	☐	☐	☐	☐
2 →	☐	☐	☐	☐
3 →	☐	☐	☐	☐
4 →	☐	☐	☐	☐
5 →	☐	☐	☐	☐

Your Key *Internal* Stakeholders
3 Years from Now (6–10)

Stakeholders	Marginal	Nonsupportive	Mixed-Blessing	Supportive
6 →	☐	☐	☐	☐
7 →	☐	☐	☐	☐
8 →	☐	☐	☐	☐
9 →	☐	☐	☐	☐
10 →	☐	☐	☐	☐

Tool 6.2. Assessing External Relationships.

Instructions: Using the stakeholders listed in Tool 1.1, check the appropriate box to indicate how your organization assesses these *external* relationships *now* or will assess them *3 years from now.*

Overall, how would you describe each of the following stakeholders when they are "external"?

Your Key *External* Stakeholders
Now (1–5)

Stakeholders	Marginal	Nonsupportive	Mixed-Blessing	Supportive
1 →	☐	☐	☐	☐
2 →	☐	☐	☐	☐
3 →	☐	☐	☐	☐
4 →	☐	☐	☐	☐
5 →	☐	☐	☐	☐

Your Key *External* Stakeholders
3 Years from Now (6–10)

Stakeholders	Marginal	Nonsupportive	Mixed-Blessing	Supportive
6 →	☐	☐	☐	☐
7 →	☐	☐	☐	☐
8 →	☐	☐	☐	☐
9 →	☐	☐	☐	☐
10 →	☐	☐	☐	☐

Tool 6.3. Priorities on Reducing Threat in Specific Relationships.

Instructions: Using the relationship with key stakeholders you have listed in Tool 1.1, check the appropriate box to indicate the strategies used by your organization for navigating key web relationships.

What priority does your organization put on reducing the level of actual or potential threat in each web relationship?

Relationship with Your Key *Internal* Stakeholders *Now* (1–5)

Stakeholders	Very Low	Very High
1 →	☐	☐
2 →	☐	☐
3 →	☐	☐
4 →	☐	☐
5 →	☐	☐

Relationship with Your Key *Internal* Stakeholders *3 Years from Now* (6–10)

Stakeholders	Very Low	Very High
6 →	☐	☐
7 →	☐	☐
8 →	☐	☐
9 →	☐	☐
10 →	☐	☐

Relationship with Your Key *External* Stakeholders *Now* (1–5)

Stakeholders	Very Low	Very High
1 →	☐	☐
2 →	☐	☐
3 →	☐	☐
4 →	☐	☐
5 →	☐	☐

Relationship with Your Key *External* Stakeholders *3 Years from Now* (6–10)

Stakeholders	Very Low	Very High
6 →	☐	☐
7 →	☐	☐
8 →	☐	☐
9 →	☐	☐
10 →	☐	☐

Tool 6.4. Priorities on Enhancing Cooperation for Specific Relationships.

Instructions: Using the key stakeholders you have listed in Tool 1.1, check the appropriate box to indicate the strategies used by your organization for navigating key web relationships.

What priority does your organization put on enhancing the level of actual or potential cooperation in each web relationship?

Relationship with Your Key *Internal* Stakeholders *Now* (1–5)

Stakeholders	Very Low	Very High
1 →	☐	☐
2 →	☐	☐
3 →	☐	☐
4 →	☐	☐
5 →	☐	☐

Relationship with Your Key *Internal* Stakeholders *3 Years from Now* (6–10)

Stakeholders	Very Low	Very High
6 →	☐	☐
7 →	☐	☐
8 →	☐	☐
9 →	☐	☐
10 →	☐	☐

Relationship with Your Key *External* Stakeholders *Now* (1–5)

Stakeholders	Very Low	Very High
1 →	☐	☐
2 →	☐	☐
3 →	☐	☐
4 →	☐	☐
5 →	☐	☐

Relationship with Your Key *External* Stakeholders *3 Years from Now* (6–10)

Stakeholders	Very Low	Very High
6 →	☐	☐
7 →	☐	☐
8 →	☐	☐
9 →	☐	☐
10 →	☐	☐

Tool 6.5. Generic Internal Stakeholder Tactics.

Instructions: Check the appropriate box to indicate what your organization's overall or "generic" tactic is *now* or will be *3 years from now.*

Overall, how would you describe your tactics for each of the following when they are internal stakeholders?

Your Key *Internal* Stakeholders *Now* (1–5)

Stakeholders	Involve Trustingly	Collaborate Cautiously	Defend Proactively	Monitor Effectively
1 →	☐	☐	☐	☐
2 →	☐	☐	☐	☐
3 →	☐	☐	☐	☐
4 →	☐	☐	☐	☐
5 →	☐	☐	☐	☐

Your Key *Internal* Stakeholders *3 Years from Now* (6–10)

Stakeholders	Involve Trustingly	Collaborate Cautiously	Defend Proactively	Monitor Effectively
6 →	☐	☐	☐	☐
7 →	☐	☐	☐	☐
8 →	☐	☐	☐	☐
9 →	☐	☐	☐	☐
10 →	☐	☐	☐	☐

Tool 6.6. Generic External Stakeholder Tactics.

Instructions: Check the appropriate box to indicate what your organization's over-all or "generic" tactic is *now* or will be *3 years from now.*

Overall, how would you describe your tactics for each of the following when they are external stakeholders?

Your Key *External* Stakeholders
        Now (1–5)

Stakeholders	Involve Trustingly	Collaborate Cautiously	Defend Proactively	Monitor Effectively
1 →	☐	☐	☐	☐
2 →	☐	☐	☐	☐
3 →	☐	☐	☐	☐
4 →	☐	☐	☐	☐
5 →	☐	☐	☐	☐

Your Key *External* Stakeholders
        3 Years from Now (6–10)

Stakeholders	Involve Trustingly	Collaborate Cautiously	Defend Proactively	Monitor Effectively
6 →	☐	☐	☐	☐
7 →	☐	☐	☐	☐
8 →	☐	☐	☐	☐
9 →	☐	☐	☐	☐
10 →	☐	☐	☐	☐

Tool 6.7. Resources for Collaborating with Stakeholders.

Instructions: Using the key stakeholders you have listed in Tool 1.1, check the ap-propriate box to indicate the strategies used by your organization for navigating key web relationships.

To what extent does your organization spend time and other resources to collabo-rate cautiously with each of the following stakeholders in joint problem solving or other joint activities?

Your Key *Internal* Stakeholders
        Now (1–5)

Stakeholders	Very Little	Very Great
1 →	☐	☐
2 →	☐	☐
3 →	☐	☐
4 →	☐	☐
5 →	☐	☐

Your Key *Internal* Stakeholders
        3 Years from Now (6–10)

Stakeholders	Very Little	Very Great
6 →	☐	☐
7 →	☐	☐
8 →	☐	☐
9 →	☐	☐
10 →	☐	☐

Your Key *External* Stakeholders
        Now (1–5)

Stakeholders	Very Little	Very Great
1 →	☐	☐
2 →	☐	☐
3 →	☐	☐
4 →	☐	☐
5 →	☐	☐

Your Key *External* Stakeholders
        3 Years from Now (6–10)

Stakeholders	Very Little	Very Great
6 →	☐	☐
7 →	☐	☐
8 →	☐	☐
9 →	☐	☐
10 →	☐	☐

Tool 6.8. Resources for Involving Key Stakeholders.

Instructions: Using the key stakeholders listed in Tool 1.1, check the appropriate box to indicate the strategies used by your organization for navigating key web relationships.

To what extent does your organization spend time and other resources to involve trustingly each of the following stakeholders in your decision making?

Your Key *Internal* Stakeholders
Now (1–5)

Stakeholders	Very Little	Very Great
1 →	☐	☐
2 →	☐	☐
3 →	☐	☐
4 →	☐	☐
5 →	☐	☐

Your Key *Internal* Stakeholders
3 Years from Now (6–10)

Stakeholders	Very Little	Very Great
6 →	☐	☐
7 →	☐	☐
8 →	☐	☐
9 →	☐	☐
10 →	☐	☐

Your Key *External* Stakeholders
Now (1–5)

Stakeholders	Very Little	Very Great
1 →	☐	☐
2 →	☐	☐
3 →	☐	☐
4 →	☐	☐
5 →	☐	☐

Your Key *External* Stakeholders
3 Years from Now (6–10)

Stakeholders	Very Little	Very Great
6 →	☐	☐
7 →	☐	☐
8 →	☐	☐
9 →	☐	☐
10 →	☐	☐

Tool 6.9. Resources for Defending Your Organization.

Instructions: Using the key stakeholders you have listed in Tool 1.1, check the appropriate box to indicate the strategies used by your organization for navigating key web relationships.

To what extent does your organization spend time and other resources to defend proactively against potentially threatening actions from each of the following stakeholders?

Your Key *Internal* Stakeholders
Now (1–5)

Stakeholders	Very Little	Very Great
1 →	☐	☐
2 →	☐	☐
3 →	☐	☐
4 →	☐	☐
5 →	☐	☐

Your Key *Internal* Stakeholders
3 Years from Now (6–10)

Stakeholders	Very Little	Very Great
6 →	☐	☐
7 →	☐	☐
8 →	☐	☐
9 →	☐	☐
10 →	☐	☐

Your Key *External* Stakeholders
Now (1–5)

Stakeholders	Very Little	Very Great
1 →	☐	☐
2 →	☐	☐
3 →	☐	☐
4 →	☐	☐
5 →	☐	☐

Your Key *External* Stakeholders
3 Years from Now (6–10)

Stakeholders	Very Little	Very Great
6 →	☐	☐
7 →	☐	☐
8 →	☐	☐
9 →	☐	☐
10 →	☐	☐

Tool 6.10. Identify Suboptimal "Fits" of Diagnoses and Tactics (Internal Stakeholders).

Instructions: Are your key stakeholders putting your organization at risk, missing opportunities, and/or wasting resources on low-priority relationships? If so, check the box that indicates the "fit" of your stakeholders and your organization.

Your Key
Internal **Stakeholders**
Now (1–5)

Have suboptimal "fits" led to one of the following:

Stakeholders	Putting the organization at risk?	Missing opportunities?	Wasting resources on low-priority relationships?
1 →	☐	☐	☐
2 →	☐	☐	☐
3 →	☐	☐	☐
4 →	☐	☐	☐
5 →	☐	☐	☐

Your Key
Internal **Stakeholders**
3 Years from Now (6–10)

Stakeholders	Putting the organization at risk?	Missing opportunities?	Wasting resources on low-priority relationships?
6 →	☐	☐	☐
7 →	☐	☐	☐
8 →	☐	☐	☐
9 →	☐	☐	☐
10 →	☐	☐	☐

Tool 6.11. Identify Suboptimal "Fits" of Diagnoses and Tactics (External Stakeholders).

Instructions: Are your key stakeholders putting your organization at risk, missing opportunities, and/or wasting resources on low-priority relationships? If so check the box that indicates the "fit" of your stakeholders and your organization.

Your Key
External **Stakeholders**
Now (1–5)

Have suboptimal "fits" led to one of the following:

Stakeholders	Putting the organization at risk?	Missing opportunities?	Wasting resources on low-priority relationships?
1 →	☐	☐	☐
2 →	☐	☐	☐
3 →	☐	☐	☐
4 →	☐	☐	☐
5 →	☐	☐	☐

Your Key
External **Stakeholders**
3 Years from Now (6–10)

Stakeholders	Putting the organization at risk?	Missing opportunities?	Wasting resources on low-priority relationships?
6 →	☐	☐	☐
7 →	☐	☐	☐
8 →	☐	☐	☐
9 →	☐	☐	☐
10 →	☐	☐	☐

CHAPTER SEVEN

LINKING YOUR ORGANIZATIONAL WEB

*Horizontal Integration
Among Physicians*

Leaders attempting to take strategic and web navigation actions confront the increasingly difficult questions of which medical group partner or partners to take sides with, whether to take sides at all, or whether to go it alone. Strategic thinking and web navigation action on these types of interorganizational relationships among physician organizations will be crucial to the success—and most probably the survival—of medical groups over the next five years.

In this chapter, we continue to flesh out the concept of the strategic web and to look in detail at the group's internal relationships—its own organizational web. We will examine the new realities that result from the attempted linking of physicians and physician organizations that is resulting from the wide range of strategic alliances, joint ownerships, and acquisitions of medical practices and medical groups. Specifically, we will introduce and discuss in detail what we call the composite medical group.

Here we focus on physician integration as a type of horizontal integration of similar organizational entities, that is, medical practices and medical groups. In the next chapter, we will look at vertical integration, that is, bringing different organizational entities together in a way that increasingly ties together the "production process" of healthcare—that links outpatient care in medical practices, inpatient care in hospitals, and managed care organizations as key buyers and payors.

In the present chapter, we examine physician horizontal integration by looking at which interorganizational relationships with other medical groups our responding medical groups were pursuing in the past and what they will do in the future. We put these relationships in the context of the core set of internal relationships within a composite medical group using our case study of the System Medical Group (SMG) in Integrating System A.

Also in this chapter, we develop a new typology of physician integration based on whether the "integrated" interorganizational relationships are tightly or loosely linked or "coupled," as described by Karl Weick (1982). Tight linkages (coupling) lead to more effective coordination and control but leave organizations vulnerable to inflexibility and high bureaucratic overhead. Loose linkages or coupling have the opposite outcomes.

We call these types of physician integration Physician Non-Integration, Virtual Physician Integration, Acquired Physician Integration, and Mixed Physician Integration. We report on the exact nature of these types of physician integration and then report the relative prevalence of each in the past and the future.

THE ORGANIZATIONAL WEB AND ITS CHALLENGES

Extensive horizontal integration among physicians is occurring (Coddington, Moore, and Fischer, 1996). In our example, SMG is now a large, multispecialty medical group that is part of an emerging integrated system. Nevertheless, SMG is made up of many small, formerly independent, primary and specialty care medical groups, as well as loosely integrated aggregates of individual primary care physicians and specialists.

We discussed the evolving strategic web in Chapter One and discussed our longitudinal case study of Integrating System A. Figure 7.1 shows the portion of the overall strategic web that focuses on the organizational web for the medical group that is part of that integrating system. We refer to this group as the System Medical Group (or SMG), and it is shown linked to the lower right corner of the triangle representing System A's key organizational components. We have designated this relatively new but increasingly common form of organization a *composite medical group*.

With capital borrowed from System A, SMG was constructed primarily out of four small or medium-size medical groups that were the strategic partners with the hospital and its emerging system mentioned earlier. They were Multispecialty Group A, Primary Care Group C, Surgical Group D, and Regional Primary Care Group F. These practices were acquired, and the physicians became employees of SMG, which was set up as a 501(a) foundation.

Aggregates of similar physicians who were solo practitioners or were in two- or three-person partnerships were also brought into the group. They are shown in Figure 7.1 as the Pediatricians and the OB/GYNs, together with other solo Primary Care Physicians (PCPs) or Specialist Physicians (SPPs). The group had between seventy-five and one hundred physicians at the time of the study.

Figure 7.1. The System Medical Group's Organizational Web (A Composite Medical Group Created Through Practice Acquisition by Integrating System A).

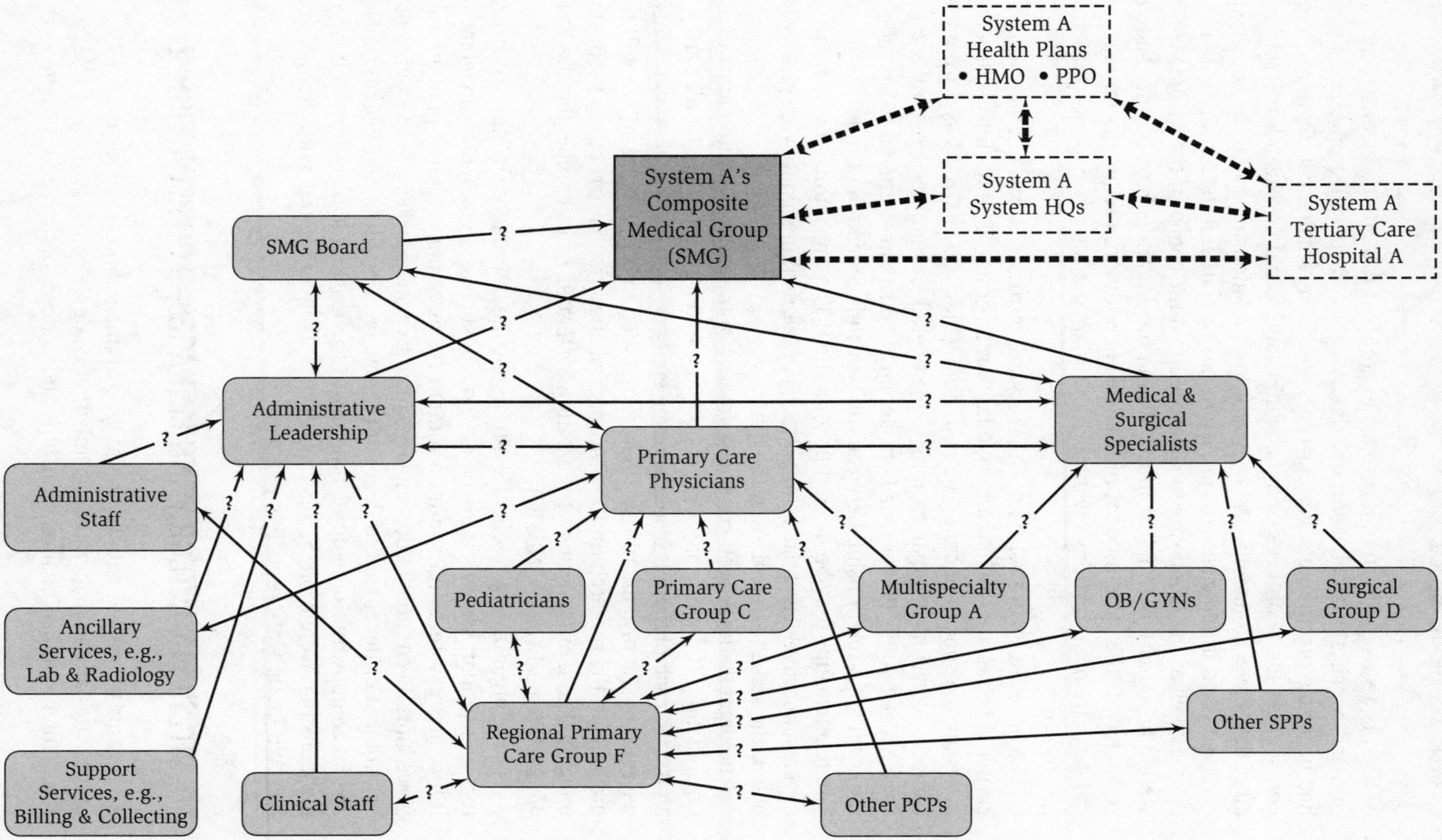

SMG is a specific form of a composite group. It is a 501(a) medical foundation and consists of a collection of primary care and specialist physicians who
had been solo practitioners, various types of existing small medical groups, support services for all of these, and the administrative and physician leadership for
all of the above, along with SMG's board. Each relationship had to be managed.

The dashed triangle shows the system health plan and the tertiary care hospital, as well as the composite medical group. In the center of the triangle is the
system headquarters. Implicit in the system headquarters box, but not shown
separately, is the system board of trustees. In addition, the boards for each of
the separate organizations (system health plan and tertiary care hospital) are
not shown.

The boxes in Figure 7.1 have either square or rounded corners. The square-
cornered boxes are the overall organization or group. The rounded-cornered
boxes are the subcomponent groups of each. One-headed arrows lead from the
component groups or organizations to the overall stakeholder group or organization. The two-headed arrows between any two square-cornered boxes reflect
the reality of a relationship between the two and some kind of mutual impact.
The relationships may be desired or undesired. The impact may be supportive
or nonsupportive. The relative importance of the relationship may be greater to
one of the stakeholders than to the other.

The organizational web consists primarily of the internal components of an
organization. If a medical group, a hospital, and a health plan are all parts of
an IDS/N, each of them is also a separate entity or strategic business unit. When
we refer to the organizational operational web in our examples, we will be
drawing on the research on the SMG organization that is part of the vertically
integrated core of the system (Integrating System A) or its competitor, the Network B Medical Group (NBMG).

For the organization to operate effectively, the internal organizational structure and support systems must be developed, such as a common management
information system and common human resource management policies and
procedures. Even more important, administrative and physician leadership must
be acquired or developed to deal with a new level of administrative and managerial complexity that is foreign to any of the existing leaders from the organizations that were brought together; each is likely to see the world from his or
her own group's or specialty's perspective.

PHYSICIAN INTEGRATING LINKAGES—LOOSE OR TIGHT?

An organization's ultimate level and type of integration is the result of a series
of activities and managerial decisions that coalesce into a pattern of relationships. Interorganizational relationships and, indeed, organizations themselves,

can be formed or designed in many ways. A major characteristic of all those relationships and organizational designs is whether the pieces are loosely or
tightly linked or coupled (Weick, 1982).

Loose linkages result in flexibility, decentralization of authority, and autonomy among individual units or partners. Tight linkages provide for centralization of decision making and for control and coordination among multiple units
or partners. Integration in healthcare is made up of a mixture of these relationships, with inherently tighter or looser linking.

In our study, the responding medical groups reported their own organizations as

- Being part of an informal strategic alliance with a medical group—
  changing from 30 percent in the past to 25 percent in the future.

- Being part of a formal strategic alliance with a medical group—from 23
  percent to 59 percent.

- Being part of a multiprovider system made up of similar kinds of
  organizations—from 24 percent to 49 percent.

- Jointly owning facilities or other organizations with a medical group—
  from 11 percent to 31 percent.

- Having acquired medical practices or a medical group—from 37 percent
  to 49 percent.

- Having been acquired by a medical group—from 1 percent to 6 percent.

Effective physician leadership remains a key to success both in horizontal relationships among physician organizations and in vertical integration of medical
groups with hospitals, MCOs, and IDS/Ns themselves. The groups we surveyed
reported optimistically that being part of a system with strong physician leadership, as exemplified by significant physician economic linkages, control over use
of services, and involvement in governance groups, will change from 45 percent
in the past to 72 percent in the future.

Types of Physician Horizontal Integration

First, we divided our respondent groups into whether or not they had formal
strategic alliances with other medical groups, that is, had loosely linked relationships with other physician groups. Then, we looked at whether or not they were
acquiring medical practices or medical groups, that is, had tightly linked physician groups. This typology allowed us to classify each organization's physician
integration as one of four types: Physician Non-Integration (having neither loosely
linked strategic alliances with nor tightly linked acquisition of other groups), Virtual Physician Integration (participating only in formal strategic alliances without

acquiring medical practices or groups), Common Ownership Physician Integration (acquiring medical practices or medical groups without any formal strategic alliances), and Dual Physician Integration (having both loosely linked and tightly linked relationships with other medical groups).

Figure 7.2 also indicates the percentage of our respondents' organizations who are in each of the four cells in the past and in the future. In the past, Non-Integration was the dominant type of physician integration, representing 53 percent of the organizations. Acquired Integration was the second most prevalent type of physician integration in the past, with a distant 24 percent. Although together they represented nearly one-fourth of all groups, the least prevalent types of physician integration in the past were Mixed Integration (13 percent) and Virtual Integration (10 percent).

However, our respondents expect some significant shift in the future. Non-Integration is expected to decline in half from 53 to 26 percent. Mixed Integration and Virtual Integration, which incorporate the use of formal strategic alliances, are the major beneficiaries of the shift away from Non-Integration and from an exclusive reliance on acquisition. Mixed Integration increases from 13 to 35 percent of the organizations. Virtual Integration is expected to increase from 10 to 24 percent. Acquired Integration declines from 24 to 15 percent. As a result of these shifts, the Mixed and Virtual types of physician integration will be the most prevalent in the future.

Figure 7.2. Evolving Types of Physician Horizontal Integration.

Does Your Medical Group Have Formal
Strategic Alliances with Other Medical Groups?

	Yes	No
Has (or Will) Your Medical Group Acquired Medical Practices with Other Medical Groups? Yes	**Hybrid Physician Integration** *Past:* 13% **Future:* 35%	**Common-Ownership Physician Integration** Past: 24% Future: 15%
No	**Virtual Physician Integration** Past: 10% Future: 24%	**Physician Non-Integration** Past: 53% Future: 26%

*Percent of organizations fitting each type in the past

**Percent of organizations expected to fit each type in the future

Physician Non-Integration

Physician Non-Integration means having neither loosely linked nor tightly linked relationships with other groups. Non-Integration includes medical groups that participate only in informal strategic alliances without the formality that gives some meaningful structure that will permit virtual organizations to operate. Such medical groups either see these loose relationships as adequate, are unwilling to sacrifice their autonomy further, or are not seen by others as highly attractive formal partners. They know they might not be always dealing with bad guys, but they are basically pessimistic about what they can do together. The mirror image of the web optimist, they have little regard for the positive side of the relationship. They believe that almost all relationships are risk-laden.

These groups' leaders appear unwilling or unable to think systematically about the threat and cooperation potentials inherent in the web relationships surrounding them and, therefore, cannot establish a pattern of priorities to reduce those threats or to enhance cooperative potential in the relationships.

Virtual Physician Integration

Virtual Physician Integration medical groups have formal strategic alliances without actually acquiring other medical practices or groups. They focus primarily on creating loose linkages with other physician organizations. Even though they know they might not be always dealing with good guys, they are optimistic about what they can do together, with little regard for the dark side of the relationship. They believe that almost every relationship can be made into a win-win for both parties.

These organizations certainly do not miss opportunities that others might, but they can put their medical groups at risk through ignoring or downplaying the implications, for example, of growing dependence on their partners and having limited control, as would be true if they had been acquired by those partners.

For example, their partners can be acquired by other medical groups for horizontal integration or by hospitals or insurance companies for vertical integration. Less extremely, their partners can form other formal or informal alliances with the group's competitors or terminate the agreement when the formal contract runs out.

Growing dependence can leave a group highly vulnerable strategically. At the same time, the groups forming virtual integration with other medical groups maintain considerable strategic flexibility and do not incur the fiscal burdens and risks of acquisitions.

Common Ownership Physician Integration

Acquired Physician Integration medical groups have not relied on formal strategic alliances but have instead acquired other medical practices or groups. They focus primarily on creating tight linkages with other physician organizations.

By acquiring their potential partners, these organizations avoid the danger of putting their medical groups at risk of growing dependence on strategic alliances partners while only having limited control. This form of integration is the mirror image of virtual integration, and the advantages and disadvantages are opposite.

Although these groups do not have growing dependence on partners not under their control, they do not have the same strategic flexibility as those groups forming virtual integration with other medical groups through formal alliances. Acquired Integration groups may be also highly vulnerable strategically. They not only incur the fiscal burdens and risks of acquisitions, but they may not be able to successfully move from the on-paper integration written up by lawyers to the reality of a well-governed, cost-effective, and (least likely) synergistic physician organization.

Dual Physician Integration

Medical groups whose type of physician integration is "hybrid" have both loosely linked and tightly linked relationships with other medical groups. Does this mean they are unwilling to recognize that there are both good guys and bad guys in the world? No, it does not. It reflects the most sophisticated view of the emerging world of web relationships: most relationships will have both opportunities and threats in them. The advantage of hybrid integration is that it attempts to balance the control found in acquisition with the flexibility inherent in loose linkages through alliances.

FROM INDEPENDENCE TO A MIX OF TYPES OF INTERDEPENDENCE

We have looked at the overall patterns of change in types of physician integration. But that leaves unclear which organizations changed and where they went, if they left. Here, we will examine all of the medical groups reporting non-integration in the past and see what percentage of them stayed, as well as what percentages went where.

Less than half (22 percent) of the 53 percent of organizations with prior non-integration expected to remain that way in the future. Of the other organizations that were at the lowest level of interorganizational linkage in the past, 16 percent expected to have Virtual Physician Integration, only 4 percent to move to acquired physician integration, and 11 percent to Mixed Integration in the future.

Mixed Physician Integration is of particular interest here because of its unique combination of both loose and tight linkage. One might ask whether this kind of integration is

- Merely a transitional way-station until more formally integrated linkages are created that have the appropriate management information systems and organizational and governance structures.

- The ultimate hybrid organization of the future that combines the strengths of both loose and tight linkages, providing adequate control and coordination without loosing strategic and operational flexibility.

Our data seem to indicate that medical group executives do not see it as a transitional type of integration for their own organizations. If our responding organizations are correct, a large number of medical groups may attempt to create the sophisticated physician organizations that, in fact, combine the two types of linkage to balance control with flexibility. For example, the competing network's composite medical group called Network B Medical Group (NBMG) followed just this approach.

NBMG was the primary medical group competitor of SMG. NBMG used acquisition only to form the core of the new group. All acquisitions were of primary care physician practices and small groups both in the urban area and, perhaps most important, throughout the vast rural region surrounding the urban center. This acquisition of primary care physicians was done to provide a tightly linked core for managed care contracting that would operate under centralized control through a common governance structure and linked information systems.

However, NBMG did not leave relationships with key specialists to traditional referral relationships nor informal strategic alliances. Instead, they created a virtual multispecialty medical group by establishing formal alliances with key specialist groups that would then coordinate all care within their specialty area. Medical directors were appointed and fees paid to those medical groups to play that role from NBMG with the corresponding feeding of covered lives by NBMG's primary care physicians to these loosely linked partners. They, in turn, became the gatekeepers for those type of specialists throughout the region. In the future, these linked groups will control the specialty capitation dollars from Network B through their formal alliances with NBMG, which will control the primary care dollars and serve as the gatekeepers for the network's covered lives generated by its joint ownership in the growing network-specific HMO.

Of course, trying to manage and lead an organization with both loose and tight linkages that are crucial to its success represents a significant management challenge. Relationships that were traditionally external are now basically internal—but without a common hierarchy and chain of command. In addition, the web navigation skills needed to manage that type of loosely linked interdependence are not necessarily the same as those needed by a traditional chief operating officer or groupwide medical director within a physician organization with common ownership.

INTERDEPENDENCE WITHIN THE ORGANIZATIONAL WEB

SMG represents an increasingly typical medical group within the evolving strategic web for the medical group industry. Composite medical groups, such as the one shown in Figure 7.1, are constructed of several small existing medical groups, some limited partnerships, and a large number of solo practitioners. The strategic impetus—and the capital—may well come *not* from the physician owners of the original practices but from local, regional, or national hospitals, hospital systems, insurance companies, large existing medical groups, or integrating health systems.

In Figure 7.3, we present a more analytical look within any horizontally integrating medical group. This figure is based on a medical group built through acquisition. That is, it represents what is now a single organization that is attempting to integrate the acquired practices. This acquisition could have been accomplished nearly overnight, as in some composite medical groups, or could have occurred over a long period of time.

Figure 7.3 is, nevertheless, a highly simplified model of the complex set of relationships involved. It graphically focuses on some of the complex array of horizontal and vertical relationships within the system physician organization that can have an effect on an organization. This complexity would be even greater if the group were a composite built from an aggregate of organizations (including individual medical practices) that were not part of the same organization before.

This simplified model reminds us, first, that there is a set of overall formal leaders, made up of administrators and physicians, who are responsible for the group as a whole. The dominant role of physician leaders in medical groups—as physician-driven organizations—creates an important difference from most other healthcare organizations.

Second, we distinguish those leaders from the ones at the operating unit level. In an academic medical center, those units would probably be departments. In other multispecialty groups, they could be organized either by geography or services offered (for example, whoever is in a family healthcare clinic with family practitioners, pediatricians, and obstetricians) or organized by specialty (for example, pediatricians, or general surgeons.)

Third, we look at the physicians themselves as separate from the organizational hierarchy. As autonomy-oriented professionals, their desired and their actual role in decision making is a potential source of organizational web challenges within each specialty area, as well as between and among specialties.

Key Vertical and Horizontal Interdependent Relationships

Shown in Figure 7.3 are the four key vertical and horizontal relationships we outline later in this section:

Figure 7.3. Interdependence in Key Vertical and Horizontal Relationships Within the Horizontally Integrating Medical Group.

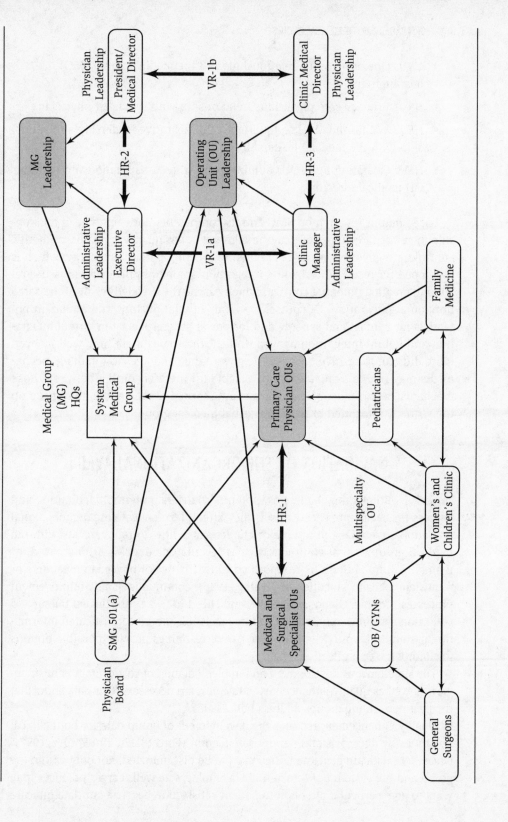

- *VR-1:* Operating unit's relationship with the medical group (MG) headquarters

- *HR-1:* Primary care physicians' relationship with specialist physicians

- *HR-2:* Within the MG headquarters, administrative leadership's relationship with the medical leadership

- *HR-3:* Operating unit (OU) administrative director's relationship with the OU medical director

Based on our research on SMG and its competitors, for each type of relationship there are three types of issues to address: issues related to relative authority, control, and governance; issues related to creating potential synergy, which is the hoped-for result of horizontal integration among physicians; and issues related to creating potential conflict, which can be the dreaded result of the same horizontal integration. Of course, the kinds of relationships and attendant potentials for conflict and synergy and for power struggles exist in virtual integration and hybrid integration as well. In fact, the issues there may well be even more difficult to resolve because the governance and decision-making mechanisms may not be available or not accepted if there is conflict between those mechanisms and those within the separate formal organizations that make up the virtually integrated or partially virtual medical group.

NAVIGATION OF THE ORGANIZATIONAL WEB

Table 7.1 outlines the challenges, potential barriers, potential facilitators, and choices for healthcare executives as they attempt to navigate the organizational operational web. One of the major challenges is how to reduce costs with the medical group so that contracts with MCOs may be developed, increased, or maintained. In addition to group purchasing, the use of physician extenders or multiskilled health practitioners (Fottler, 1996), continuous quality improvement processes (Counte, Glandon, Olescke, and Hill, 1992), a sophisticated billing and collection system to minimize accounts receivable, and a sophisticated information system to identify the excessive use of resources provide possible options for improving cost-effectiveness.

The simultaneous development and implementation of cost-containment strategies, as well as quality-enhancement strategies, are necessary. Our data show that the best-performing groups address both issues.

Quality enhancement requires the development of group data for both clinical outcomes by diagnosis and patient satisfaction (Ford, Bach, and Fottler, 1997). Once these data are generated, they need to be disseminated, not only within the group and the system but to external stakeholders as well. Larger practices may want to give particular attention to patient satisfaction because our data indicate

Table 7.1. The Organizational Web: Challenges, Barriers, Facilitators, and Choices Confronting Healthcare Executives As They Navigate This Web.

Challenges	Potential Barriers	Potential Facilitators	Choices
1. How to reduce group costs	1. Individual practitioner culture	1. Common and sophisticated information system	1. Selection of strategic priorities for group
2. How to enhance group income	2. Inadequate collection system	2. Sophisticated billing and collection system	2. Resource allocation decisions within group
3. How to align group and individual physician incentives	3. Power shifts from specialists to primary care physicians	3. More sophisticated group managers	3. Selection of cost-containment and quality-enhancing strategies
4. How to increase group patient satisfaction	4. Individual measures and reviews	4. MCO patient "steering" to group	4. Structuring or restructuring of the group
5. How to assure group quality of patient	5. Lack of differentiation vis-à-vis competitors	5. System volume discounts on purchases	5. Centralization vs. decentralization of authority and control
6. How to reduce conflict and enhance group cooperation in the group	6. Lack of adequate information systems	6. Effective physician leadership to integrate clinical and managerial systems	6. Selection of group executives to manage internal and external stakeholders
7. How to enhance operational synergy of group components	7. Different perspectives concerning the desirability of different types of change	7. Determination of how much integrative interstructure (such as information systems) to create	
8. Lack of integration of different types of physicians	8. Determination of how much to compete with other practices within the system		
9. Selection of key stakeholders related to achieving strategic priorities			
10. Selection of generic management strategies and specific tactics for each stakeholder			

this as the area where their performance is inferior to that of their smaller counterparts. Perhaps their interactions with patients are more impersonal.

It is important for all medical groups to develop strategic priorities and then to manage in a way that is consistent with these priorities. This means their resource allocation decisions and their selection and management of key stakeholders have to be consistent with their strategic priorities. For example, it would make no sense for a group to develop a strategic priority to enhance group income through capitated managed care contracts and then fail to assign this activity to anyone.

It is also important that the management of key stakeholder relationships be consistent from one part of the organization to another. For example, the credentialing of physicians should not vary within the system. There should also be a fit between the medical group's diagnosis of a particular web relationship and the generic tactic and specific actions used to manage those relations. For example, operating unit stakeholders who are part of a supportive relationship with the medical group headquarters should be trustingly involved in the group's decision making.

The structuring of the medical group and centralization or decentralization are related but distinct concepts. The structuring has to do with the linkages that are developed. In Figure 7.1, the composite medical group has internal linkages with a variety of formerly separate and autonomous medical groups, as well as with physicians who were in solo practice. The apex of this organizational structure is the medical group headquarters and the board.

The structure could exist with tight coupling and centralization of authority and control at the top or with loose coupling and decentralization of power and control within the medical group itself. Given how little is known about structuring the ideal healthcare organization and the lack of evidence that daily operational decisions can be effectively centralized, it makes sense to decentralize most decisions with the exception of major capital expenditures.

The selection and development of executives for medical groups is a crucial decision. As noted in our data, this was a particular problem in the academic practices and the smaller practices. Some people argue that many medical practice executives are not as "professionalized" in educational credentials as those in hospitals where a specialized master's degree in education has been expected for a generation.

New administrative and physician executives could be recruited from M.S.H.A. programs or M.B.A. programs, whereas existing executives could have their skills upgraded through executive degree programs and short courses. The focus of all of these programs for executives at the operational level should be on internal operations and managing the immediate relationships within the organizational web as noted in Figure 7.3.

The determination of how much integrative infrastructure to create will probably be made at the MG level with input from lower levels in the organization, including the OUs. An example of the this type of decision would be a large investment in information systems to provide an electronic patient medical record that would be accessible at all points in the group's array of urban and regional clinics. Another example would be a decision to employ one or more case managers or case coordinators. The purpose would be to link the various subparts of the organization, better coordinate services, and improve the quality of care for the patient.

LEADERSHIP IMPLICATIONS

Medical groups will be in the process of undergoing major organizational changes in their degree of autonomy. For example, 78 percent of responding organizations described themselves as a free-standing business in the past, but only 38 percent expect to be so in the future. With medical groups losing autonomy, what are they gaining as they become part of these new organizational forms?

This movement away from free-standing businesses and toward horizontal and vertical memberships illustrates the tremendous changes occurring within the medical group industry. Whole organizational forms such as solo practices are disappearing. New organizational forms such as composite medical groups are evolving to conduct business in ways foreign to many existing healthcare executives. These new organizational forms facing medical group executives in the future will require new and more sophisticated managerial tools to manage intraorganization relationships in order to ensure profitability and survival.

Web navigation, the subject of Chapter Six, is designed to help executives better manage specific organizational relationships, including individuals, groups, and organizations that have a stake in the decisions of the organization. Each horizontally integrated medical group must assess its emerging organizational web in order to effectively develop arrangements and manage relationships that are mutually beneficial. As the medical group industry evolves into one in which larger, horizontally integrated medical groups replace the independent practitioner, how will individual physicians participate in these horizontally integrated groups and alliances, and what role can they expect to play? Which kind of organization will likely become the most powerful competitively—large, tightly linked medical groups, virtual medical groups, a mixture, or even small, stand-alone, single-specialty groups? Perhaps the more hierarchical nature of large, tightly linked medical groups (compared to the less complex, small medical group or a loosely linked virtual organization) means that those executives will have more relevant managerial capability in managing the day-to-day and the strategic issues encountered in the overall changing strategic web of medical groups. Will these large, tightly linked, horizontally integrated emergent forms of medical groups have too complex a set of internal relationships? Will that complexity render the groups incapable of creating synergy? Or will they simply have increased costs resulting from acquisition debt and the additional layers of management needed to coordinate more complex organizational forms?

Although the outlook for medical groups is not altogether optimistic, it is not completely pessimistic either. This new era of horizontal integration presents both risks and opportunities. However, survival of the medical group depends on the ability of its executives to learn how to effectively manage these new and emerging relationships within their organizational web, as well as in the rest of their strategic web.

By moving aggressively and wisely and by using appropriate strategic and web navigation priorities and tactics, an executive can ensure survival and possibly growth for the medical group. One approach to managing the internal organizational web is through the creation of mutually beneficial interdependencies or arrangements, ranging from limited formal strategic alliances to acquisitions that create different forms of integration such as those we have discussed here.

The implications for medical group leaders are summarized in seven key leadership challenges: how to reduce the horizontally integrated medical group's costs, enhance the group's income, align group and individual physician incentives, increase satisfaction of the group's patients, manage internal conflict and enhance internal cooperation, ensure quality of patient care, and enhance operational synergy.

STEPS FOR NAVIGATING YOUR ORGANIZATIONAL WEB

To effectively navigate your organizational web, we recommend the following steps, supported by Toolkit 7:

- Assess your group's horizontal physician linkages in terms of how loose or tight each one is and how they are likely to change in the next three years.

- Determine your group's current physician integration type and whether it will likely change in the next three years. Use Tool 7.1.

- Identify the key vertical and horizontal interdependent relationships within your organizational web (see Figure 7.1) using Tool 7.2. At a minimum, the following should be addressed:

    VR–1: Operating unit's relationship with the medical group (MG) headquarters

    HR–1: Primary care physicians' relationship with specialist physicians

    HR–2: Within the MG headquarters, administrative leadership's relationship with the medical leadership

    HR–3: Operating unit (OU) administrative director's relationship with the OU medical director

- Using Tool 7.4 or 7.3, develop lists of challenges, potential barriers, potential facilitators, and choices facing your group's executive leadership team. In your analysis, parallel the general challenges, barriers, facilitators, and choices reported in Table 7.1 using Tool 7.3. In order to meet *each* of your group's organizational web challenges, there are ten key leadership actions to be taken. In turn, each of these actions should be addressed in two time frames—*what to do immediately* and *what over the next three years.* Use Tool 7.4 to help you formulate the specific actions you will recommend for your group in meeting key challenges.

- Design and build the specific administrative infrastructure you will recommend for your group to provide the optimal balance of control through tight linkages (for example, common ownership) and flexibility through loose linkages (for example, virtual organizations) that will ensure that your group can effectively navigate its organizational web.

TOOLKIT 7

Navigating Your Group's Organizational Web

Tool 7.1. Overall Type of Physician Horizontal Integration.

Instructions: Based on Figure 7.2, what kind of horizontal integration does your group have? Does your group have a formal strategic alliance, indicating a loosely linked relationship? Is your group acquiring a medical practice or medical group's strategy, indicating a tightly linked relationship? Assess your group's horizontal physician linkages in terms of how loose or tight each one is and how likely they are to change in the next three years.

Your organization:

Now	3 Years from Now	Physician Integration
☐	☐	1. *Physician Non-Integration*—Having neither loosely linked strategic alliances with nor tightly linked acquisitions of other groups
☐	☐	2. *VIrtual Physician Integration*—Participating only in formal strategic alliances without acquiring medical practices or groups
☐	☐	3. *Common Ownership Physician Integration*—Acquiring medical practices or medical groups without any formal strategic alliances
☐	☐	4. *Hybrid Physician Integration*—Having both loosely linked and tightly linked relationships with other medical groups

Tool 7.2. Key Vertical and Horizontal Interdependent Relationships.

Instructions: Identify the key horizontal and vertical relationships within your organizational web and the issues that result from them. The interdependence among the different subgroups within your organization is important for your medical group to recognize. Use Figure 7.3 as a reference for this tool.

VR-1: Medical group operating unit's relationship with the medical group headquarters

Relative Authority and Control
Challenges/Opportunities
1._____
2._____
3._____
4._____
5._____

Potential Synergy
Challenges/Opportunities
1._____
2._____
3._____
4._____
5._____

Potential Conflict
Challenges/Opportunities
1._____
2._____
3._____
4._____
5._____

HR-1: Primary care physicians' relationship with specialist physicians

Governance
Challenges/Opportunities
1._____
2._____
3._____
4._____
5._____

Potential Synergy
Challenges/Opportunities
1._____
2._____
3._____
4._____
5._____

Potential Conflict
Challenges/Opportunities
1._____
2._____
3._____
4._____
5._____

HR-2: Within the medical group headquarters, administrative leadership's relationship with the medical leadership

Relative Authority and Control
Challenges/Opportunities
1._____
2._____
3._____
4._____
5._____

Potential Synergy
Challenges/Opportunities
1._____
2._____
3._____
4._____
5._____

Potential Conflict
Challenges/Opportunities
1._____
2._____
3._____
4._____
5._____

HR-3: Operating unit (OU) administrative director's relationship with the OU medical director

Relative Authority and Control
Challenges/Opportunities
1._____
2._____
3._____
4._____
5._____

Potential Synergy
Challenges/Opportunities
1._____
2._____
3._____
4._____
5._____

Potential Conflict
Challenges/Opportunities
1._____
2._____
3._____
4._____
5._____

Tool 7.3. Organizational Web Challenges, Barriers, Facilitators, and Choices.

Instructions: Parallel the general challenges, barriers, facilitators, and choices reported in Table 7.1 with those that apply specifically to medical groups.

Specific Challenges	Barriers
1.＿＿＿＿＿＿＿＿＿＿＿＿	1.＿＿＿＿＿＿＿＿＿＿＿＿
2.＿＿＿＿＿＿＿＿＿＿＿＿	2.＿＿＿＿＿＿＿＿＿＿＿＿
3.＿＿＿＿＿＿＿＿＿＿＿＿	3.＿＿＿＿＿＿＿＿＿＿＿＿
4.＿＿＿＿＿＿＿＿＿＿＿＿	4.＿＿＿＿＿＿＿＿＿＿＿＿
5.＿＿＿＿＿＿＿＿＿＿＿＿	5.＿＿＿＿＿＿＿＿＿＿＿＿

Facilitators	Choices
1.＿＿＿＿＿＿＿＿＿＿＿＿	1.＿＿＿＿＿＿＿＿＿＿＿＿
2.＿＿＿＿＿＿＿＿＿＿＿＿	2.＿＿＿＿＿＿＿＿＿＿＿＿
3.＿＿＿＿＿＿＿＿＿＿＿＿	3.＿＿＿＿＿＿＿＿＿＿＿＿
4.＿＿＿＿＿＿＿＿＿＿＿＿	4.＿＿＿＿＿＿＿＿＿＿＿＿
5.＿＿＿＿＿＿＿＿＿＿＿＿	5.＿＿＿＿＿＿＿＿＿＿＿＿

Tool 7.4. Planning Tool for Implementing Key Needed Actions.

Instructions: Complete this exhibit *for each of the challenges* facing your group in order to plan the implementation of needed actions for each.

Web: Organizational

Challenge: ＿＿＿＿＿＿＿＿＿＿＿＿＿＿＿＿＿＿＿＿＿＿

Your Group's Strategic Navigation and Web Navigation Types (based on your strategic and web navigation priorities from Tools 3.4 and 5.3). Check the most appropriate *now* and *in 3 years.*

Now	In 3 Years	
＿＿	＿＿	Strategic Entrepreneur
＿＿	＿＿	Strategic Engineer
＿＿	＿＿	Strategic Ostrich
＿＿	＿＿	Strategic Navigator

Now	In 3 Years	
＿＿	＿＿	Web Entrepreneur
＿＿	＿＿	Web Engineer
＿＿	＿＿	Web Ostrich
＿＿	＿＿	Web Navigator

Tool 7.4. Planning Tool for Implementing Key Needed Actions, cont'd.

1. What actions do you recommend for your group in meeting this challenge? Be specific!

   Immediately?
   Over the next 3 years?

2. In what ways do your recommended actions support your group's overall strategic intentions and other tactical actions?

   Immediately?
   Over the next 3 years?

3. What is your specific plan for implementing each of the proposed actions?

   Immediately?
   Over the next 3 years?

4. What are the most significant factors that could undermine the implementation process, and how can they be dealt with?

   Immediately?
   Over the next 3 years?

5. What resources will be required for implementation, and are they available?

   Immediately?
   Over the next 3 years?

6. How cost-effective are your recommendations? If they are not cost-effective, what alternative actions can you take?

   Immediately?
   Over the next 3 years?

7. Which physician and/or administrative managers will have the lead role in implementing these particular actions?

   Immediately?
   Over the next 3 years?

8. Do the responsible managers have the necessary abilities and authority to effectively implement these actions? What will you do to improve their abilities and ensure their authority?

   Immediately?
   Over the next 3 years?

9. What other group or system managers or other personnel—as internal stakeholders—should be involved in the implementation process?

   Immediately?
   Over the next 3 years?

10. If the implementation process does not work as planned, what contingency approach will you go to next? Why will it work if this process did not?

    Immediately?
    Over the next 3 years?

CHAPTER EIGHT

ASSESSING YOUR
NETWORK/SYSTEM WEB

Vertical Integration and Its Variants

Much of the emerging healthcare literature champions the development of integrated healthcare networks and systems as *the* fundamental strategy for facing the uncertain future created by healthcare reform. Managers, seeking to position their organizations for optimal strategic responsiveness to a still poorly understood future, have turned to linkages with others who have been competitors or adversaries. Thus, particularly over the past several years, hospitals, physicians, and health plans have been creating the kinds of vertically integrated networks and systems discussed by Fottler and Malvey (1995); Kaluzny and Zuckerman (1995); Blair, Fottler, Paolino, and Rotarius (1995); Coddington, Moore, and Fischer (1996); and Shortell and others (1996).

New relationships are forming among key hospital, physician, and health plan stakeholders. Partnerships among any two of these, as well as potentially powerful integrated healthcare organizations, are being created. In this chapter, we continue to develop the concept of the strategic web and to look in detail at the organization's relationships with the key potential components of any IDS/N: physicians, hospitals, managed care organizations, and the IDS/N itself.

Leaders attempting to take strategic action also confront the increasingly difficult questions of which partner or partners and (increasingly) which integrated network or system to take sides with, whether to take sides at all, or whether to go it alone instead. Strategic thinking and action on these types of interorganizational relationships will be crucial to organizational success over the next five years.

In the present chapter, we examine which interorganizational relationships healthcare organizations were pursuing in the past and which they will pursue in the future. We put these relationships in the context of what the core set of relationships in an integrated system or network are, using our case study of Integrating System A.

In the last chapter, we looked at physician integration as a type of horizontal integration among similar organizations. In this chapter, we will look at vertical integration, as the different parts of the process of healthcare delivery are brought together in a coordinated form. That coordination can result from very tight linkages (for example, common ownership) or through loose linkages that create virtual organizations. Tight linkage leads to more effective coordination and control but leaves organizations vulnerable to inflexibility and high bureaucratic overhead. Loose linkage has the opposite outcomes.

We will identify four new types of medical group integration in terms of the tightness or looseness of their interorganizational relationships and then report the relative prevalence of each in the past and the future. We call these types of integration Non-Integration, Virtual Integration, Full System Integration, and Transitional Integration.

THE NETWORK/SYSTEM WEB AND ITS CHALLENGES

IDS/Ns typically have organization structures that vertically integrate medical group practices, physicians, hospitals, and health plans, such as managed care organizations, in order to provide a coordinated continuum of health services for a defined population. This healthcare organization often is willing to be held clinically and financially accountable for the outcomes and health status of the population served (Shortell and others, 1993). A key principle of IDS/Ns is the alignment of incentives to encourage cooperation rather than adversarial relationships among physicians, hospitals, and health plans (Coddington, Moore, and Fischer, 1994, 1996).

Coddington, Moore, and Fischer (1996) have looked at two key dimensions of the emerging, multiple forms of integrated systems that their case studies demonstrated: *integration among physicians* (horizontal integration such as exists in our case study's composite medical group) and *integration between hospitals and physicians* (partial vertical integration). Integration between physicians and the system, discussed by Shortell and his colleagues (1996), represents still another type of partial vertical integration. These models show the range of possible patterns of relationships that exist or are still emerging in healthcare markets throughout the United States. Both research teams recognized the complexity of integrating the health plan or MCO as the third potential type of integration partner. One question is whether or not prescribed organizational strategy can lead to sustainable competitive advantage. We argue that networks, which are one type of intangible resource, can be developed and may lead to sustainable competitive advantage. We will illustrate how stakeholder relationships among healthcare organizations exist within various types of complex networks. Further, we will show how these networks can lead to competitive advantage.

The analyses and discussions that follow show a common theme emerging regarding the delivery of healthcare services in the United States: the emergence of a relatively new organizational structural form—the integrated delivery system/network (IDS/N). IDS/Ns are complex, multifaceted organizations that are growing in importance in the healthcare industry. The emergence of these multiorganizational forms requires that all healthcare industry organizations—medical group practices, hospitals, payor organizations, suppliers—adapt to the ever-increasing demands placed on them as the industry experiences revolutionary changes.

In addition to extensive horizontal and vertical integration among physicians, integration of managed care organizations is occurring as well (Coddington, Moore, and Fischer, 1996; Shortell and others, 1996). The network/system web consists primarily of the internal organizational components of the integrated system itself. This may include one or more of the following: medical groups, hospitals, health plans, and the central headquarters of the system. Figure 8.1 shows the network/system web, with the organizational web shown on a separate box in the lower right-hand corner. We discussed the overall evolving strategic web in Chapter One and discussed our longitudinal case study of Integrating System A. SMG is now a large, multispecialty medical group that is part of an emerging integrated system.

The lower right-hand portion of the figure shows a box representing the organizational web, which was presented earlier in Figure 7.1. This expansion in Figure 8.1 beyond the traditionally "internal" parts of the organization shown in Figure 7.1, although simplified, shows various components of the broader network/system web that are also now internal to the organization that the medical group is in.

The core of the system is formed around four key components: system headquarters and its board, tertiary care Hospital A and its board, health plans and their boards, and the medical group and its board.

Other key information about System A is as follows. It was started by Hospital A. The system board and executive leadership are all from the hospital board and existing hospital executives. Tertiary Care Hospital A has more than nine hundred beds. Thirty-five rural hospitals and rural health clinics are affiliated with the hospital. Hospital A is a joint owner with several other large hospitals of their own HMO. The HMO has twenty thousand covered lives after eighteen months in operation. The hospital has formed its own PPO. The hospital created a composite system medical group (SMG) of more than seventy-five physicians through practice acquisition. SMG physicians are made up of several small, limited liability partnership groups and solo practitioners. SMG

Figure 8.1. Integrating System A's System Web (A Simplified Model of Owned and Affiliated Components).

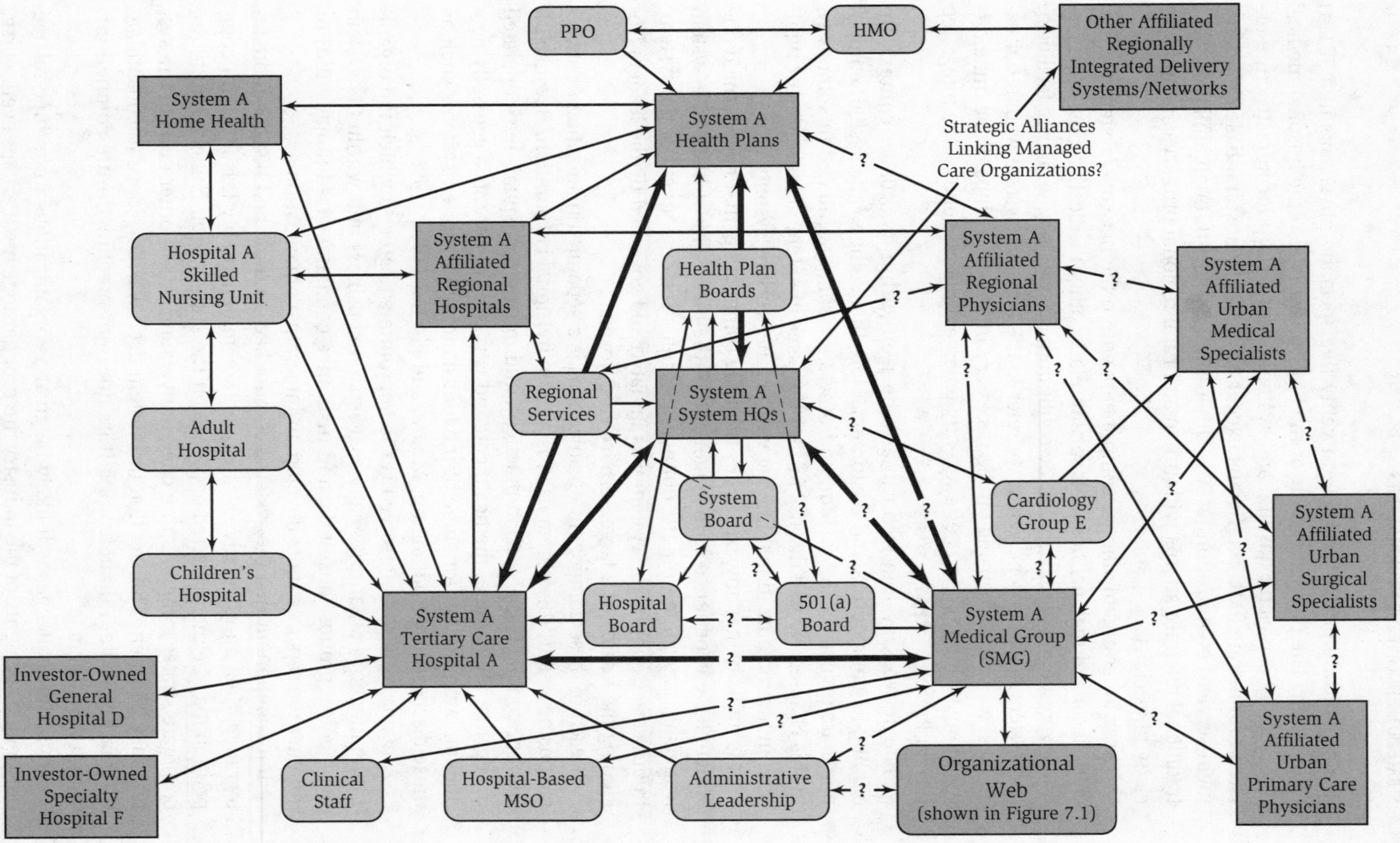

consists of fifty primary care and twenty-five specialty physicians in a 501(a) foundation. The physician chair of the SMG board is also the hospital medical director and serves on hospital and system boards. No prior infrastructure existed to integrate SMG physicians except for a small, hospital-based management services organization (MSO). Other linkages exist through affiliations and traditional referral patterns with urban and rural-regional primary care and specialty physicians.

These other organizational components within the network/system web include local and regional hospitals, health plans, other medical groups, organizations representing other parts of the continuum of care (long-term care facilities), and system headquarters. When we refer to the network/system web in our examples, we will be focusing on the necessary interrelationships of the quite different organizational parts of a recently emergent phenomenon—the integrated system itself.

The network/system web can also be seen within its broader context, including its competitors and customers. Note that some of the system components are owned by the system, and others are simply affiliated in some way. In this chapter, we will discuss further the issue of extent of looseness or tightness in interorganizational linkage within a network or system.

It is unlikely that any executives from the components that have formed one system have experience in managing all of the pieces. Most likely, the system leadership has come from the dominant or initiating component of the system. In our case example, the system was initiated and governed by the leaders (including the board) of a large, tertiary care hospital.

If each of these component organizations is a separate organization or strategic business unit, the system itself is a multidivisional corporation. Because insurance companies, physician practices, and inpatient hospitals have operated in separate segments of the healthcare industry, this represents a generally new phenomenon, except for some of the longstanding integrated systems such as those discussed by Coddington, Moore, and Fischer (1994, 1996).

A major issue to be resolved is the appropriate degree to which the organization functions organizationally as a separate business unit within the system (as medical groups, hospitals, and insurance companies traditionally did) or whether the separate units develop an integrative organization.

If it is important that the system act more like a system and become more integrative, then an integrative strategy with commensurably less interunit competition may be the preferred approach. If the system itself is incidental to the corporate strategy, then a more competitive approach to other units in the system may be taken. The fact that the system itself was developed to consolidate the market and eliminate competitors does not preclude future competition within the system.

Thus, the challenges will likely be great as organizations from three related but unique segments of the industry are brought together. Perhaps even worse, many leaders of each of these types of organizations see the other two types as untrustworthy or even hostile—if not outright enemies. Pressures for integration do, indeed, make for interesting bedfellows.

VERTICAL INTEGRATING LINKAGES—LOOSE OR TIGHT?

As we discussed when we looked at horizontal integration among physicians, loose linkages result in flexibility, decentralization of authority, and autonomy among individual units or partners. Tight linkages provide for centralization of decision making and control, as well as coordination among multiple units or partners. Vertical integration in healthcare is made up of a mixture of these relationships with inherently tighter or looser linking.

To achieve either loose or tight vertical integration, there must be relationships of medical groups with their three potential partners: hospitals, managed care organizations, and the networks/systems themselves. The "Facing the Future" study findings for several types of integrating relationships with each will be presented next, by potential partner. For each partner, the relationships are listed from the loosest to the tightest form.

Medical Groups' Integrating Relationships with Hospitals

In our study, the responding medical groups reported the following changes in their own organizations:

- Being part of an informal strategic alliance with a hospital—from 48 percent in the past to 32 percent in the future
- Being part of a formal strategic alliance with a hospital—from 29 percent to 71 percent
- Jointly owning facilities or other organizations with a hospital—from 17 percent to 34 percent
- Owning an acquired hospital—from 4 percent to 8 percent
- Having been acquired by a hospital—from 6 percent to 11 percent

Medical Groups' Integrating Relationships with Managed Care Organizations

The responding medical groups reported their own organizations as

- Having discounted fee-for-service contracts with managed care organizations—from 92 percent in the past to 68 percent in the future.
- Having capitated contracts with managed care organizations—from 48 percent to 89 percent.
- Owning a managed care organization—from 11 percent to 28 percent.

Medical Groups' Integrating Relationships with Networks and Systems

The respondents indicated their medical group as

- Being part of a multiprovider system made up of different kinds of organizations—from 15 percent in the past to 50 percent in the future.

- Being part of a loosely integrated delivery network made up of medical practices, hospitals, and managed care organizations—from 41 percent to 29 percent.

- Being part of a fully integrated delivery system made up of medical practices, hospitals, and managed care organizations—from 11 percent to 68 percent.

In sum, our respondent executives apparently expect their organizations to develop more formal linkages and affiliations and to become more vertically integrated in the future.

TYPES OF VERTICAL INTEGRATION

We divided our respondents' organizations into whether they were (1) part of a network or system where relationships among the organizations were overall loosely linked or (2) part of a network or system where relationships among the organizations were overall tightly linked or (3) part of neither or (4) part of both.

Figure 8.2 shows the resulting four cells of the types of integration of our respondents' organizations. This typology allows us to assign each organization to one of four integration types: The Transitional Integration organization (participating in both loosely coupled and tightly coupled systems/networks), the Full System Integration organization (participating only in tightly coupled systems/networks), the Virtual System Integration organization (participating only in loosely coupled systems/networks), and the Non-Integration organization (participating in neither loosely coupled nor tightly coupled systems/networks).

Figure 8.2 also indicates the percentage of our respondents' organizations that are in each of the four cells in the past and in the future. In the past, Non-Integration was the dominant type of integration, representing 50 percent of the organizations in our study. Virtual System Integration was the second most prevalent type of integration in the past, with 39 percent. The least prevalent types of integration in the past were Full System Integration (9 percent) and Transitional System Integration (2 percent).

However, our respondents expect some significant shift in the future. First, Non-Integration is expected to decline from 50 to 16 percent. Second, the Full

**Figure 8.2. Evolving Types of Network/System Integration—
Integration of Medical Practices, Hospitals, and Managed Care Organizations.**

Your Medical Group Is Part of a
Loosely Integrated Delivery Network

		Yes	No
Your Medical Group Is Part of a Fully Integrated Delivery System	Yes	**Transitional System Integration** **Past:* 2% ***Future:* 12%	**Full System Integration** *Past:* 9% *Future:* 56%
	No	**Virtual System Integration** *Past:* 39% *Future:* 16%	**System Non-Integration** *Past:* 50% *Future:* 16%

*Percent of organizations fitting each type in the past

**Percent of organizations expected to fit each type in the future

System Integration and (to a lesser degree) Transitional System Integration are the major beneficiaries of the shift away from the Non-Integration category. The Full System Integration type of integration increases from 9 to 56 percent of the organizations. Transitional System Integration increases from 2 to 12 percent. Third, Virtual Integration declines from 39 to 16 percent. As a result of these shifts, the Full System Integration type of integration is predicted to be the most prevalent in the future, followed equally by continued Non-Integration (or, alternatively, lack of integration) and the Virtual Integration form, with Transitional System Integration last.

System Non-Integration

System Non-Integration means having neither loosely linked nor tightly linked relationships with other groups. Non-Integration includes medical groups that see themselves as going it alone or having only dyadic relationships. For example, they may have informal or formal alliances with hospitals but are not part of a broader, vertically integrated network. Such medical groups either see these loose relationships as adequate, are unwilling to sacrifice their autonomy further, or are not seen by emerging networks/systems as highly attractive formal partners.

These groups' leaders may think that independence has been or will be an effective position in the future. Alternatively, they may be unwilling or unable to think systematically about the threat and cooperation potentials inherent in the network/system web relationships surrounding—but not including—them and, therefore, cannot establish a pattern of priorities to reduce threats or to enhance cooperative potential in the relationships.

Virtual System Integration

Virtual System Integration medical groups are part of a loosely integrated delivery network. As with physician integration (discussed in Chapter Seven), these organizations certainly do not miss opportunities that others might, but they can put their medical groups at risk through ignoring or downplaying the implications, for example, of growing dependence on their partners with limited centralized direction and control, as is true in being part of a more fully integrated (tightly linked) system.

Lack of tight linkages among their multiple potential partners can leave these medical groups highly vulnerable strategically. For example, their partners can be acquired by hospitals or insurance companies or more fully integrated systems for vertical integration. At the same time, groups forming virtual vertical integration through loosely integrated networks maintain considerable strategic flexibility and do not incur the fiscal burdens and risks of common ownership-based systems.

Full System Integration

Full System Integration medical groups are part of what they see as a "fully integrated delivery system." They focus primarily on creating tight linkages with hospitals and MCOs.

This form of integration is the mirror image of virtual integration, and the advantages and disadvantages are opposite. Although these groups do not have growing dependence on partners not under their control, they do not have the same strategic flexibility as those groups participating in virtually integrated networks.

Full Integration groups may be highly vulnerable strategically. They not only incur the fiscal burdens and risks of the overhead needed to coordinate and control multiple partners' behavior, but they may not be able to successfully move from paper organizational charts of the new system to the reality of a well-governed, cost-effective and (least likely) synergistic fully integrated system.

Transitional System Integration

Medical groups whose type of system integration is "transitional" have both loosely linked and tightly linked relationships with networks/systems. This could reflect the most sophisticated view of the emerging world of network and system web relationships, because most relationships will have both opportunities and threats in them. However, the medical groups reporting in our study see this type as unstable and simply a transitional form to full, tightly linked system integration. The advantage of mixed integration is that it attempts to balance the control found in acquisition with the flexibility inherent in loose linkages through alliances.

Academic practices were predominantly part of loosely integrated networks in the past and expect to be among the most highly integrated in the future. They are particularly distinct in specific interorganizational relationships in several ways. Together with large (nonacademic) medical groups, they are more likely to own an MCO than either small or medium-size groups. They are most likely to have informal and formal strategic alliances with hospitals. Again, they are like large medical groups in jointly owning facilities with a hospital or in having acquired a hospital, which is much rarer for smaller groups. They are most likely to have informal alliances with medical groups. Academic practices are as likely to have formal medical group alliances or to have joint ownership with a medical group as are nonacademic, large organizations. They have acquired or will acquire medical practices or medical groups about as frequently as medium-size groups but much less so than large organizations.

The size of nonacademic medical groups is highly related to their types of integration in the past and in the future. Smaller groups have been the most independent; they have had the least organizational linkage and will be the lowest in future full integration, although they will, as a whole, become more involved in tightly coupled relationships. Large nonacademic groups have been the most integrated in the past and will be so in the future. Medium-size groups are, of course, in the middle.

The extent of managed care penetration only affected *future* levels of discounted fee-for-service contracts. Current managed care penetration also predicts the belief among those with less managed care now that they will be more likely to be acquired by another medical group in the future.

FROM SOLO INDEPENDENCE
TO SYSTEM INTERDEPENDENCE

In Figure 8.2 we show the overall patterns of change in types of integration. But that leaves it unclear which organizations changed and where they went, if they left. Here, we will look at all of the organizations in the Non-Integration type in the past and see what percentage of them stayed, as well as which percentages went where. Those organizations at the lowest level of interorganizational linkage—Non-Integration—in the past expected to be part of Full System Integration (38 percent), Virtual System Integration (25 percent), and Transitional System Integration (12 percent) in the future. One-quarter of organizations with prior Non-Integration expected to continue in Non-Integration in the future.

Thus, there is *both* stability and change in the types and levels of integration (linkage) in our responding organizations. The majority of those currently not integrated will move to higher levels of loose or tight linkages. Apparently, our respondents believe that being more fully integrated, primarily through tight linkages, will be more effective than either independence or loose linkage in the future.

As with Mixed Dual Integration in Chapter Seven, Transitional System Integration is of particular interest here because of its unique combination of both loose and tight linkages.

It is clear from our data that what we term Transitional System Integration is, in fact, merely a transitional way-station until integrating systems are truly fully integrated with the appropriate management information systems and organizational and governance structures.

In contrast to what we found with physician horizontal integration, at the system level this mix of tight and loose linkages does *not* appear to be the ultimate hybrid organization of the future that combines the strengths of both loose and tight linkages—providing adequate control and coordination without losing strategic and operational flexibility.

For example, System A was at the time of the study in this transitional phase, with a combination of very loose linkages (based on loose informal or informal alliances) and very tight linkages (based on common ownership through acquisition). For the system to move ahead, it will be necessary to create truly integrated administrative and governance structures. This integrative infrastructure will link its three major medical group, hospital, and MCO components not only with each other but with a common system headquarters and governing board using a linked information system.

An organization's ultimate level and type of integration is the result of a series of activities and managerial decisions that coalesce into a pattern of relationships. The specific choices that can and must be made will be clearer in the next section, which looks at the range of interorganizational relationships whose characteristics imply loose, moderate, or tight linkage—and thereby the level of interdependence.

INTERDEPENDENCE WITHIN AN EMERGING INTEGRATED SYSTEM

System A represents at least one major type of integrating system within the healthcare industry. The strategic impetus and the capital came from the dominant hospital for a region, but it could also have come from hospital systems, insurance companies, large existing medical groups, or other integrating health systems.

In Figure 8.3, we identify several key horizontal and vertical relationships that reflect the interdependence of system integration. This figure shows these relationships from the point of view of the system medical group. Other relationships exist among other parties, for example, between the system hospital organization and the system managed care organization.

Figure 8.3 focuses on some of the complex array of horizontal and vertical relationships within the core of the network/system web organization that can have an effect on the system medical group.

Key Interdependent Relationships of the System Medical Group with the System Board

We focus on five key vertical and horizontal relationships in Figure 8.3:

- VR-1: SMG's relationship with its board
- VR-2: SMG board's relationship with the system board
- VR-3: SMG's relationship with the system headquarters
- HR-1: SMG's relationship with the system MCO
- HR-2: SMG's relationship with the system hospital organization

Figure 8.3. Interdependence in Key Vertical and Horizontal Relationships for the System Medical Group in the Core of an Integrating System.

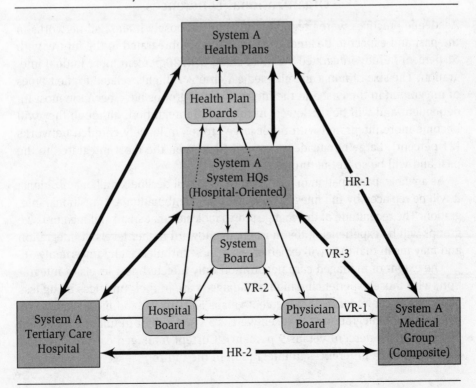

Based on our research on SMG and its competitors, for each type of relationship three types of issues appear: those related to (1) relative authority, control, and governance; (2) to creating potential synergy, which is the hoped-for result of horizontal integration among physicians; and (3) to creating potential conflict, which can be the dreaded result of the same horizontal integration.

Because of our interest in authority and governance relationships, we will address specific instances of all of these for each of the three vertical relationships. We will not present any details about the horizontal issues among partners within the system.

Several key issues emerge within this vertical relationship between the medical group and its own board. This could have been discussed in Chapter Seven when we talked about horizontal integration within the system medical group's organizational web. We have chosen to present it here as a basis on which to look at the other governance and authority relationships; these would not have existed had there not been vertical integration.

Namely, were there not a system, the medical group board would have been the ultimate governing body, and there would have been no authority structure outside the medical group itself. Instead, the SMG board is linked to the system board just as the administrative and physician leaders are linked to the executives in the system's headquarters.

Organizational Differences

Academic practices were predominantly part of loosely integrated networks in the past and expect to be among the most highly integrated in the future, with 61 percent in fully integrated systems, along with 20 percent more in dual integration. The size of nonacademic medical groups is highly related to their types of integration in the past and the future. Smaller groups have been the most independent and will be the lowest in future full integration, although they will become more integrated with other large groups in loosely coupled networks (21 percent). Large nonacademic groups have been the most integrated in the past and will be so in the future.

As a whole, participation in virtual integration will decline for all organizations; it will be replaced by full integration alone or in combination as transitional integration. The magnitude of the change scores indicates that small and medium-size groups will be experiencing the most change toward higher levels of integration and may mean that they will experience the most turbulence and uncertainty.

The extent of managed care penetration only affected past levels of integration, with those experiencing higher managed care in their practices being less likely to be non-integrated (44 percent versus 55 percent) and more likely to be part of virtual integration (42 percent versus 37 percent) or in full or transitional integration (14 percent versus 9 percent). Current managed care penetration does not predict differences in integration in the future.

ORGANIZATIONAL CHOICES
DETERMINE INTERDEPENDENCE

Perhaps one of the most perplexing questions that any manager has to deal with is to determine what factors are responsible for the competitive success of an organization. The field of strategic management has long been concerned with explaining why differences in performance exist among different organizations. An important recent perspective is called the *resource-based view of the firm*. Resources that are valuable, rare, and difficult to imitate or to substitute for can provide an organization with the ability to create and sustain a competitive advantage (Barney, 1991).

Interorganizational relationships can be classified as tangible resources, along with land and capital. Whether relationships resources will help attain and sustain a competitive advantage remains problematic, however.

Each relationship resource must meet three key criteria: Is the relationship valuable? Is the relationship rare? Can the relationship be imitated by competitors or substituted for?

Virtual integration is formed from loosely linked relationships such as informal strategic alliances with hospitals or medical groups or discounted fee-for-service managed care contracts. Even being part of a loosely integrated network will decline in our responding organization's future. Alternatively, more tightly coupled relationships will grow. These more tightly coupled linkages will, of course, raise many autonomy, governance, and control issues, both for the system and for its component organizations.

Loosely integrated delivery networks (the prime example of virtual organizations) have the overall pattern of primarily loosely coupled relationships. For example, organizations in such networks are most likely to indicate that they have informal strategic alliances with hospitals and medical groups. Discounted fee-for-service managed care contracts are so loosely coupled that virtually everyone has had them in the past, although that will be less true in the future.

Being part of a loosely integrated network will not only decline in our responding organization's future, but those organizations with this loosely coupled integration will also experience the most overall change (as seen in the percentage change scores).

More tightly linked relationships will grow for those who have had non-integration and for those in virtual integration. These will increasingly catch up to what fully integrated system organizations have now, although in some areas considerable difference will remain. This may be a greater change than they may be aware of, as they will be moving from primarily linked autonomy to a coordinated and controlled structure.

ORGANIZATIONAL SKILLS
AND ABILITIES FOR INTEGRATION

However, having valuable, rare, and inimitable relationship resources is not enough. The organization that can manage those relationships successfully on an ongoing basis may be able to attain, manage, and take advantage of tangible resources that would otherwise not be possible. This managing ability is itself an intangible resource. The stakeholder management approach is designed to facilitate the development of this key intangible resource for your organization. Here we focus on the relationships themselves.

As mentioned before, relationships are basically tangible *resources,* although they are somewhat unobservable by outside parties. The full possibilities of the relationship may not be clearly known or understood by the participants. The abilities of organizational leaders to assess potential relationships, to make strategically consistent decisions on interorganizational linkages, and then to manage those relationships provides the key intangible resources to an organization.

Although others may observe that a relationship exists, and perhaps know why that relationship exists, details of the relationship may be unobservable. For example, the relational dynamics among all the individuals and the loyalties that develop may not truly be known to any of the parties involved. Competitive advantage may come from highly developed, even unique, abilities to initiate and sustain relationships with stakeholders.

For example, all organizations, in order to exist, will have stakeholder relationships; however, some organizations manage these relationships better than others. So, it may not be the relationships themselves that are unique but rather the ability to organize them and make the most efficient use of them.

The next question is about the relationship between our types of integration and their potentially valuable but intangible skills and abilities that should enhance their effective integration and interorganizational relationship management. We asked our respondents to indicate their organization's current skills and abilities compared to competitors in their local markets. The integrating organizational capabilities we examined were as follows:

- Ability to work collaboratively with medical groups
- Ability to work collaboratively with hospitals
- Ability to work collaboratively with managed care organizations
- Skills in planning and organizing to coordinate the actions of multiple organizations
- Skills in negotiation and conflict management to manage the diverse interests of multiple organizations

- Skills in creating a common vision and purpose to manage and coordinate multiple organizations
- Leadership skills for managing fully integrated systems/networks
- Information system skills and capabilities to support decision making

The most consistent finding across the seven "soft skills," but not for the more technical information skills and capabilities (which includes hardware installation and management), is that those in fully integrated systems (or in transitional integration) reported the highest levels of capabilities. The differences among independent and loosely integrated organizations were nonexistent.

It seems that fully integrated organizations disproportionately had or have developed the skills needed to make integration more successful. Those with no experience or loosely linked experience have less of what is needed to prepare for their own future, which they have indicated will include more integration, primarily of the tightly coupled kind. Also, crucial leadership skills for integration show the greatest difference among the integration types and may indicate who will be most likely to be in control of emerging systems in the future.

We looked at the effect of academic practice, organizational size, and the percentage of managed care in the local market on our integrating skills and abilities. High managed care penetration only affected the reported ability to work collaboratively with MCOs.

Medical group size did not predict the ability to work collaboratively with hospitals, skills in planning and organizing for coordination, skills in negotiating and conflict management, or information skills. However, size did predict the ability to work collaboratively with medical groups and with managed care organizations, skills in creating a common vision and purpose, and leadership skills for managing fully integrated systems or networks.

Larger organizations performed better than smaller ones in all areas where there were differences. However, the strongest and most consistent finding was that academic organizations reported much lower capabilities than nonacademic ones—of all sizes—along all skills and abilities needed for integration. For example, only 10 percent of academic organizations saw themselves as superior to their competitors in leadership skills, but 20 percent of small groups, 31 percent of medium-size groups, and 38 percent of large groups reported superior capabilities. This pattern was consistent.

INTEGRATING MECHANISMS AND KEY STAKEHOLDERS

We examined five integrating mechanisms:

- Negotiating contracts with key stakeholders
- Forming strategic partnerships with key stakeholders

- Changing risk-sharing methods to integrate financing and delivery of care (for example, capitation and subcapitation)

- Developing electronic interfaces and pooling data among strategic partners to develop and disseminate information concerning patient care outcomes

- Developing performance standards to evaluate membership in provider networks

In each case, if the respondent organization was or will be using these mechanisms, we also asked them to select the single most important stakeholder they must manage effectively so that tactic is deemed successful.

Among the integrating mechanisms, the most prevalent in the past were to negotiate contracts with key stakeholders, followed by forming strategic partnerships with key stakeholders. In the future, developing electronic interfaces among strategic partners will be most prevalent but negotiating contracts, forming strategic partnerships, and changing risk-sharing methods will be nearly as common.

Examining the most prevalent integrating mechanisms, we note some significant differences in the most important stakeholders required for each. The negotiation mechanism was implemented through physicians and managed care organizations in the past. However, future negotiations will be implemented though IDS/Ns and MCOs. The forming of strategic partnerships involved physicians, patients, hospitals, and, to a lesser extent, MCOs in the past. In the future, these partnerships will be primarily through IDS/Ns and, to a much lesser degree, MCOs.

A generalization regarding integrating mechanisms is that making them work will be done increasingly through IDS/Ns and somewhat by MCOs and, therefore, that physicians and hospitals will be much less important in the future.

Organizational Differences

As might be expected, organizations that are part of more fully integrated systems have used more of these tactics in the past than those who have been independent, with loosely integrated organizations in the middle. However, no differences in the use of these mechanisms are expected in the future, where all organizations will be using many more.

High managed care penetration only affected reported past use of these mechanisms, not future use. Academic practices reported use of integrating mechanisms equivalent to medium-size, nonacademic groups in the past. Larger groups used more of the mechanisms and smaller ones less than academic practices. The same pattern is expected in the future.

NAVIGATION OF THE NETWORK/SYSTEM WEB

Here, we see the complex relations between the group and other units in the system. Table 8.1 shows the challenges, barriers, facilitators, and choices confronting healthcare executives as they negotiate the network/system web. The network/system web provides a picture of the various pieces of the system, excluding the external stakeholders of the system. This includes components that are both owned and affiliated.

Although the system managerial challenges and choices are similar to those at the organizational level, there are some differences. Obviously, system-level managers need to consider how the various pieces of the system fit together and the degree to which they exhibit "systemness." In other words, the emphasis at the system level is on integration rather than operations.

It is important that system executives identify strategic system priorities and that there be synergy between those priorities and those of the system units. In other words, the strategic priorities of the units need to reinforce and not be in conflict with the strategic priorities of the system. The resource allocation decisions, quality and cost initiatives, and stakeholder diagnosis and management priorities of the system also need to reinforce the system's strategic priorities.

Some integration is better than no integration. Independent organizations may well be loners in the future, unable to survive in a hostile and rapidly changing environment. In addition, intended increases in integration must be complemented through reinforcing tactical actions such as developing and implementing crucial integrating mechanisms if the potential success of the original good idea—to become more integrated—is to be achieved. Although some integration is good, too tightly linked integration may create strategic dinosaurs that are unable to change with the new demands of the next century, which is soon upon us.

System executives need to have a background and experience that gives less emphasis to operations and more to managing various stakeholders across organizational boundaries (interorganizational relationships). Of particular interest is the system determination of how much emphasis to give to new acquisitions as opposed to internal operations of existing units. At this juncture, there is a great emphasis on acquisition in order to increase market share and reduce competition. However, over the longer term, emphasis needs to shift to increasing efficiency and effectiveness within each of the system units. This means measuring and improving cost-effectiveness, clinical outcomes, and patient satisfaction.

Integration of competitive strategies between subunits in the system presents a major challenge to system managers. For example, the hospital may want to help fill their beds by signing a Medicaid contract. However, physicians may refuse to serve Medicaid patients because they consider them unattractive. In this case, system executives will need to overcome the physician resistance

Table 8.1. The Network/System Web: Challenges, Barriers, Facilitators, and Choices Confronting Healthcare Executives As They Navigate This Web.

Challenges	Potential Barriers	Potential Facilitators	Choices
1. How to reduce system costs	1. Individual practitioner culture	1. More sophisticated system managers	1. Selection of strategic priorities for system
2. How to enhance system income	2. Lack of consistency in policies across the system	2. Internal referrals within the system	2. Resource allocation decisions within system
3. How to align system and individual physician incentives	3. Lack of management expertise in managing particular products or stakeholders	3. System volume discounts on purchases	3. Selection of systemwide cost-containment and quality-enhancing strategies
4. How to increase system patient satisfaction	4. Lack of systemwide electronic medical records	4. Effective system management to integrate separate units	4. Structuring or restructuring of the system
5. How to increase system quality of patient care	5. Lack of differentiation vis-à-vis competitors	5. Centralized information systems accessible throughout the system	5. Centralization versus decentralization of authority and control
6. How to reduce conflict and enhance cooperation in the system	6. Lack of strategic priorities and strategic focus	6. Selection of system executives to manage internal and external stakeholders	
7. How to enhance operational synergy of system components	7. Conflicts between the system board and individual unit boards	7. Determination of how much integrative interstructure to create	
8. Lack of integration of different types of physicians	8. Determination of how much to emphasize new acquisitions vs. improvement in operations of existing system units		
9. Selection of key stakeholders, generic management strategies, and specific tactics to manage each			

through various incentives if synergy is to be achieved. The determination of how much network or system integrative infrastructure to create will probably be made at the system headquarters level, with input from the original partners—who are now themselves at lower levels in the organization.

An example of this type of decision would be a large investment in information systems to provide an electronic patient medical record that would be accessible at all points in the system—during patient hospital stays, while visiting primary care physicians, and when being treated by a specialist. Simultaneous information would be going to the system's own MCO, who has contracted to provide the complete continuum of care for these covered lives from key payors—employers, Medicare, and Medicaid.

Another example would be a decision to design an effective, interlinked set of boards for governance. It would be essential that these boards effectively represent all the key parties of the new system. The purpose would be to link the various subparts of the organization, better coordinate services, and improve the quality of care for the patient.

If the other parts of the system (specifically, the medical group and the MCO) are simply treated as if they were now departments of the large tertiary care hospital rather than ongoing system partners, the governance structure will not be effective, except as an attempt to gain and maintain control over two groups often seen at odds with hospitals—physicians and insurance companies.

This is a real danger for medical groups in hospital-dominated systems. Counterpart dangers could also exist for hospitals in those network/system webs built by medical groups or insurance companies that did not include full partnership for all parties in the new systems. If a tightly linked system core also has loosely linked affiliations, the problem of how to effectively include system/network partners in decision making and in system gains will be even more difficult to resolve.

LEADERSHIP IMPLICATIONS

As the healthcare industry evolves into one in which systems and networks replace the independent providers such as medical groups, physicians, and hospitals, how will provider organizations (medical groups and hospitals) participate in these systems and networks, and what role can they expect to play? Which kind of organization will likely become the controlling element in IDS/Ns—hospitals, medical groups, or managed care organizations? Perhaps the more hierarchical nature of hospitals (compared to the less complex generic medical group)suggests that hospital executives have more experience in managing day-to-day, as well as in strategic issues that arise in complex organizational forms such as the IDS/Ns. As the new, radical healthcare organizational forms emerge, strategic web navigation will prove to be invaluable, as medical group leaders make strategic decisions and implement them. As hospitals see their current organizational forms (for example, as inpatient, tertiary care facilities with expensive but empty beds) losing their position as the dominant provider organization in healthcare, will executives attempt to move their hospitals into a new position within the healthcare industry—as the parent company of an IDS/N? Will such a likely movement enhance the probability that the hospital executive will have the IDS/N "corporate" job in the future? (In many areas, hospitals have had more capital with which to invest in the infrastructure of IDS/Ns.)

Whatever the reasons, in our earlier survey (Blair, Fottler, Paolino, and Rotarius, 1995), medical group panel experts believed their medical groups will wield less power and influence over IDS/Ns, whereas hospital panel experts believed their hospitals will wield that power and influence.

Even though increasing integration is nearly inevitable, it does not mean that synergy through consolidation will occur. Indeed, horizontal and vertical integration may well produce far more increases in administrative overhead and co-ordination staff and other costs than is saved through the nearly mythical synergy. Whatever the specific nature of their integrated relationships with other organizations, healthcare executives will need to improve their skills and abilities dramatically if they are to effectively participate and to manage the levels and types of tight integration that are expected.

This new era of IDS/Ns presents both risks and opportunities for healthcare organizations. Although our results indicate that medical groups will be more integrated in the future, medical groups do have vital, and perhaps never totally replaceable, functions to perform as members of IDS/Ns.

However, survival of the medical group depends on the ability of executives to learn how to effectively manage the many new and emerging relationships and stakeholders. Executives can take lessons learned from dealing with organizational stakeholders such as MCOs and apply that knowledge to understand how to deal with relatively unknown organizations such as IDS/Ns. Because even though MCOs are still relatively new organizational stakeholders in the healthcare industry, their executives generally have more experience dealing with them than dealing with IDS/Ns.

For example, the uncertainty that medical groups will face as they attempt to deal with IDS/Ns will be similar to, or greater than, the uncertainty they feel as they try to manage their current relationships with MCOs. Leaders should be able to use their experiences with MCOs as a point of reference to aid in understanding the magnitude of the impact of IDS/Ns.

One outcome of these new interorganizational relationships including systems and networks is that leaders of healthcare organizations must manage relationships with a growing number of active, powerful, and sometimes competing stakeholders who exert an influence on every healthcare management issue; these stakeholders must be recognized and evaluated for their potential to support or threaten the organization and its competitive goals.

The key leadership implications for the network/system web are brought together in seven basic challenges. They are how to reduce system overhead and coordination costs, enhance system income, reduce conflict among system component organizations, enhance cooperation among system components, increase systemwide patient satisfaction, ensure systemwide quality of patient care, and enhance the operational synergy of system components.

STEPS FOR NAVIGATING YOUR NETWORK/SYSTEM WEB

To effectively navigate your network/system web, we recommend the following steps, supported by Toolkit 8:

- Identify the key individual, group, and network/system stakeholders that make up your network/system web. (Are these included in the key internal stakeholders you identified in Chapter One using Tool 1.1?)

- Assess your group's vertical network/system linkages in terms of how loose or tight each one is and how they are likely to change in the next three years.

- Determine your group's current system integration type and whether your type of system integration will likely change in the next three years. Use Tool 8.1.

- Identify the key vertical and horizontal interdependent relationships within your network/system web similar to Figure 8.3 using Tool 8.2. As a minimum, address these vertical relationships:

    VR-1: SMG's relationship with its board

    VR-2: SMG board's relationship with the system board

    VR-3: SMG's relationship with the system headquarters

- Using Tool 8.3, develop lists of challenges facing your organization, potential barriers, potential facilitators, and choices facing your group's executive leadership team.

- Use Tool 8.4 to help you formulate the specific actions you will recommend for your group in meeting key challenges.

- Design and build the specific administrative infrastructure you will recommend for your group to provide the optimal balance of control through tight linkages (for example, common ownership) and flexibility through loose linkages (for example, virtual organizations) that will ensure your group can effectively navigate its organizational web.

TOOLKIT 8

Navigating Your Group's Network/System Web

Tool 8.1. Type of Network/System Integration.

Instructions: What kind of linkage does your medical group possess? Is your organization part of a network or system where relationships are loosely linked or part of a network system where relationships are tightly linked? Indicate the type of integration of your organization *now* and how it will be *3 years from now.*

Your organization:

Now	3 Years from Now	Network/System Integration
☐	☐	1. *System Non-Integration*—Having neither loosely linked nor tightly linked relationships with other groups
☐	☐	2. *Virtual System Integration*—Medical groups that are part of a loosely integrated delivery network
☐	☐	3. *Full System Integration*—Medical groups that are part of a fully integrated system
☐	☐	4. *Transitional System Integration*—Having both loosely linked and tightly linked relationships network/systems

Tool 8.2. The Core of an Integrating System (Interdependence Within the Triad Plus One from the Perspective of the System Medical Group).

General Instructions: For the network or system your organization is the "SMG" member of, fill in the appropriate actual names of the core SMG, hospital, MCO and system HQs members in the boxes. In the other boxes with rounded corners, fill in the names of the board(s) that govern the different parts as well as the network/system board. Insert NA if an organization (or board) does not apply to your network/system.

Assessment Instructions: For each vertical and horizontal relationship, insert + or − on each of the three lines to indicate whether the relationship is positive or negative in terms of decision making/governance, conflict, and synergy. If any of these three aspects of the relationship is "neutral" or "has no impact on this particular relationship" use a 0. Insert NA if this relationship (or any aspect) does not apply to your organization.

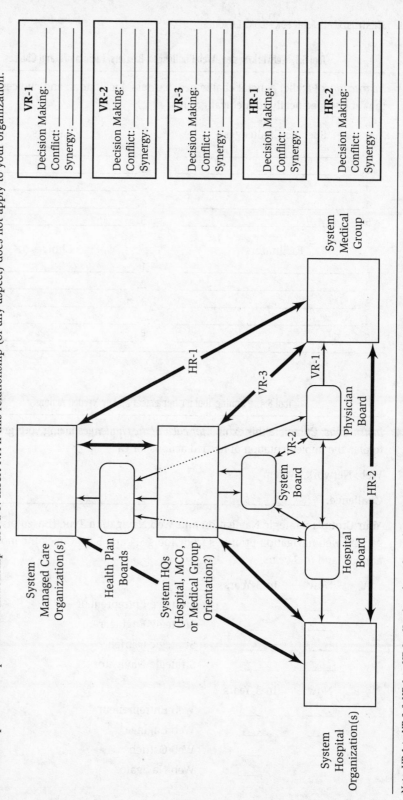

Note: VR-1 to VR-3 & HR-1 to HR-2 = Key *interdependent relationships* to be assessed, clarified, and managed to resolve issues of the appropriateness of decision-making/governance processes, the extent of current or potential conflict, and the extent of current or potential synergy.

Tool 8.3. Network/System Web Challenges, Barriers, Facilitators, and Choices.

Instructions: Parallel general challenges, barriers, facilitators, and choices with those that apply specifically to medical groups.

Specific Challenges

1._____
2._____
3._____
4._____
5._____

Barriers

1._____
2._____
3._____
4._____
5._____

Facilitators

1._____
2._____
3._____
4._____
5._____

Choices

1._____
2._____
3._____
4._____
5._____

Tool 8.4. Planning Tool for Implementing Key Needed Actions.

Instructions: Complete this exhibit *for each of the challenges* facing your group in order to plan the implementation of needed actions for each.

Web: Network/System

Challenge: _____

Your Group's Strategic Navigation and Web Navigation Type (Based on your strategic and web navigation priorities from Tools 3.4 and 5.3). Check the most appropriate *now* and *in 3 years.*

Now	In 3 Years	
____	____	Strategic Entrepreneur
____	____	Strategic Engineer
____	____	Strategic Ostrich
____	____	Strategic Navigator

Now	In 3 Years	
____	____	Web Entrepreneur
____	____	Web Engineer
____	____	Web Ostrich
____	____	Web Navigator

Tool 8.4. Planning Tool for Implementing Key Needed Actions, cont'd.

1. What actions do you recommend for your group in meeting this challenge? Be specific!

   Immediately?
   Over the next 3 years?

2. In what ways do your recommended actions support your group's overall strategic intentions and other tactical actions?

   Immediately?
   Over the next 3 years?

3. What is your specific plan for implementing each of the proposed actions?

   Immediately?
   Over the next 3 years?

4. What are the most significant factors that could undermine the implementation process, and how can they be dealt with?

   Immediately?
   Over the next 3 years?

5. What resources will be required for implementation, and are they available?

   Immediately?
   Over the next 3 years?

6. How cost-effective are your recommendations? If they are not cost-effective, what alternative actions can you take?

   Immediately?
   Over the next 3 years?

7. Which physician and/or administrative managers will have the lead role in implementing these particular actions?

   Immediately?
   Over the next 3 years?

8. Do the responsible managers have the necessary abilities and authority to effectively implement these actions? What will you do to improve their abilities and ensure their authority?

   Immediately?
   Over the next 3 years?

9. What other group/system managers or other personnel—as internal stakeholders—should be involved in the implementation process?

   Immediately?
   Over the next 3 years?

10. If the implementation process does not work as planned, what contingency approach will you go to next? Why will it work if this process did not?

    Immediately?
    Over the next 3 years?

CHAPTER NINE

MANAGING WITHIN YOUR COMPETITIVE AND EXTENDED WEBS

In this chapter, we will examine the competitive web using the evolving competitive web of System A as an example. We will consider the challenges, barriers, facilitators, and choices facing the system. Then we will apply Michael Porter's (1985) competitive analysis to medical practices and illustrate it with examples. Finally, we will outline how to manage each of the competitive forces, including those in the extended web.

THE COMPETITIVE WEB

Figure 9.1 shows the web from a medical group's perspective. Both the organizational web and the network/system web are shown in separate boxes at the bottom of the figure. For the first time, stakeholders external to the organization and system are shown. Organizations that are not part of the system (indicated by nonshaded boxes and question marks on the relationship arrows) are shown because the survival of the unit may depend on multiple sources of patient income. A refusal of a particular subcomponent to negotiate contracts with external stakeholders could jeopardize its survival. Multiple sources of dependence are preferable to fewer sources of dependence.

Our case example reflects a composite medical group of nearly one hundred physicians brought together by a hospital system in the process of integrating further to include physicians and managed care organizations. That system is

Figure 9.1. The Competitive Web (Shown from the System Medical Group's Perspective).

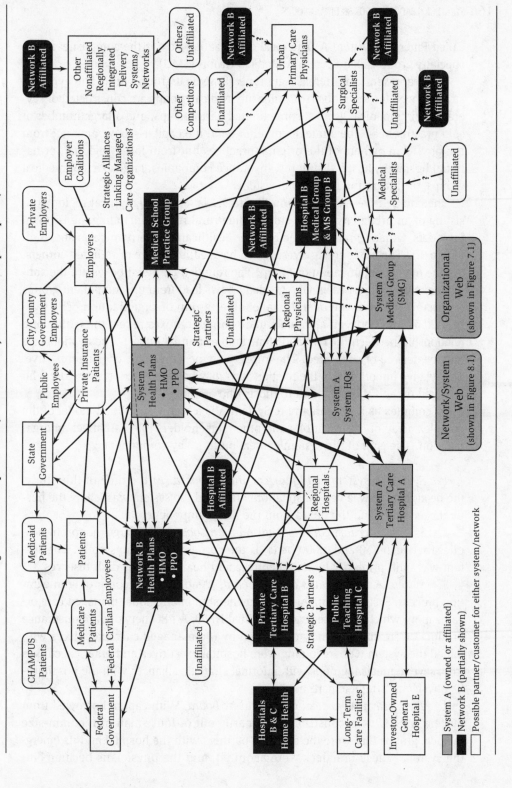

System A (owned or affiliated)

Network B (partially shown)

Possible partner/customer for either system/network

called Emerging System A. The focal organization here is the composite, multi-specialty group called System A Medical Group (SMG).

SMG represents an increasingly typical medical group within the evolving strategic web for the industry. Composite medical groups are constructed of several existing medical groups, some limited partnerships, and a large number of solo practitioners. The strategic impetus—and the capital—may come *not* from the physician owners of the original practices but from local, regional, or national hospitals, hospital systems, insurance companies, large existing medical groups, or integrating healthcare systems.

The competitive web shown in Figure 9.1 is for a geographical region consisting of an urban city and its surrounding rural region, including the regional providers. Other segments of the broader healthcare industry are also shown in Figure 9.1. The boxes themselves, which have either square or rounded corners, are the overall organization or group. The rounded-cornered boxes are the subcomponent groups of each. One-headed arrows lead from the component groups or organizations to the overall stakeholder group or organization. The two-headed arrows between any two square-cornered boxes reflect the reality of a relationship between the two and some kind of mutual impact. The relationships may be desired or undesired. The impact may be supportive or nonsupportive. The relative importance of the relationships may be greater to a stakeholder who is linked organizationally than to those who are not.

As complex as it appears to be, System A is a highly simplified model of the complex array of organizations and other stakeholders that can affect an organization. The core of the system centers on four key components:

1. *System A system headquarters and its board.* At the time of this study, the headquarters was very hospital-oriented, and the system was led by the hospital executives and the board from the next component.

2. *System A tertiary care Hospital A and its board.* This large, nonprofit hospital (between 750 and 1,000 beds) is the cornerstone of the system. The system was built primarily by its executives and board using its cash reserves.

3. *System A health plans and its boards.* As part of the continuing integration process, System A bought partial ownership in a regional managed care organization, which was a federally qualified HMO. A PPO network and insurance products were subsequently developed by the managed care executives who joined the system. Others joining were hospital executives and other executives from several medical groups with informal strategic alliances with the hospital—its physician "strategic partners."

4. *The System A medical group and its board.* With capital borrowed from System A, SMG was constructed primarily out of four small or medium-size medical groups that were the strategic partners with the hospital and its emerging system. These practices were acquired, and the physicians became em-

ployees of SMG, which was set up as a 501(a) foundation. Aggregates of similar physicians who were solo practitioners or in two- or three-person partnerships were also brought into the group.

Table 9.1 shows the challenges, barriers, facilitators, and choices confronting the healthcare executive in the competitive web. A key issue in navigating both the competitive web and the extended strategic web is how the system executive team can proactively provide external stakeholders with information relevant to their needs (Rosenthal and Harper, 1994). However, to date individual consumers as potential patients have had minimal input in reporting initiatives (Hibbard and Jewett, 1996; Ribnik and Carrano, 1995) with the exception of patient satisfaction survey data. Among the external stakeholders targeted for report card information are employers and employer coalitions, third-party payors, legislators, patients, local and trade media, system boards, CEOs, system managers, and accreditation and regulatory agencies (Dearmin, Brenner, and Migliori, 1995; Nerenz, Zajac, and Rosman, 1993).

Healthcare executives usually make assumptions about the type of information and its format that various stakeholders desire (Dearmin, Brenner, and Migliori, 1995). These assumptions include beliefs that (1) individuals want information about patient satisfaction and comparative performance in order to select among providers; (2) large purchasers (business and MCOs) want information about plan financial performance, efficiency, and effectiveness to guide purchasing decisions; and (3) accrediting agencies want information about compliance with existing standards. Yet, it is important for system executives to query their key stakeholders in a systematic fashion to identify indicators responsive to stakeholder preferences.

At the system level, the choice is how to recruit or develop specialists to manage the wide range of external stakeholders. These activities include collaboration, negotiation, need identification, service provision, and the evaluation of the management of each stakeholder. Another choice is to what degree of autonomy should subunits of the system be allowed in negotiating contracts with external stakeholders.

THE STRATEGIC ATTRACTIVENESS OF THE MEDICAL GROUP INDUSTRY

Several structural elements within the environment affect the level of competition in an industry (Porter, 1980; Autrey and Thomas, 1986). More specifically, the strategic attractiveness of any industry and the intensity of competition to be found there are affected by competitive rivalries among existing firms, risk of entry by potential competitors, bargaining power of suppliers, bargaining power of buyers, and threat of substitute products.

Table 9.1. The Competitive Web: Challenges, Barriers, Facilitators, and Choices Confronting Healthcare Executives As They Navigate This Web.

Challenges	Potential Barriers	Potential Facilitators	Choices
1. How to communicate system performance to external stakeholders	1. Lack of common information system	1. System can suboptimize one component in order to enhance another	1. Resource allocation for new acquisitions versus internal operations
2. How to negotiate contracts and other collaborative activities with other external stakeholders	2. Lack of common measures of success for different system components	2. One-stop shopping for all services within the system	2. Resource allocation decisions within system
3. What contracts (if any) to sign with unaffiliated organizations	3. System leadership that only understands "their" type of organization	3. Common electronic medical records	3. Recruitment and development of specialists to negotiate with key external stakeholders
4. How to determine what external stakeholders are key	4. Different goals and priorities for different system components	4. Effective system information system	4. Provision of system performance information to key external stakeholders
5. How to enhance system market share and financial returns	5. Training and rotation of managers across system components	5. Centralization versus decentralization of various functions	
6. Team building between component organizations	6. Degree of autonomy for system components in identifying and negotiating with external stakeholders		

Porter's focus was not on the individual organization. He was concerned with whether the industry (or a specific segment of the broader industry) was strategically "attractive." If managers were to determine that an industry is attractive to move into or to stay in (a corporate strategy decision), then Porter suggested one of four "generic strategies": cost leadership, differentiation, cost focus, and differentiation focus as a competitive strategy for a particular organization or for a particular strategic business unit focused on that industry or industry segment (Porter, 1985). Various studies of the hospital industry using Porter's competitive analysis have been conducted (Sheldon and Windham, 1984; Baliga and Johnson, 1986; Autrey and Thomas, 1986). Whitehead and others (1989) modified and applied these general notions to the managed care industry, as did Blair and Fottler (1990) and Topping and Fottler (1990).

Medical groups have greater organizational complexity than solo practices or limited partnerships and are also able to make a common, group decision on strategic issues. The part of the healthcare industry that medical groups compete in is clearly different from other industry segments within healthcare, such as the hospital industry or the pharmaceutical industry. Among specialists in medical groups, it is common to further segment the medical group industry into specialty versus multispecialty or primary care versus referral specialty segments.

The medical group segment of this industry is growing as integration systems and networks stimulate increasing physician integration through consolidation of individual and small groups of physicians into medical groups that have different organizational structures and sets of governance issues (Savage, Taylor, Rotarius, and Buesseler, 1997).

The competitive situation is changing as well (Coddington, Moore, and Fischer, 1994; Delmar, 1995; Blair, Fottler, Paolino, and Rotarius, 1995). Medical groups face

- *Rivalry* from each other.
- *Threat from new medical group entrants,* particularly the more recently formed and capitalized composite medical groups built through practice acquisition by integrating networks and systems.
- *The bargaining power of suppliers,* specifically physicians, which is changing as available alternatives for physicians change. Physicians are suppliers in two ways. First, they can choose to provide direct labor and expertise (including the sale of their private practice) to a medical group, an existing rival, one of the new entrants created by an integrated delivery system or network (IDS/N), or a substitute like a network of ambulatory clinics that is provided by hospitals or hospital systems. Second, they are providers of patient referrals that can go to a specific medical group or any of its rivals, new entrants, or substitutes.
- *The growing bargaining power of buyers,* as more alternatives are available to them. Managed care organizations and employers are increasingly making aggregate buying decisions; they decide who can provide the services available from

medical groups and what the price will be. In addition, patients are making buying decisions that affect medical groups. Patients make choices of health plans (and their associated medical group providers), and they choose among medical group or other physician service providers within the network for that plan.

• *Threat from medical group substitutes.* Hospitals can organize their own physician networks and build a chain of ambulatory facilities on their own campuses and throughout the community or region. These can provide cost-effective, medical group substitutes.

Amid this growth and change, major questions for medical groups are as follows:

• Do they have viable strategies both now and for the future?
• Can they survive extensive change in the overall industry?
• If they survive, what organizational form will they have and with what level of autonomy?

STAKEHOLDER PERSPECTIVES ON THE MEDICAL GROUP INDUSTRY

Stakeholders exert an influence on every issue and must be recognized and evaluated for their potential to support or threaten the organization and its competitive goals. Stakeholders attempt to affect those decisions and actions in order to influence the direction of the organization so that it is consistent with the needs and priorities of the stakeholders themselves.

An organization usually cannot choose its own stakeholders—stakeholders choose themselves. They have stakes in organizations because of the content or process of organizational decisions and actions. They can choose to identify their particular stakes in the organization's decisions and act on the implications for them, or they can choose not to.

Typically, stakeholders decide to exercise their right to "protect their stake" on an issue-by-issue basis. For example, physician employees are usually thought of as a supportive stakeholder group to a medical group organization, regarding most strategic and operational issues. However, regarding the issue of increasing the physician employees' productivity in terms of total numbers of patients seen per day, medical group leaders would likely find that their usually supportive stakeholder has just become less supportive. In other words, a stakeholder's view of the organization and its degree of supportiveness (or nonsupportiveness or even hostility) for the organization's decisions is contingent on the specific issue at hand.

Although Porter's competitive analysis looks at the power potential of key stakeholders, how that power might be used is not well developed within this approach. We argue that the amount of collaboration provided by key stakeholders is just as important as any other power stakeholders have, if not more so.

Both power and collaboration are relevant to our analysis because they affect something fundamental for the stakeholder: the potential to threaten the organization or to cooperate with it (Blair and Fottler, 1990). Stakeholder supportiveness affects how and whether power is used by stakeholders, thus ultimately determining the strategic vulnerability of medical groups.

MANAGING EACH OF THE COMPETITIVE FORCES

In this section, we will review how medical practices have or could manage each of the seven key stakeholders within their competitive web. First, we will examine physicians as direct competitors of medical practices and as suppliers of services to medical practices. Second, we consider hospitals as potential substitutes. Third, we analyze the expectations of patients, MCOs, and employers as buyers of the services of medical practices. Finally, we examine IDS/Ns as existing or potential entrants to the market.

Physicians as Competitors and Suppliers

Our respondents did not view physicians in competitive solo or group practice as having a high potential for either threat or cooperation in the future. This is undoubtedly due to the fact that these competitive physicians do not directly control reimbursement or incomes for a medical group (only 20 percent viewed them as controlling key resources in the future). However, physicians as suppliers to the medical practice pose little threat in the future but offer a high degree of potential for cooperation, as viewed by our executive respondents.

About 84 percent of our respondents viewed their supplier physicians as having a high potential for cooperation in the future. In particular, 78 percent expected these physicians to form a coalition with their organization in the future. In addition, medical practices that believe they do a better job than their competitors in managing their competitors and their supplier physicians also tend to see high potential for cooperation and lower potential for threat from each of these two stakeholder groups.

A major competitive challenge for medical groups in relating to their competitor physicians is the emergence of physician "report cards." For example, Governor Lawton Chiles recently signed a bill that will give Florida patients access to their doctors' medical and criminal records ("Florida," 1997b). The Florida Medical Association, which originally opposed the legislation, decided to support it after changes were made to let doctors review, make factual corrections, and update their profiles before they were made public. About fifty thousand doctors will be profiled, and the reports will be made available on the Internet and in public libraries in 1999. Information on convictions, settled malpractice suits, disciplinary actions, and bankruptcies will be included in these reports.

Obviously, these report cards will be expanded in the future to include such variables as cost-effectiveness, clinical outcomes, and complaints to medical societies. Medical practices need to carefully assess their physicians, including both their currently affiliated and potential partners, in order to determine their competitive attractiveness. Decisions concerning where to receive care may well be more data-driven in the future (Slovensky, Fottler, and Houser, 1988).

Although our respondents viewed supplier physicians as nonthreatening (as noted earlier), in some cases physicians affiliated with a particular medical practice or medical plan could withdraw their services as a response to a perceived competitive threat. Salt Lake City-based Intermountain Health Care (IHC) has twenty-three hospitals and three health plans with about 320,000 enrollees ("Intermountain Health Care," 1994). Sensing that the IHP was positioning itself to secure a significant portion of the managed care market and exclude them from its plans, almost a quarter of the physicians in Logan, Utah, have withdrawn from the system. They hope their defection will make IHC a less desirable insurance option to local employers and thus stem its growth.

Two recent developments made physicians feel their practices were at risk. First, IHC introduced the area's first HMO, which excluded many area physicians. Second, physicians received notice that they could no longer send IHC patients to Western Surgery Center, an outpatient facility owned by a group of local doctors. This facility is the only competitor to the Logan Regional Hospital (owned by IHC). The physicians remain optimistic that the situation will be resolved in their favor; meanwhile, IHC is threatening to bring in other physicians in the area to "fill the gap." This case illustrates the fallacy of assuming your supplier physicians will be supportive, even when they perceive your behavior as threatening.

The major managerial challenge for medical groups in relating to both competitor and supplier physicians is knowing how to collaborate with each. The most important requirement of a managed care environment is having single-signature authority to provide a range of services. A particular IDS/N or medical practice could own, lease, or contract for these services. Because total ownership and control is beyond the financial means of most organizations, contracts offer the best option. The key criterion for deciding with whom to contract for what is to determine what is the most cost-effective setting for each service.

Collaboration with competing IDS/Ns and medical practices is not a widespread trend but has begun to emerge on the West Coast (Tokarski, 1997). The size and composition of the market can serve as a starting point to determine whether an IDS/N or medical group should attempt to offer a given service and, if so, whether it should own or contract for it. Core services will vary, depending on whether the organization is in a metropolitan market or a rural area. Organizations in rural areas need to focus on outpatient services by forming strong bonds with local physicians. Mergers in rural areas also make sense as a way to reduce costs, offer more complete care services, and gain critical mass for possible managed care contracts. Alternatively, metropolitan markets can theoretically support a full continuum of services for populations enrolled in managed care services.

Instead of trying to own it all, control it all, and do it all, IDS/Ns and medical practices could create an elaborate web agreement with members of their own organizational network and with competitors. This means they could compete with the latter in some areas while collaborating in areas where each has something unique to contribute.

The ideal physician partners are those who will contribute to building or making the organization part of a strong system of care in the market—those with both high quality and low cost or those in a market that has not seen much collaborative activity (McManis, 1994). Although most IDS/Ns and medical practices would like to see themselves as the center of a system or an equal partner in an affiliation, honest self-assessment is a prerequisite to affiliation discussions. Small medical practices, those without documented quality or cost-effectiveness, and those in areas that have seen a great deal of collaboration will have limited bargaining power and limited choices.

A strong motivation to succeed or a fear of being left out will enable some competitors to collaborate in some areas for their mutual benefit. However, past history cannot always be overcome. Rivalries can be so bitter that it would take a complete change of leadership on both sides and a discarding of institutional memory to get the parties to talk to each other.

A "clinic without walls" form of organization is becoming an increasingly common first step in the process of physician medical practice integration and consolidation (Johnson and Schryver, 1994). In this type of arrangement, the medical practices of many physicians are combined in one common practice enterprise. A clinic without walls can provide the marketing and bargaining clout, economics of scale, and related advantages of a large medical practice, such as management expertise. This is accomplished through standard flexibility that enables physicians to maintain an acceptable level of individual practice identity and control. This type of arrangement could also be expanded to include other currently unaffiliated medical groups.

Clinics without walls bring together the resources of many previously unrelated medical practices in a single organization. This enables the group to amass resources and acquire the infrastructure that is necessary to participate in managed care contracts. Most important, a clinic without walls may serve to prepare and facilitate eventual physician participation in larger IDS/Ns. It may enable physicians to address the key issues of incentives and cultural change in a more gradual, controlled fashion.

Hospitals as Substitutes

Our respondents evaluated the potential threat by hospitals as providers of substitutable services for those of medical practices to be relatively low in the past and in the future. Still, 30 percent felt hospitals could and would pose a competitive threat in the future. Less than one-third thought hospitals would be more powerful than their own organizations in the future, controlled needed resources, or would form a coalition excluding their organization.

However, the major change was the high percentage who believed the potential for cooperation was high and would be higher still in the future. About two-thirds anticipated a high potential for cooperation with hospitals in the future. In particular, they expected to form a coalition with one or more hospitals in the future. Those who believed they managed hospitals much better than other medical practices in their local market were more likely than other medical practices to see a high level of potential cooperation with hospitals in the future. Better management of hospitals apparently involves more cooperation and collaboration with them.

Managed care organizations such as HMOs have viewed hospitals as major sources of excess expenditures of healthcare costs. Hospital administrators have responded to increased pressure to reduce costs by shortening lengths of stay and shifting expensive procedures from inpatient to outpatient locations. As the numbers of community hospitals, inpatient days, and inpatient utilization have declined, these decreases have been offset by a dramatic increase in hospital outpatient visits and outpatient surgical procedures (Shua-Haim and Gross, 1997). This shift is creating great friction between hospitals and traditional, office-based private practitioners in solo or group medical practices.

Medical practices are joining together in larger, multispecialty groups and are offering a variety of services that are attracting contracts with HMOs. These outpatient services include same-day hernia repair, cataract removal, colonoscopy with biopsies, and laparascopic surgery of the abdomen. Preliminary data suggest that the shift to outpatient procedures results in significant cost savings without sacrificing quality of care, as judged by patient satisfaction, morbidity, or mortality (Shua-Haim and Gross, 1997). The Health Forecasting Group in Alameda, California, predicts that hospitals will move toward specialized ambulatory centers for arthritis, diabetes, cardiology, oncology, orthopedics, and cancer in the twenty-first century (American Group Practice Association, 1992).

Hospitals are frantically attempting to compete with medical practices by building similar and sometimes larger facilities. When this approach is unsuccessful, hospitals offer to purchase the physician practices and their facilities and then employ physicians as full-time, salaried employees. When physicians become salaried by a hospital, they may have less incentive to stay one step ahead of the competition by attending conventions and reading journals to learn the most up-to-date treatments. This tendency, if valid, may suggest that hospital-based ambulatory care may be at a disadvantage in competing with medical practices unless their physicians are accountable for their performance.

One example of the competitive thrust of hospitals has been the recent provision of ambulatory services in shopping malls. In 1995, Evanston and Glenbrook hospitals unveiled a four-hundred-square-foot center for breast and mammography at the Nordstrom store in Old Orchard Shopping Center in Skokie, Illinois (Morrall, 1995). These hospitals had learned, during four focus group sessions, that traditional channels were not reaching their target audience of women. Focus group members suggested making the tests more accessible and convenient in a setting that is less sterile and more inviting.

The center is on the store's first level behind the beauty section, and it complements breast cancer services already offered by the store. Women awaiting appointments carry beepers and can shop while they wait. The store has marketed the center to consumers by hanging prominent in-store signs and passing out brochures. The hospital is marketing the service through local television, radio stations, and newspapers. Obviously, these types of hospital ambulatory services in shopping malls pose a competitive threat to medical practices.

Not all hospitals attempt to compete directly with medical practices; some have taken the path of collaboration and established new relationships with medical practices. For example, alliances and contracts of all kinds can allow a hospital and certain medical practices to share the costs and benefits of providing specific services. In addition, whole departments and units, entire medical practices, hospitals, and systems have merged.

Sometimes, hospitals do compete intensely with medical groups. Sometimes, they are more cooperative and collaborative. And sometimes, they pursue both strategies simultaneously.

Many hospitals continue to try to convert independent physicians into salaried employees, despite the potential negative implications for overall performance (efficiency, customer focus, quality) when incentives are lacking. However, a growing number of nonprofit hospitals have begun adopting the infrastructure of physician practice management (PPM) companies to their own needs by joining with medical practices to form management service organizations (MSOs) (Bianco and Schine, 1997). Like PPMs, MSOs are physician-driven companies that use advanced business methods to rationalize medical practice. Unlike PPMs, MSOs are privately held entities in which ownership is generally split 50–50 between doctors and hospitals. One of the largest MSOs involving 2,500 physicians was formed by North Shore Health Systems, a nonprofit hospital group on New York's Long Island.

Recently, McManis and Associates held an executive forum for leaders of medical practices to discuss some of the key trends and issues they face today (McManis, Pavia, Ackerman, and Connelly, 1996). All participants agreed that the hospital has become a cost center as opposed to a revenue producer. However, it is often necessary to have a hospital as a partner to achieve cost-effectiveness, coordination of patient care, access to capital, and bargaining power in dealing with MCOs. It is important to choose a hospital partner whose leaders understand medical practices and are willing to compromise in order to meet the professional and autonomy needs of physicians.

Patients as Buyers

Patients are important buyers of the services of medical practices, not only because of their direct purchases but also because they can influence MCOs and employers to include (or not include) a particular provider in a health plan. Only a minority of our respondents (26 percent) viewed patients as posing a threat in the future. However, almost two-thirds thought medical practices would have a high potential for cooperation with patients in the future. Less than a majority of respondents expected patients to be more powerful than their own organization, to control needed resources, and to form a coalition with their organization. These results raise a question as to how these organizations could achieve the high potential for cooperation with patients that they forecast for the future.

Medical practices need to attain and enhance patient satisfaction to generate business through word-of-mouth recommendations from present patients (Ford, Bach, and Fottler, 1997), who might recommend the practice to other potential patients or recommend to employers and MCOs that a particular provider be included in its health plan or list of preferred providers.

One way to keep patients happy is to keep employees happy. Stephen Strasser, president and CEO of Health Care Research Systems of Columbus, Ohio, notes that "satisfied employees who like their work will generate satisfied patients" (Sherer, 1997, p. 10). In his 1992 study of the impact of nurses' and physicians' attitudes on patient satisfaction, he found that nurse satisfaction was more important than physician attitudes in predicting overall patient satisfaction. Another recent study explored the relationship between employee satisfaction and patient loyalty, based on a survey of more than seven hundred patients and two hundred nursing staff members at a one-thousand-bed hospital in the Midwest (Atkins, Marshall, and Javalgi, 1996). The authors found a strong relationship between nurse satisfaction and patients' intent to return in the future or to recommend the hospital to others.

How can you tell if your employees are satisfied enough to keep patients happy? Both employees and patients should be surveyed periodically to identify employee attitudes and match them against patient feedback (Fottler, Crawford,

Quintana, and White, 1995). Carson Dye, a consultant with Findley, Davis, Inc. of Toledo, Ohio, recommends that employees be surveyed every twelve to eighteen months using traditional measures (satisfaction with supervisors, co-workers, and compensation package) as well as nontraditional measures (whether they feel they have personal control over their work environment, pride in the organization, and influence) (Sherer, 1997). Dye also suggests using positive feedback from patients to reward employees by posting complimentary letters from patients on well-displayed bulletin boards.

Most healthcare executives in general and medical practice executives in particular believe they provide high-quality customer service to satisfied patients. However, a comparison with the customer service available from other industries, such as the hospitality industry, indicates otherwise. For example, when an out-of-town couple visited a New York hospital so the wife could be treated, her husband stayed in the nearby Pierre Hotel (Montague, 1995). Despite an ongoing hospital focus on customer satisfaction, the patient's husband was dissatisfied with its service orientation. He complained to the hospital's administrators that their customer service did not begin to compare to what he had experienced at the Pierre Hotel. He suggested that they treat patients more like guests.

In response to this criticism, hospital staff in the human resources, building services, food and nutrition, and admitting departments met with their counterparts at the Pierre Hotel (Montague, 1995). The hospital came away from this meeting with a number of concrete ideas for improvement, including

- A mentoring program patterned after the hotel's program that paired new employees with veterans.

- Keeping employee locker rooms, break rooms, and bathrooms as clean as its guest area to enhance employee morale and customer service.

- Screening prospective employees more carefully to select those who are oriented to good customer service.

- Setting up a customer service program for its physicians, nurses, residents, interns, and laboratory technicians.

Years ago, healthcare organizations would have rejected the criticisms and suggestions. However, in an era of managed care, medical practices and other health service organizations can stay in business only if their patient-customers are satisfied, or more than satisfied, with both the technical quality of care and the customer service.

In addition to patient satisfaction, a number of other patient-related challenges and issues face medical practice executives. First, the aging population will mean increased demand for the services of medical practices. However, the population of uninsured and underinsured employees implies that those practices may have to restrict access to services and be prepared for more patient complaints about fees, as well as more negative community relations. The growth of malpractice suits requires medical practices to engage in defensive medicine and implement practice guidelines. Third, the increased competition for the premium dollar will mean increased marketing expenses and total expenses to market the practices' services to patients and third-party payors. Fourth, the two-income family now requires service at convenient (for them) times and places. This means extended hours and higher labor costs to staff services over a longer work day.

In managing patients, it is crucial that existing patients be retained and new patients be recruited for the medical practice. These challenges must not only be addressed and managed as suggested, but the challenges and the medical practice's responses must be communicated to patients and other affected key stakeholders, including employees. When communicating with patients, their insecurities and concerns must be addressed (Miles, 1996). Patients may feel that because the organization is in transition, their care may also be in transition. The medical practice needs to develop a comprehensive and detailed communication plan in order to combat rumors.

MCOs as Buyers

Managed care organizations (MCOs) are important to medical practices because they account for an increasing proportion of all insured patients and can choose the providers they will include in their health plans. Not surprisingly, our medical practice respondents forecast a higher potential for both cooperation and threat from MCOs in the future. In particular, approximately 70 percent of these respondents believe that MCOs control key resources, are more powerful than their own organization, and have the potential to form a coalition with the organization.

In competing for contracts, MCOs are under continual pressure to lower or maintain their premiums. This means they continually seek to lower their reimbursements for services provided by medical groups and other providers. If medical groups are not "at risk" in agreeing to provide capitated services to a given population, they will be at the mercy of the MCOs, who will seek repeated discounts by playing one medical group off against another. This will be a particular problem for small groups that have no clout with MCOs. Small groups are also ill-equipped to deal with the complex paperwork that managed care requires.

To deal with this challenge, a growing percentage of medical groups are signing contracts with MCOs that put the groups at risk. One report by Marion Merrill Dow found that 54 percent of group practices had contracts that put them at risk in 1993, up 50 percent from 1992 (Jaklevic, 1997). These contracts accounted for 20 percent of medical practice revenue, up from 12 percent in 1992. A reasonable estimate of the percentage of medical practices with at-risk contracts in 1998 would be 70–80 percent. In addition, the report found that 89 percent of medical group practices had managed care contracts with HMOs and PPOs, up from 56 percent in 1992.

The MCOs themselves are currently under political attack from consumers and all levels of government because of real and alleged abuses. Governor Lawton Chiles of Florida has recently signed a bill creating the nation's first annual report card on HMOs ("Florida," 1997b). The first report cards on the state's forty HMOs will be available in 1998 and will rate HMOs on a scale from excellent to poor in the categories of quality of care, accessibility, member satisfaction, and cost to plan members. The law also prohibits HMOs from imposing gag orders on doctors and other healthcare providers.

The Massachusetts Joint Committees on Health Care and Insurance have endorsed a sweeping bill that would curtail the power of managed care entities ("Massachusetts," 1997). The new legislation would allow physicians, not MCOs, to determine appropriate lengths of inpatient stays and what medical equipment is necessary for treating a patient. The bill would cap financial bonuses at 5 percent of a doctor's annual salary. It would also require reimbursement for "reasonable" emergency care, establish a binding appeals process, establish plans to issue fines for failing to meet periodic reporting requirements, and allow members to seek out-of-network care for higher premiums.

In response to the growing concern regarding financial incentives given by MCOs to physicians treating Medicare and Medicaid patients, the U.S. Department of Health and Human Services (DHHS) has issued new rules on physician incentive plans (Wagner, 1996). Plans must now disclose physician incentive plans to the Health Care Financing Administration (HCFA) or the state Medicaid agency and also provide a summary of these plans to enrollees.

All of this legislation and regulation has had the effect of redirecting the power of MCOs to impose controls on the provision of care provided by medical groups. However, it does not eliminate the market power of MCOs to impose lower reimbursements on medical groups and play one off against another in markets made up of many competitive, unorganized medical groups. This is why medical groups are merging with each other and selling out to physician practice management companies (PPMs) such as MedPartners, which are themselves consolidating.

We are now beginning to see alliances and affiliations between MCOs and PPMs. In 1997, MedPartners and Aetna U.S. Healthcare (an HMO) announced an agreement under which many of the insurer's fourteen million healthcare customers will gain access to eleven thousand physicians affiliated with MedPartners (Bianco and Schine, 1997). This is the first nationwide alliance between an HMO and a PPM and will likely pressure other MCOs to follow suit. Medical groups can also "cooperate" with MCOs by signing contracts to deliver specified services to a given population for a specified price. They can also join IDS/Ns that include one or more HMOs.

Employers as Buyers

Employers are concerned with high healthcare costs, the complexities of the healthcare industry, and government mandates concerning employee benefits. The result has been employers shopping for lower prices and (to a lesser degree) improved service. They are also contracting directly with providers, including medical groups. As noted in Chapter One, employers are expected to be key stakeholders of medical groups in the future.

There are several reasons for the growing importance of employers to medical practices. First, the number of self-insured companies has been growing steadily, and self-insured companies tend to look most actively for innovative ways to control their costs and develop innovative relationships with providers. Second, there is increasing corporate dissatisfaction with both traditional health plans and MCOs. Third, there is growing willingness by medical practices to experiment in dealing directly with employers. Fourth, the growing emergence of buyer coalitions has put additional pressure on medical groups to search for ways to contain costs while maintaining or improving quality (Signorelli, 1994).

One of the newest and most significant drivers of healthcare change in many markets is the consolidation of purchasing strength via coalitions usually led by employers (Lipson and De Sa, 1996). A few local coalitions have developed substantial market strength in negotiating healthcare prices with insurers and providers. Regional and statewide employer coalitions have strengthened the ability of local purchasers to negotiate better prices and value with health plans and providers. State-level purchasing alliances have had only modest influence on local markets, but they are an important new source of information about premium prices for small employers.

Three factors strongly relate to the coalition influence on the local healthcare market: (1) membership composition and size, (2) extent of collective purchasing activity, and (3) the extent of competitive bidding (Lipson and De Sa, 1996). If a community's largest and most influential employers participate in a coalition, it is more likely to have market clout. The more lives represented by a coalition (relative to the size of the market), the greater the market power. If state employee benefit plans or Medicaid programs participate in a coalition, the impact of the coalition is enhanced because these purchasers buy for hundreds of thousands of people. However, when corporate leaders belonging to a coalition have close ties to the industry through membership on boards, the coalition's influence may be blunted.

Even when a purchasing coalition has many large, influential members, its impact may be diminished if its members do not purchase coverage as a group (Lipson and De Sa, 1996). Coalitions that jointly contract with health plans are able to strike better deals on price and documentation of quality. Coalitions in

Des Moines, Minneapolis, and St. Louis that purchase insurance collectively for its members appear to have made the most progress toward improved health benefits for their members in terms of lower prices and greater documentation of quality.

The use of competitive bidding is the third and final factor affecting the influence of employer coalitions (Lipson and De Sa, 1996). The Gateway Purchasing Association member companies in St. Louis buy health benefits through a competitive bidding process from MCOs. Health plan bids were initially estimated to be an average of 12 percent lower than premiums charged to the participating employers in the previous year. These savings were lower than they might have been in St. Louis and elsewhere because coalition employers allowed their employees other choices.

Most employer coalitions have little interest in changing the healthcare system; they are simply looking for a low-cost vendor to contain their health costs (Lipson and De Sa, 1996). The vast majority of coalitions are shifting costs to employees, switching from indemnity to managed care plans, and aggressively negotiating with insurers and health plans. Fewer coalitions—but many of the larger ones—are trying to influence employee choice by redesigning employer contributions, using quality data to make provider selections, or contracting with providers directly to eliminate the middle-man role in a health plan.

Only a few of the larger groups will consider direct contracting with employers or coalitions because they cannot offer one-stop shopping unless they are part of an IDS/N. Direct contracting between employers and IDS/Ns will be discussed in the next section.

Medical practices could create their own health plans and market their services directly to employers. Several medical groups have attempted this without great success in California (Enthoven and Singer, 1996). HMOs that are owned or operated by medical groups make up a small proportion of HMO business in California. Medical groups are limited to aggressively marketing their own health plans for fear that other plans will stop marketing their provider services in retaliation. It is also reasonable to question whether a medical-practice-run network would push medical groups aggressively enough to reduce costs and monitor quality. Finally, insurance carriers have very large capitalization, whereas medical groups have very low capitalization. This makes it difficult for medical groups to comply with solvency requirements for HMOs and to compete effectively.

IDS/Ns as Buyers

Our respondents reacted to IDS/Ns as new market entrants the way they did to MCOs as buyers. That is, they view the IDS/N as an entity that is high in both potential threat and potential cooperation. More specifically, they view it as more powerful than their own organization, as controlling key resources, and as offering a high potential to form a coalition with their organization.

Some questions medical groups should ask before they decide to merge with or form an alliance with an IDS/N are as follows:

- Do the purchasers of its services want the likely results of integration in our local market?

- Will working as part of an IDS/N increase the medical practice's ability to provide value to our consumers while working in a manner we find acceptable? (Sherman, 1996).

An IDS/N will need to produce improvements in medical quality and efficiency to add value to the community. The result does not automatically flow from the act of integration. A centralized organization can be a burden to productive activity and an obstacle to creating value. Other industries are moving away from higher levels of integration in their quest for quality and efficiency improvement (Sherman, 1996).

A medical practice choosing to join an IDS/N will need to take steps to ensure that the group will maintain an acceptable degree of autonomy within the system. It will need the ability to accept accountability for quality and efficiency and to retain control of how its physicians deliver healthcare to patients. The practice will need to have the status of partners or owners of the IDS/N rather than an employee status. This means sharing in the financial gains and losses (Sherman, 1996).

A medical practice within an IDS/N will also need to shift its focus from revenue production to the production of higher-quality, cost-effective care for the IDS/N. Therefore, the focus of medical practice executives will need to evolve from incentive based on the number of visits or procedures performed by each physician to the ability to manage resources and deliver quality healthcare under a limited budget (Sherman, 1996).

Medical practices that are part of IDS/Ns can contract directly with employers to provide their services to a given population on a capitated basis. Direct contrasting will eliminate some middle-man costs and may also alleviate some political or community concerns (Matthews, 1997). The benefits of direct contrasting are that it builds a long-term relationship with key customers, locks in market share, provides customized health plans and delivery networks, provides immediate clinical care, and secures quality.

IDS/Ns and their associated medical practices need to know their local market and segment employers in that market by size and ownership. Typically, large employers are self-funded. Small employers are often costly to service. Multi-location employers may make decisions only at the corporate level. Employer coalitions are very price-sensitive.

THE EXTENDED WEB

Figure 9.2 shows the extended web. The organizational web, the network/system web, and the competitive web are shown as boxes at the bottom of the figure. The extended web includes both the state and federal governments in their various roles as legislator, regulator, and payor. In addition, various other national health plans, healthcare delivery organizations, and physician practice management companies (for example, MedPartners and PhyCor) are also web participants. Key stakeholders in this group affect the medical practice indirectly through other members of its network/system web, including system headquarters, MCOs, and hospitals.

Table 9.2 summarizes challenges, barriers, facilitators, and choices related to the extended web. A key concern for healthcare leaders is how to develop system units and executives to manage all of these regional and national stakeholders, with their disparate information needs. At present, MCOs are receiving close scrutiny from Congress because of the perception and reality that patient care has been shortchanged in order to reduce utilization and improve profitability. The problem needs to be addressed not only through political lobbying but through development of protocols for the management of patient care, with input from physicians delivering care at the unit level. If these problems are not addressed, adverse legislation could be passed that would freeze current practice and preclude productivity improvements.

PPMs promise to alter the balance of power in healthcare over the next ten years as greatly as HMOs did in the past ten years (Bianco and Schine, 1997). Thousands of doctors in medical practices across the country are joining forces under the PPMC banner, giving rise to a new type of enterprise: publicly traded, professionally run, ultra-acquisitive, for-profit corporations assembled from heretofore independent medical practices.

Peter Stamos, director of Stanford's Comparative Health Research Center, predicts that the PPM industry could raise its revenues from $12 billion in 1996 to $60–100 billion in 2001 (Bianco and Schine, 1997). Jason Rosenbluth, analyst for Volpe, Whelan, Brown in San Francisco, believes that PPMCs will become the new center of the healthcare universe. The industry provides a countervailing force to MCOs. It strengthens physician hands in negotiating terms with HMOs, PPOs, and other third-party payors. It also reduces the power of MCOs to infringe on physician medical authority by requiring advanced authority for simple procedures and refusing to pay for costly procedures. Finally, it brings investment capital and management expertise that can help a medical practice provide and document high-quality, cost-effective care.

However, many physicians who acknowledge the benefits of professionalizing their management practices are reluctant to join forces with a PPMC because

Figure 9.2. The Extended Web (The System Medical Group's Ability to Manage Extended Web Relationships Becomes Increasingly Dependent on the Emerging System).

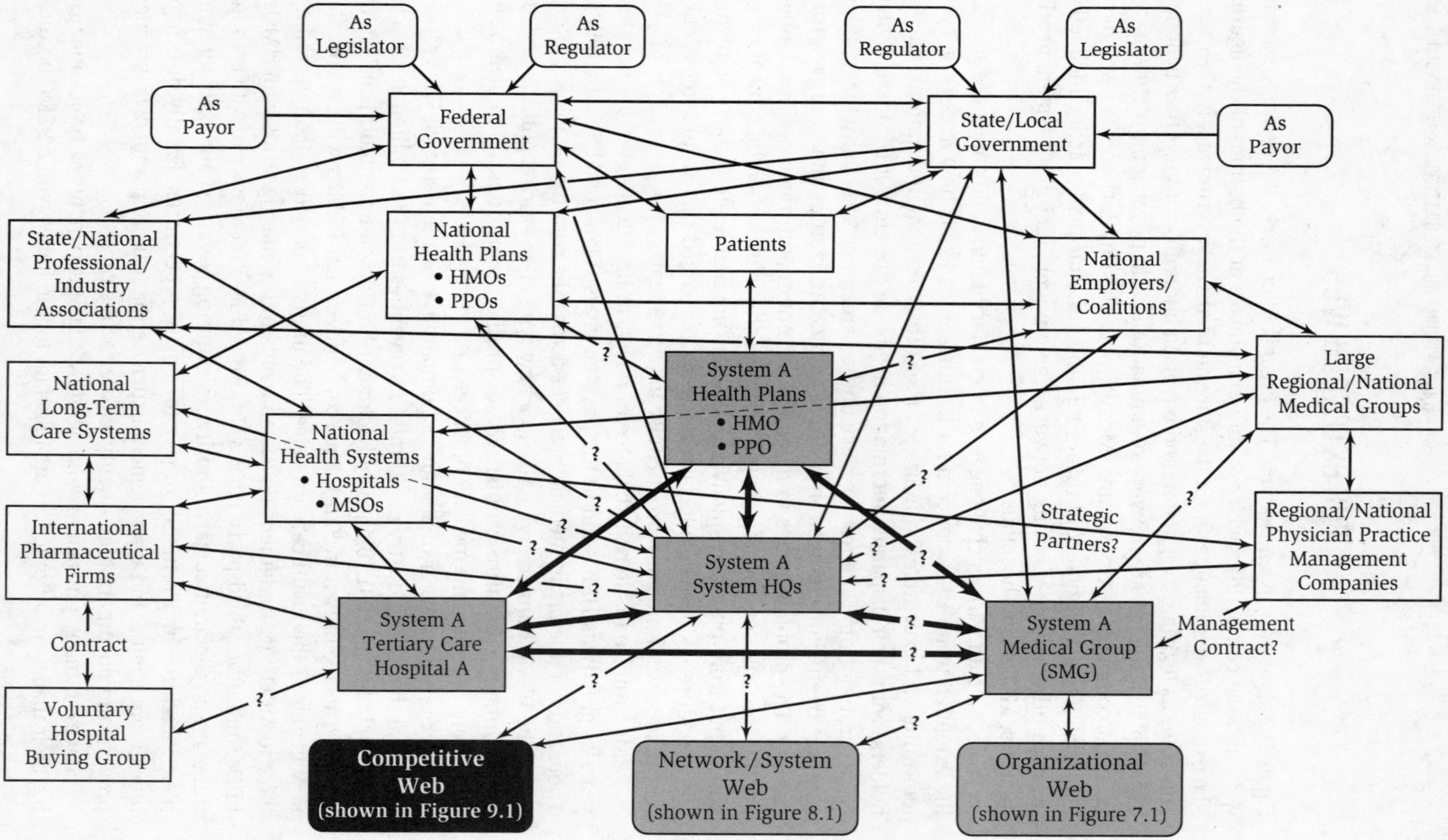

Table 9.2. The Extended Web: Challenges, Barriers, Facilitators, and Choices Confronting Healthcare Executives As They Navigate This Web.

Challenges	Potential Barriers	Potential Facilitators	Choices
1. How to manage federal and state governments in their role as legislator, payor, and regulator	1. Lack of system executive experience in political realm	1. One-stop shopping allows negotiation with regional and national stakeholders	1. Development of system units to manage national and regional stakeholders
2. How to manage other regional and national stakeholders (including IDS/Ns)	2. Lack of system executive experience in dealing with national or regional organizations	2. Selection of system executives with experience in managing national and regional stakeholders	2. Resource allocation decisions within system
3. How to manage national medical groups and national physician management companies	3. Shifting goals and priorities of national stakeholders	3. Sophisticated information system	3. Recruitment of system executives with the appropriate skills, knowledge, and experience to implement 1 and 2 above
4. What information to generate and disseminate to national stakeholders	4. Inadequate reimbursement from government programs	4. Identification and provision of information needs to national stakeholders	
5. Changing stakeholder expectations			

of concerns that they may lose their independence and autonomy (Bianco and Schine, 1997). In the long run, they fear that their best interests and those of their patients will be subjugated to investors' desire for profit. Typically, the PPMC buys the assets of the physician group, including its clinic building, equipment, accounts receivable, and so on (Bianco and Schine, 1997). However, the physicians continue as employees of their own professional corporation, which signs a long-term service contract with the PPMC. The physicians retain full sovereignty over medical policy and physician personnel matters, including pay. Nonphysician clinic employees are transferred to the payroll of the PPMC, which recapitalizes the practice and manages its business affairs in exchange for an annual fee of 15–20 percent of practice income. The PPMC reduces overhead by 10–20 percent, consolidates purchasing, and invests in new information systems. The goal is that the PPMC and its affiliated physicians prosper together or not at all.

The obvious challenge for a medical practice is to find ways to become more integrated, gain market power, and achieve economies of scale. In addition to selling out to a PPMC, they could also merge with or affiliate with a system owned by a hospital, a health plan, or another (nonprofit) multispecialty group practice. By a wide and increasing margin, employee physicians prefer to work for other doctors in physician-owned group practices rather than to be employed by PPMCs, MCOs, or hospitals (Bianco and Schine, 1997). However, even the largest and most sophisticated multispecialty practices have concluded that they lack the capital, management skills, or nerve to go it alone in the current managed care environment. PPMCs offer a solution to most of these problems in exchange for a lower level of independence and autonomy.

All levels of government affect the medical practice and all other components of a system. Currently, local governments and local communities are raising questions about the value of integration and are asking, What's in it for us? (Scott, 1997). Recently, Florida's attorney general Bob Butterworth brought a lawsuit asking a private hospital to justify its merger plans in terms of community impact. Three class-action lawsuits have been filed against Marshfield (Wisconsin) Clinic accusing the 450-physician practice of overcharging consumers after a local court found it had violated antitrust laws.

State governments make many decisions concerning the allocation of resources (for example, healthcare versus education) that affect the adequacy of its reimbursement to providers. A shift of spreading priorities from healthcare to other sectors could, for example, result in inadequate Medicaid reimbursement rates to providers. This could result in physician unwillingness to provide service to Medicaid patients and create access problems and a negative community reaction to the medical practice. Alternatively, it could result in cost-shifting to private-pay patients, with the consequent negative reaction of patients and employers. An increasing use of long-term care services by the Medicaid population could result in a shift in resources from medical practices to long-term care services.

The state government could impose regulations on medical practices to control their Medicaid costs or to enhance quality of care or consumer information. Such initiatives may reduce the physician's autonomy in choosing the best treatment for a given patient or create adverse publicity for the medical practice. For example, the Massachusetts legislators recently ordered the governor to give consumers continued access to disciplinary and malpractice information on the state's 27,000 physicians ("Massachusetts," 1997). There will also be a Board of Directors in Medicine to license and discipline physicians. If the general public becomes concerned about the market power, limited access, social inequity, quality of care, or excessive changes of IDS/Ns, a state health services commission might be established to protect the public interest and allocate health resources in that state. All of these actual or potential state initiatives could affect a medical practice or the system or network of which it is a part.

The federal government, like state governments, affects medical practices and their associated IDS/Ns through its spending priorities. Its resource-based relative value system (RBRVS) for reimbursing physicians obviously affects the salaries of physicians in primary care as opposed to the specialties, as well as within the various specialties. The regulations of provision of care and human resources practices is another federal initiative that affects medical practices. Finally, the federal government's changing interpretation of antitrust law affects mergers in various markets.

Medical practices might respond to federal initiatives in any number of ways. They might shift their dependence from federal Medicare patients to private-pay patients. They could allow physicians to determine their own plan for compensating physicians within the practice, or they could recruit more primary care physicians. They might set up a system to monitor government policy changes and to check for compliance with regulations, either within the medical practice or the IDS/N of which it is a part.

Medical groups could enlist antitrust lawyers prior to implementing any merger that is likely to have a significant impact on a local market. National and regional employers or coalitions are also key stakeholders in the extended web. Regional employer purchasing coalitions are using their purchasing power to push for improved quality and cost-effectiveness (Hayes, 1996). They are also establishing new criteria for selection of providers. One example is the Buyers' Health Care Action Group (BHCAG) of Minnesota (Hayes, 1996). Their selection criteria include an emphasis on quality management and improvement tools such as practice guidelines—a management process driven by physicians rather than administrators. There is a focus on health maintenance and improvement activities such as self-care, nutrition, and preventive care. An automated medical record is another criteria. Member satisfaction is stressed. HEDIS (Health Plan Employer

Data Information Set) measurements for mammography screening rates, low birth weights, and immunization rates are required. The criteria also specify management competencies as indicated by a continuous quality improvement process that looks at outcomes and develops protocols, as well as an internal system to measure and monitor provider performance.

For IDS/Ns, the BHCAG also specifies the following contractual requirements for its partners (Hayes, 1996). The system must be accountable for the full continuum of care and develop standard measures, identify and eliminate instances of unnecessary care and inspection, and create provider-defined "best practice" standards and guidelines. Finally, the health plan must provide appropriate incentives to reward improved performance and outcomes. Although these requirements are not typical now, medical practices and IDS/Ns should be aware that they could well be typical in the future.

National health plans are another key stakeholder in the extended web to which both medical practices and IDS/Ns must relate. While employers have been resisting higher insurance premiums, national and regional HMOs have been caught in a profit squeeze because their cost of drugs has been increasing as much as 10–20 percent a year ("Prescription Drugs," 1997). One reason for the cost increase is that patients are using more prescriptions and each prescription has become more expensive over time. In response, HMOs are imposing additional hurdles for physicians if they want to have the broadest choices among today's top medicines. In addition, as states impose additional reporting requirements on HMOs in the form of report cards ("Texas," 1997), the HMOs are likely to require better documentation of outcomes, patient satisfaction, and cost-effectiveness from providers with whom they contract.

One of the most controversial issues relating to regional and national MCOs is their "gag rules." These rules prohibit physicians from discussing with patients either their own (the doctors') financial arrangements with MCOs or the healthcare options that are available but not covered by patients' plans. Recently, the Florida Physician's Association threatened to sue certain national MCOs in Florida because of these rules (Galuszka, 1996). Unexpectedly, Humana broke ranks and volunteered to drop the restrictions. This is a case of a national HMO backing down in the face of political pressure from local physicians who were in a position to seriously harm the HMO's reputation.

State and national professional and industry associations are also key. The single most powerful of these associations is the Joint Commission on Accreditation of Healthcare Organizations (JCAHO). The joint commission has recently announced that it will include healthcare outcomes in its accreditation process for the first time (JCAHO, 1997). This action is in response to pressure from purchasers, consumer groups, all levels of government, and the general public.

The initiative is titled ORYX and is supported by sixty performance measurement systems with which JCAHO has contracted (JCAHO, 1997). Health plans, integrated systems, and provider-service organizations must choose a minimum of ten separate measures from one or more of five specified consensus-based measure sets in 1997. In 1998, each network must choose twenty separate measures, and by 1999 each group must choose thirty separate measures. The important point is that, in addition to government regulation and control, private regulatory agencies like JCAHO also can pose significant opportunities and threats through their regulatory role. Medical practice executives are well advised to anticipate and proactively manage relationships with these stakeholders.

A final key stakeholder in the extended strategic web are the national health-care systems. Richard Scott, past CEO of Columbia/HCA, recently spoke at a Medical Group Management Association conference (Pope, 1996) and discussed his perception of the advantages and efficiency benefits to be gained by physicians who link with his company. Columbia/HCA is moving away from the purchase of practices and working to "integrate" physicians by contract, using management service organizations (MSOs) and integrated practice associations (IPAs).

Scott stressed his company's ability to measure quality, patient satisfaction, and cost and then report these data to relevant stakeholders. He also recommended that physician practices link with his company because of its success in aligning incentives with their affiliated physicians (unlike most MCOs). From the perspective of the medical practice executive, a national health system (Columbia/HCA) or a national health plan (for example, Kaiser) offer other options for partnership arrangements in addition to the PPMs and the physician-led, nonprofit physician networks discussed previously.

LEADERSHIP IMPLICATIONS

Many leadership implications emerge from our analysis in this chapter. First, we have noted that being part of a system or network is an advantage in managing stakeholders in the extended web because they may have political expertise not usually found in the smaller medical practice, and employers prefer one-stop shopping. Managing key stakeholders in the extended web also requires a sophisticated information system not usually found in a non-integrated medical practice. Establishing a political unit within the system or network is necessary in order to monitor and manage the dependence on government as legislator, regulator, and payor. And finally, the system or network must develop and report indicators of cost-effectiveness, quality of care, outcomes, and patient satisfaction for the joint commission, employers, or employer coalitions, MCOs, and all levels of government.

Medical practice executives need to develop and document data on quality, patient satisfaction, and cost-effectiveness and communicate it to all the stakeholders in the competitive web, including members of its own system or network, competitors supplying similar services, patients, MCOs, and employers. They also need to carefully assess their physicians in terms of quality of care, patient satisfaction, cost-effectiveness, malpractice claims, broad certifications, and so forth. Then, these data should be used to market the practice through report cards. However, they need to avoid actions that will trigger a physician backlash such as restrictions on "the practice of medicine" or "cookbook medicine." Physician-developed protocols can be useful tools for communication and process improvement.

Medical practices could sign contracts to deliver capitated services with organizations both inside and outside their IDS/N. These contracts should put them "at risk" in order to avoid continual HMO pressure to reduce prices. A clinic without walls may be a reasonable first step in medical practice integration because it provides some market advantages without significantly compromising physician autonomy. Management service organizations jointly owned with hospitals are another option for medical practice executives because they allow higher degrees of physician and practice autonomy than do buyouts. Even more important than the structural form of collaboration is the choice of a hospital partner who understands medical practices and is willing to meet the professional and autonomy needs of physicians. All affiliations should be viewed from the perspective of their impact on physician and practice autonomy.

Finally, medical practice executives should try to enhance patient satisfaction by enhancing the satisfaction and commitment of the partners and the other employees. Areas for improvement can be identified through periodic patient-satisfaction and employee-attitude surveys. Positive feedback from patients can be used to reward employees. Modeling a medical practice on the way services are delivered in the finer hotels is one way to improve customer service. Continual communication with patients and employees is necessary at all times, but particularly during times of major change.

STEPS FOR NAVIGATING
YOUR COMPETITIVE AND EXTENDED WEBS

To effectively navigate your competitive web, the following steps are suggested:

- Identify key group and organizational stakeholders that make up your group's competitive web.

    Refer to Tool 1.1. How are those identified here represented among your top key stakeholders?

    Determine if subgroups or additional stakeholders need to be added.

- Develop specific lists of each of the following, using Tool 9.1:

    Challenges within your competitive web

    Barriers within your competitive web

    Potential facilitators for navigating your competitive web

    Choices concerning strategies and tactics within the competitive web for the executive leader

To effectively navigate your extended web, the following steps are recommended. They are supported by Tool 9.1.

- Identify the key groups, organizations, or associations that make up the external web.

    Which (if any) are key stakeholders to your organization?

    What groups or organizations within the other webs serve as facilitators to the extended web stakeholders?

    Assess your group's specific challenges, barriers, facilitators, and choices by completing Tool 9.2.

- Using Tool 9.3, assess how successful you were in navigating the competitive and extended webs.

TOOLKIT 9

Navigating Your Group's
Competitive and Extended Webs

Tool 9.1. Competitive Web Challenges, Barriers, Facilitators, and Choices.

Instructions: Parallel the general challenges, barriers, facilitators, and choices reported in Table 9.1 with those that apply specifically to medical groups.

Specific Challenges

1._____
2._____
3._____
4._____
5._____

Barriers

1._____
2._____
3._____
4._____
5._____

Facilitators

1._____
2._____
3._____
4._____
5._____

Choices

1._____
2._____
3._____
4._____
5._____

Tool 9.2. Extended Web Challenges, Barriers, Facilitators, and Choices.

Instructions: Parallel the general challenges, barriers, facilitators, and choices reported in Table 9.2 with those that apply specifically to medical groups.

Specific Challenges	Barriers
1._____	1._____
2._____	2._____
3._____	3._____
4._____	4._____
5._____	5._____

Facilitators	Choices
1._____	1._____
2._____	2._____
3._____	3._____
4._____	4._____
5._____	5._____

Tool 9.3. Planning Tool for Implementing Key Needed Actions.

Instructions: Complete this exhibit *for each of the challenges* facing your group in order to plan the implementation of needed actions for each.

Web: Competitive or Extended

Challenge: _____

Your Group's Strategic and Web Navigation Type (based on your strategic and web navigation priorities from Tools 3.4 and 5.3). Check the most appropriate *now* and *in 3 years.*

Now	In 3 Years	
____	____	Strategic Entrepreneur
____	____	Strategic Engineer
____	____	Strategic Ostrich
____	____	Strategic Navigator

Now	In 3 Years	
____	____	Web Entrepreneur
____	____	Web Engineer
____	____	Web Ostrich
____	____	Web Navigator

Tool 9.3. Planning Tool for Implementing Key Needed Actions, cont'd.

1. What actions do you recommend for your group in meeting this challenge? Be specific!

   Immediately?
   Over the next 3 years?

2. In what ways do your recommended actions support your group's overall strategic intentions and other tactical actions?

   Immediately?
   Over the next 3 years?

3. What is your specific plan for implementing each of the proposed actions?

   Immediately?
   Over the next 3 years?

4. What are the most significant factors that could undermine the implementation process, and how can they be dealt with?

   Immediately?
   Over the next 3 years?

5. What resources will be required for implementation, and are they available?

   Immediately?
   Over the next 3 years?

6. How cost-effective are your recommendations? If they are not cost-effective, what alternative actions can you take?

   Immediately?
   Over the next 3 years?

7. Which physician and/or administrative managers will have the lead role in implementing these particular actions?

   Immediately?
   Over the next 3 years?

8. Do the responsible managers have the necessary abilities and authority to effectively implement these actions? What will you do to improve their abilities and ensure their authority?

   Immediately?
   Over the next 3 years?

9. What other group/system managers or other personnel—as internal stakeholders—should be involved in the implementation process?

   Immediately?
   Over the next 3 years?

10. If the implementation process does not work as planned, what contingency approach will you go to next? Why will it work if this process did not?

    Immediately?
    Over the next 3 years?

CHAPTER TEN

BECOMING A STRATEGIC WEB NAVIGATOR

T his final chapter provides an overview, integration, and extension of our models and data analysis. First, we will integrate strategic navigation and web navigation to create five new strategic web categories: the Strategic Web Navigator, the Strategic Navigator Only, the Web Navigator Only, the Limited Navigator, and the Strategic Web Ostrich. We will focus on the two extreme categories (the Strategic Web Navigator and the Strategic Web Ostrich), which account for the majority of medical practices in the past and the future. These strategic web types will be compared with regard to their relative performance, tactics, and management of relations with stakeholders, as well as to their prevalence by practice size, academic affiliation, degree of integration, and managed care penetration in the local community.

Second, we will consider what it means to be a Strategic Web Navigator. Examples of how medical practice executives could strategically navigate their web of relationships will be discussed. Third, for those who are interested in developing their own processes for navigating each of the four web levels, we provide an agenda for one or more strategic retreats. Fourth, we provide a convenient summary of the major ideas and concepts provided in this book.

INTEGRATING STRATEGIC NAVIGATION AND WEB NAVIGATION

We have previously discussed both strategic navigation and web navigation and indicated the preferred management strategies for each. Figure 10.1 shows how the two navigation types (strategic and web) can be combined, as well as the relative prevalence of each type in the past and the future. The Strategic Navigation type is shown on the vertical axis; the Web Navigation type is shown on the horizontal axis.

Past and Future Prevalence of Strategic Web Navigation Types

At the extreme upper left corner of Figure 10.1 is the Strategic Web Navigator, which represents medical practices that are *both* Strategic Navigators and Web Navigators. Remember that a Strategic Navigator is both entrepreneurial- and

Figure 10.1. In Search of the Strategic Web Navigator—Bringing Together Strategic and Web Navigation Priorities for the Same Organization.

	Web Navigation Type		
	Web Navigator	Web Optimist/Pessimist	Web Ostrich
Strategic Navigator	**Strategic Web Navigator** *Past: 3% **Future: 10%	← Past: 4% Future: 13%	**Strategic Navigator Only** Past: 5% Future: 8%
Strategic Entrepreneur/ Engineer	↑ Past: 4% Future: 17%	**Limited Navigator** Past: 9% Future: 23%	↓ Past: 20% Future: 16%
Strategic Ostrich	**Web Navigator Only** Past: 5% Future: 3%	→ Past: 10% Future: 4%	**Strategic Web Ostrich** Past: 40% Future: 7%

(vertical axis label: Strategic Navigation Type)

*Percent of organizations fitting each type in the past

**Percent of organizations expected to fit each type in the future engineering-oriented. The Web Navigator has a high priority for both enhancing cooperation *and* reducing threats in web relationships. The arrows in the cells adjacent to the upper left cell indicate these cells, which are not pure types but which we also classify primarily as Strategic Web Navigators.

The Strategic Web Ostrich in the lower right corner represents medical practices that are both Strategic Ostriches and Web Ostriches. A Strategic Ostrich has low levels of both entrepreneurial *and* engineering orientation. The Web Ostrich has a low priority for both enhancing cooperation *and* reducing threats in web relationships. As in the case of the Strategic Web Navigator, the adjacent cells are also classified as Strategic Ostriches.

Three other categories combine strategic and web navigation. In the upper right corner are the Strategic Navigators, who are also Web Ostriches. That is, they combine an entrepreneurial orientation and an engineering orientation with an unwillingness to either reduce threat or enhance cooperation. The lower left corner represents Web Navigators Only, who are Web Navigators but Strategic Ostriches. Finally, in the middle cell is the Limited Navigator, who exhibits moderate levels of both strategic and web navigation.

If we compare and contrast the five strategic navigation types for both the past and the future, the following patterns emerge:

- Strategic Web Ostriches decline from 70 percent in the past to 27 percent in the future.

- Strategic Web Navigators increase from 11 percent in the past to 40 percent in the future.

- Limited Navigators increase from 9 percent in the past to 23 percent in the future.

- Web Navigators Only and Strategic Web Ostriches each represent relatively small percentages of medical practices in the past and the future.

It appears that in the past most medical practices (70 percent) were Strategic Web Ostriches, most of which expect to become either Strategic Web Navigators or Limited Navigators in the future. The obvious question is whether moving to the Strategic Web Navigator category will be beneficial to medical practices. Do Strategic Web Navigators perform better than the other strategic web navigation types?

Performance of Strategic Web Navigation Types

We examined the perceived competitive advantage of our five strategic web navigation types relative to clinical quality, service orientation, market share, profitability, cost-effectiveness, organizational survival, and fulfillment of stakeholder needs in the past and in the future. Results in the past indicated that the Strategic Web Navigator and the Strategic Navigator Only were superior to all other types for all performance dimensions except profitability, which showed no significant differences. In the future, our medical practice executives predict similar levels of performance for all strategic web types on all dimensions except clinical quality, where Strategic Web Navigators expect significantly better performance.

Strategic Web Navigators were significantly more likely than the Strategic Web Ostrich (with the other strategic web types in the middle) to be above average in size, a nonacademic practice, a multispecialty practice, and fully integrated.

From a management perspective, Strategic Web Navigators were significantly more likely than Strategic Web Ostriches to

- Have a strategic plan.
- Have high levels of involvement in strategic planning.
- Have strong physician leadership.
- Believe MCOs and IDS/Ns control key resources.
- Believe patients have high levels of power relative to the medical practice.
- Form a coalition with physicians, patients, hospitals, competitors, MCOs, and IDS/Ns.
- View internal physicians, patients, and IDS/Ns as supportive stakeholders in the future.
- Involve their patients in the future.
- Believe they have managed their physicians better than their local competitors in the past—and believe that will be true for the future as well.
- Modify services, pursue horizontal integration, pursue horizontal integration by contract, shift domain, form strategic partnerships with key stakeholder, and initiate or expand TQM or CQI in the future.
- Rate their ability to work collaboratively with medical groups and hospitals, their skills in negotiation and conflict management to manage multiple organizations, their skills in creating a common vision and purpose, and their leadership skills for managing fully integrated IDS/Ns as much better than their competition in the future.
- Have involved their internal patients and collaborated with competitors, MCOs, and IDS/Ns in their practices in the past.
- Have employed entrepreneurial tactics such as developing a market niche, modifying services to adapt to the local market, horizontally integrating in the local market, horizontally integrating by contract at the

national level, vertically integrating across the continuum of care, and shifting their domain in response to regulation.

- Have implemented integrating tactics such as developing electronic interfaces and past data, developing electronic interfaces and past data, developing performance standards in provider networks, and integrating financing and delivery of care.
- Have used engineering tactics such as cost-benefit analysis to consolidate duplicative services, tighten physician utilization controls, differentiate services based on technical quality, and initiate or expand TQM or CQI.

In short, our analysis shows that Strategic Web Navigators have performed better in the past and are expected to perform better in the future than all other strategic web types, but particularly the Strategic Web Ostrich. Medical practice executives should strive to become Strategic Web Navigators in the future. This means they need to be entrepreneurial in seeking out new market opportunities and attending to internal operations in order to contain their costs (they need to be Strategic Navigators). At the same time, they need to be simultaneously defending against threats from their external stakeholders and seeking out opportunities for cooperation and collaboration (they also need to be Web Navigators).

Strategic Web Navigators are different from other medical practices in their strategic navigation and web navigation priorities and in their managerial practices. In particular, Strategic Web Navigators are more likely to view IDS/Ns as key stakeholders and to manage their physicians better than others. They also tend to view their internal stakeholders more positively and are more likely to involve them in their activities or collaborate with them. Alternatively, the Strategic Web Ostrich has a greater tendency to view internal stakeholders more negatively and are more likely to monitor or defend against them. The Strategic Web Navigator also tends to implement more entrepreneurial, integrating, and engineering tactics in both the past and the future. This means they are more proactive along a number of dimensions.

PROCESS GUIDELINES FOR FORMULATING STRATEGIC WEB NAVIGATION IN MEDICAL GROUPS

This section will summarize process guidelines for formulating and implementing strategic web navigation strategies and tactics. It will outline how to do strategic web navigation. The details and rationale for each step are provided in the individual chapters. Figure 10.2 provides a conceptual framework for both this section and the one to follow.

Figure 10.2. Strategic Web Navigation.

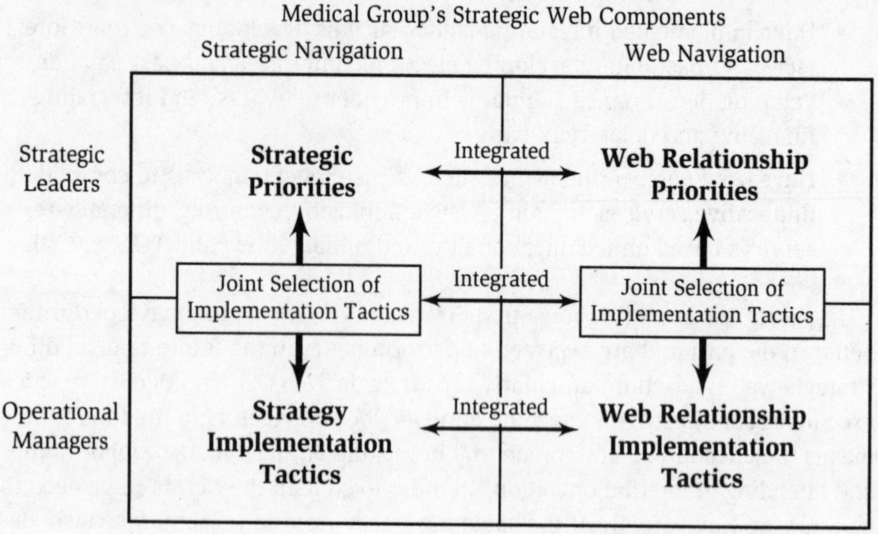

Medical Group's Strategic Web Components

	Strategic Navigation		Web Navigation
Strategic Leaders	**Strategic Priorities**	← Integrated →	**Web Relationship Priorities**
	↑		↑
	Joint Selection of Implementation Tactics	← Integrated →	Joint Selection of Implementation Tactics
	↓		↓
Operational Managers	**Strategy Implementation Tactics**	← Integrated →	**Web Relationship Implementation Tactics**

Strategic leaders need to set priorities and develop web navigation tactics. Operational managers implement strategy and web relationship tactics. This will be discussed further in our strategies retreat section.

Develop Strategic Priorities and Plans

- Create shared mission and values (determine who you are and what you do best).

- Assess external environmental opportunities and threats.

- Assess internal organizational strengths and weaknesses.

- Classify your own organization as a Strategic Navigator, Strategic Engineer, Strategic Entrepreneur, or Strategic Ostrich, based on your priority on strategic entrepreneurship, strategic engineering, or both.

- Strive to emphasize both engineering and entrepreneurship by becoming a Strategic Navigator in the future.

- Establish priorities to achieve high-quality, customer-focused, cost-effective patient care.

- Explore entrepreneurial opportunities to develop and market new services.

Develop Web Relationships, Priorities, and Plans

- Devote a high level of economic resources, effort, and time to relationship assessment and reassessment.

- Do continual environmental scanning of key internal and external relationships in all four strategic webs.

- Identify all key external and internal relationships now and in the future. Key relationships are those relevant to the implementation of the strategic priorities and plans because they control economic or noneconomic resources needed by the organization.

- Classify your own organization as a Web Navigator, a Web Optimist, a Web Pessimist, or a Web Ostrich in terms of relative emphasis on a priority to enhance cooperation, reduce threat, or both.

- Strive to both enhance cooperation and reduce threat by becoming a Web Navigator in the future.

- Assess each relationship in terms of its potential to form a supportive or nonsupportive coalition with others.

- Classify each key relationship as supportive, mixed-blessing, or nonsupportive, based on its power to threaten or cooperate with the organization.

- Link with organizations both inside and outside your IDS/N.

- Determine which stakeholder resource inputs are vital to the medical practice and which have partial or total substitutes.

- Shift dependence from nonsupportive to supportive stakeholders where feasible.

- Become associated with a larger entity rather than remain totally independent.

- Build a consensus toward integrating with other partners.

The process guidelines we have provided for the formulation of strategic web navigation require that we first develop strategic priorities and plans and then develop web relationship priorities and plans. The guidelines reflect our ideas about doing it as well as the patterns of relationships between strategic or web types and various performance measures reported earlier. Obviously, a practice that is a Web Navigator Only has failed to strategically plan, whereas a Strategic Navigator Only has to failed to consider web relationships. Only the Strategic Web Navigator has done both.

PROCESS GUIDELINES FOR IMPLEMENTING STRATEGIC WEB NAVIGATION IN MEDICAL GROUPS

The guidelines presented earlier do not cover the specific reinforcing tactical actions required to implement these strategic priorities and plans. A failure to plan for and implement reinforcing tactical actions has been the greatest failure in strategic management. Next, we present a process for implementing strategic web navigation through tactics that reinforce strategic plans and priorities. Again, these guidelines provide a convenient summary of what has already been presented in the individual chapters.

Develop Strategy Implementation Tactics

- Reinforce strategic intentions with supportive tactical actions (combine how you think and act).

- Reengineer internal systems to enhance customer value (high-quality, cost-effective patient care).

- Use TQM or CQI processes and other techniques to measure, control, and improve physician and employee use of resources, technical quality, and service orientation.

- Develop a management and clinical information system that allows the practice to define and document data on quality of care (outcomes), patient satisfaction, and cost-effectiveness.

- Communicate these data to all key stakeholders in all four webs.

- Carefully evaluate the performance of physicians in the medical practice against practice or external benchmarks in such areas as clinical quality, outcomes, patient satisfaction, complaints, cost-effectiveness, malpractice claims, and board certification.

- Reward physicians based on their performance compared to these dimensions.

- Allow physicians to be involved in development of clinical protocols, as well as measurement of the dimensions.

- Prepare and educate all staff concerning the changing market realities and the consequent need for collaborative relationships and cost-effective, high-quality patient care.

- Manage patient satisfaction by enhancing employee commitment, motivation, and job satisfaction.

- Model practice on service delivery in the better hotels.

- Continually communicate with patients and employees, particularly during periods of major change.

- Consider the viewpoints of all internal and external key stakeholders before implementing new tactical actions.

- Retain high levels of physician autonomy and independence.

- Align physician incentives to be compatible with both the medical group's goals and its parent IDS/N's objectives.

Develop Web Relationship Tactics

- View relationships as either supportive or mixed-blessing.

- Perceive a higher potential for cooperation and a lower potential for threat.

- Anticipate the goals of key stakeholders; attempt to satisfy these stakeholders by offering appropriate inducements in exchange for essential contributions.

- Implement generic relationship navigation tactics that fit the nature of the web relationship: involve trustingly in the supportive relationship; collaborate cautiously in the mixed-blessing relationship; defend proactively in the nonsupportive relationship; and monitor efficiently in the marginal relationship.

- Implement these tactics by developing specific actions and programs for each tactic and relationship combination.

- Choose web partners that can bring resources to the relationship that are complementary to those of the organization.

- Academic practices should align with primary care practices in the community.

- Smaller practices should align with larger practices in order to gain market share.

- Negotiate both clinical and business issues with web partners.

- Develop or contract for management skills to analyze, evaluate, and negotiate contracts with MCOs, IDS/Ns, hospitals, and other medical practices.

- Link contract formation and coalition formation to group strategic goals and strategies.

- Negotiate physician autonomy and control in medical practice when joining an IDS/N.

- Sign capitated contracts with MCOs that put the medical practice and its physicians at risk to preserve incentives for high-quality, cost-effective patient care.

- Larger practices and those part of an IDS/N should explore capitated and noncapitated contracts with employers to provide specified services to a given cohort of employees.

- Explore clinics without walls as the first step in medical practice integration.

- Explore and select one of the following as a second step in integration: joint ownership with hospitals (MSOs), becoming part of a network of medical practices, joining an IDS/N, or selling out to a physician practice management company.

- Avoid large capital investments in plant and equipment on new acquisitions.

- Join a virtual network of providers.

- Focus on the metropolitan area or region.

- Emphasize many managed care contracts.

- Focus on markets where the IDS/N can be first or second in market share.

- Build relationships on a foundation of trust.

This list should also provide a process for integrating strategic navigation and web navigation. This involves strategic retreats, the assignment of responsibility for implementing strategic web tactics, and follow-up and evaluation. It also requires establishing a regional "brand identity" for a given medical practice that differentiates it from competitors.

Integrate and Implement Strategic Priorities, Web Relationship Priorities, Strategy Implementation Tactics, and Web Relationship Tactics

- Plan and implement a strategic and an operational retreat on a periodic basis to discuss strategic and web navigation strategies and tactics.

- Invite strategic leaders and operational managers to attend both retreats because implementation of reinforcing tactics is crucial to the success of strategic and web navigation strategies.

- Determine which managerial and nonmanagerial employees should be involved in the implementation process.

- Assign responsibility for specific managerial and nonmanagerial employees to implement specific strategy implementation tactics and web relationship tactics.

- Hire additional managerial expertise or contract for it as necessary.
- Evaluate the success of the strategic navigation process and the web navigation process.
- Readjust strategic navigation processes and the web navigation process.
- Seek cultural integration of disparate units around a few core values to be more compatible with market realities.
- Establish a strong local or regional brand identity.
- Market the medical practice or IDS/N to third-party payors by differentiating it from competitors in terms of location, physician credentials, operational systems and capabilities, willingness to accept risk, and other factors.

Several examples may be given. First, suppose a given medical practice desires to differentiate itself from its competition by achieving the highest levels of patient satisfaction. A specified manager would be assigned responsibility for achieving the strategic goal. It could be an executive with one of a variety of titles, including medical practice manager, marketing manager, or human resource manager. With input from retreat participants (to be described later), this individual would select a series of specific tactics to implement the strategic goal. These might include, but not be limited to, selecting or improving a patient satisfaction measurement instrument and process; incorporating these into the information system; implementing reinforcing human resource tactics to build employee commitment, motivation, and service orientation; reinforcing these with redesigned reward systems; and evaluating and readjusting the system as needed. The important point here is that an operational manager is held responsible for implementing specific tactics to achieve a particular strategic objective (and is rewarded for doing so). The performance appraisal and compensation systems are designed to reinforce the strategy and achieve the objective.

Another example might be a strategic goal to produce, document, and disseminate practice data on cost-effectiveness, outcomes, and patient satisfaction to relevant key stakeholders in the form of a practice report card. Again, input into the measurement and management processes would come from various participants in a strategic retreat. A given manager would be assigned responsibility for this activity (director of information management, chief financial officer, or some similar title) with support from other managers. He or she would then implement tactics to generate these report cards, such as determining information needs of key stakeholders, collecting and compiling specific information from a variety of sources, and evaluating the effectiveness of these report cards from the *user's* point of view (Slovensky, Fottler, and Houser, 1998).

A third example might be the implementation of a strategic objective to market the medical practice's services to several MCOs and gain capitated contracts to provide these services to a given population. This strategic objective might represent the entrepreneurial orientation of a Strategic Navigator. In this case, a marketing manager would seek input from others internal and external to the organization in identifying potential MCOs. Then, the information needs of this key stakeholder could be identified and the data disseminated to them. If deficiencies in the data or the attractiveness of the practice were identified, these could be addressed. The important point is that the responsible manager would identify what would make the practice attractive as a potential provider (from the viewpoint of the MCO) and then take steps to remedy any deficiencies and provide the desired information.

USING YOUR STRATEGIC RETREATS EFFECTIVELY

A medical practice retreat is an off-site extended meeting where executives and physicians meet in an uninterrupted setting to analyze problems and opportunities together, engage in joint problem solving, and make plans to which all will feel committed as a team (Zinober, 1994). Some of the most important purposes for having a retreat are to

- Enhance communication in order to reduce misunderstanding, petty annoyances, lack of trust, unnecessary conflicts, and divergence (rather than convergence) of thinking.
- Reduce and manage stress levels.
- Reduce conflict of values among the participants through development of mutually agreeable solutions to problems.
- Improve the quality of strategic planning by focusing on values, goals, strategic priorities, and web priorities.
- Provide on opportunity for organized feedback that can be used to design a strategic plan all can support and all can work to implement.

Armed with a plan that is data-based, supported by both medical practice executives and physician partners, and understood by all, the practice can then proceed to implement the plan in a focused, goal-oriented manner. Such an approach should be educational for all attendees but should also result in higher levels of practice performance along a number of dimensions.

We advocate that each medical practice plan two strategic retreats on a periodic basis. The first would be for strategic leaders; the second would be for strategic leaders, operational managers, and others who will be involved in implementation. The first retreat would focus on strategic priorities and plans, as well as web relationship priorities and plans. It would be primarily for leaders who are (or should be) externally focused. The second would focus on implementation of these priorities and plans through both strategy implementation tactics and web relationship implementation tactics. It would include managers and others who are internally focused.

Table 10.1 provides an agenda for the first retreat for strategic leaders. These could include the top managers in the practice, as well as the physician leadership. In a smaller practice it might include all managers and all physicians. The agenda is provided as a series of questions that might be addressed by the participants—questions that could be divided into strategic navigation issues and web navigation issues. The questions reflect the process guidelines provided earlier.

Table 10.2 provides the agenda for the second retreat, which addresses implementation and integration issues. This is attended by all those who will be involved in any aspect of implementation, as well as those who attended the first retreat. It is important that both groups be in attendance in order to minimize slippage, misunderstanding, and lack of follow-through in implementation and integration. Once again, the agenda is provided as a series of sequential questions and reflects our guidelines.

LEADERSHIP IMPLICATIONS

In this book, we provide a complement to what has been learned about IDS/Ns, the process of integration, and the retreat of integration. We refer to several excellent, in-depth case studies of integrated systems such as those by Coddington, Moore, and Fischer (1996) and Shortell and others (1996). Instead of relying on a limited number of case studies, however, we conducted a systematic national survey of 686 executives from over 650 medical groups in order to determine the perceptions of their physician and nonphysician executives of their present and future.

These groups were not preselected to be examples of existing high levels of integration with other medical groups or with hospitals and managed care organizations. Some of those who were integrating were loosely coupled; others were tightly coupled. Each type of coupling has its up-and downsides.

To understand the current challenges and to predict the future choices that will need to be made, it is important to examine the entire range of situations facing healthcare organizations today. Our data allowed us to model a wide range of possibilities along the wide and varied continuum of integration rather than to merely reflect the experiences of organizations that are well along the continuum toward full integration.

We believe that our focus on medical groups as focal healthcare organizations makes its own, unique contribution to the understanding of integrated

Table 10.1. Agenda for Retreat Number One: Leadership Issues for Strategic and Web Navigation.

I. Strategic Navigation Issues
  A. How can we create a shared mission and common values?
  B. What opportunities and threats do we face in all of our relevant external environments?
  C. What internal strengths and weaknesses do we possess as an organization?
  D. What differentiates our organization from our competitors?
  E. What could differentiate our organization from our competitors in the future?
  F. Based on our mission, goals, strengths, weaknesses, environmental opportunities, and threats, what business (corporate) strategy will we pursue? What will our strategic priorities be?
  G. How can we achieve high-quality, customer-focused, cost-effective care?
  H. How can we develop and market new services and new markets?
  I. Is our organization currently a Strategic Navigator, Strategic Engineer, Strategic Entrepreneur, or Strategic Ostrich?
  J. How can we become a Strategic Navigator in the future?
  K. Have the viewpoints of all key stakeholders been considered before implementation?

II. Web Navigation Issues
  A. Are we devoting enough resources to relationship assessment and reassessment?
  B. Who are our key internal and external stakeholders in all web levels now and in the future?
  C. Why is each stakeholder key and for which particular decisions?
  D. What are our stakeholders' core values and expectations? What is the basis for our stakeholders' power vis-à-vis our organization?
  E. How stable and how positive is our relationship with stakeholders?
  F. Is the relationship with each key stakeholder likely to shift significantly from issue to issue? More positively or more negatively?
  G. What kind of cooperative behavior and action is desired from these stakeholders, and how can it be achieved?
  H. What kind of threat does the organization face from each stakeholder, and how does this organization minimize or avoid this threat?
  I. How is each key stakeholder diagnosed in terms of potential for threat and potential for cooperation?
  J. How can we shift our dependence from less supportive to more supportive stakeholders?
  K. On the basis of the above diagnoses, how is each key stakeholder classified: supportive, mixed-blessing, or nonsupportive?
  L. Is our organization currently a Web Navigator, a Web Optimist, a Web Pessimist, or a Web Ostrich?
  M. How do we link with larger organizations within and outside our IDS/N?
  N. How can we become a Web Navigator in the future?
  O. Do we have a consensus regarding how we will go about integrating with potential web partners and about who those partners should be?

Table 10.2. Agenda for Retreat Number Two:
Operational Issues for Implementing Strategic and Web Navigation Tactics.

I. Strategy Implementation Issues
  A. How can we reinforce strategic intentions with supportive tactical actions?
  B. How can we reengineer our internal systems to enhance customer value (high-quality, cost-effective patient care)?
  C. What processes (TQM/CQI) can we use to improve efficiency and effectiveness in our practice?
  D. How can we enhance patient satisfaction?
  E. How can we develop a management information system that allows us to collect and disseminate data on outcomes, patient satisfaction, and cost-effectiveness?
  F. What are appropriate performance standards for our physicians, and how should our physician compensation system be related to these standards?
  G. How will we develop clinical protocols with physician input?
  H. How can we prepare and educate our staff for the changing market realities?
  I. How can we manage patient satisfaction by enhancing employee satisfaction?
  J. Have we aligned our physician incentives with those of the practice? How?

II. Web Relationship Implementation Issues
  A. How can we meet the needs of our key stakeholders?
  B. What tactics should we implement to involve trustingly our supportive stakeholders and defend proactively against our nonsupportive stakeholders?
  C. Which potential web partners could bring complementary resources?
  D. How can we negotiate clinical and business issues with our web partners?
  E. What management skills do we lack, and how can we gain access to these skills?
  F. What capitated contracts should we sign with whom for what strategic goals?
  G. What coalitions should we form with whom for what strategic goals?
  H. How can our physician autonomy and control be preserved?
  I. Where are we now in terms of our web relationships, and where would we like to be in the future?
  J. Should we integrate vertically or virtually throughout contract?
  K. How can we secure several managed care contracts?
  L. How can we determine which decisions should be centralized and which should be made at the lowest level within the organization?
  M. How can we develop systemwide electronic medical records?
  N. Have we developed win-win approaches that build trust?

III. Strategic and Web Navigation Integration Issues
  A. Which managers and clinical personnel should implement which strategic and web tactics?
  B. Do we need to hire or contract for additional management expertise?
  C. How can we evaluate the success of our strategic navigation and web navigation strategies and tactics?
  D. Based on this evaluation, how will the strategic navigation and web navigation be modified?
  E. How can we manage cultural conflict?
  F. How can we achieve cultural integration?
  G. How can we differentiate ourselves from our competitors?
  H. How much integrative infrastructure do we need to increase integration and become more system-like?
  I. Do we have a consensus concerning how we will integrate with various potential web partners?

healthcare. Formerly solo physicians are consolidating into medical groups, and existing groups are becoming larger. Medical groups will play an increasingly important role in providing coordinated, cost-effective, high-quality medicine to the covered lives so cherished in the growing managed care environment.

Existing large, multispecialty groups will be an increasingly significant starting point for integrated healthcare in many settings. In other situations, they are essential for emerging systems. For example, many hospital-based systems are creating their own composite medical groups to harness and coordinate the energy of physicians whose practices have been acquired. In addition, looking at networks and systems from this focus provides fundamentally different perspectives than are available with hospitals or managed care organizations as the focus.

Finally, we hope we have stimulated healthcare leaders to use the tools presented here, together with others available in the literature on strategic management and the management of relationships, for example, negotiation and conflict management and leadership. More important, we hope leaders see the strategic navigation of multiple operational and strategic webs as a challenge that can be met successfully, even though it may be daunting much of the time. The webs are there, and they contain valuable resources that will sustain organizations and allow them to be successful. True leaders must be the navigators of those webs.

GENERAL CONCLUSIONS

The ultimate destination of the healthcare industry is not completely known or understood, but outlines of the emerging system are coming into clearer focus. Ultimately, we will have a series of local and regional systems that will be horizontally and vertically integrated, and the full range of services from ambulatory to tertiary care will be available within the system. Paperwork will have been eliminated; all patient information will be available electronically throughout the system. Referrals and movement from one part of the system to another will be seamless.

Obviously, we have not yet achieved this level of integration, but we are moving fast toward organized delivery systems that aspire to be truly integrated delivery systems. As a result, the strategic web of relationships in the industry is being fundamentally restructured. The survival of medical groups and other healthcare organizations will depend on the ability of their executives to effectively manage new and emerging multiple relationships at all relevant levels in the strategic web.

All of these trends are being driven by the changing environment of the healthcare industry. The environment is turbulent and will continue to be so. In the future, fee-for-service medicine is expected to decline as capitation increases; physicians will become employees to a greater degree; organizations will become more collaborative and less competitive; the system will become more payor-driven and less provider-driven; and providers will become members of more integrated delivery systems.

As a result of these shifts, the key stakeholders of medical groups are also shifting. In the past, the three key stakeholders were physicians as individual caregivers, patients, and managed care organizations. In the future, the key stakeholders are expected to be patients and managed care organizations (as in the past) but also employers and IDS/Ns. At the same time, internal stakeholders will decline in importance. This decline in importance of internal stakeholders (and the commensurate increased importance of employers and IDS/Ns) will be particularly true for those types of medical practices likely to dominate in the future (large, multispecialty, integrated).

Although medical groups that were neither loosely nor tightly coupled (they were independent) constituted about half of all medical groups in the past, they will constitute a very small minority in the future. Most medical groups will be either part of a fully integrated system or a loosely integrated network in the future. Academic practices and larger practices are more likely to be fully integrated and less likely to be independent or loosely integrated than are small, nonacademic practices.

Medical groups expect to initiate or increase a significant number of collaborative relationships in the future. First, they expect to increase their formal strategic alliances with physicians and other medical groups while acquiring other medical group practices. Second, they expect to increase their formal strategic alliances with hospitals. Third, they expect to see an increase in capitated contracts with MCOs and a decline in discounted fee-for-service contracts. Fourth, they expect to become part of a fully integrated delivery system.

Executives expect to increase their use of all of the integration mechanisms in the future. They expect to negotiate contracts with key stakeholders, form strategic partnerships with key stakeholders, change their risk-sharing methods to integrate financing and delivery of care, develop electronic interfaces and pool data among strategic partners to disseminate information concerning patient care outcomes, and develop performance standards to evaluate membership in provider networks. The latter three integration mechanisms will increase by the greatest percentage in the future. Implementation of these mechanisms will occur primarily through IDS/Ns.

A major issue for the present and future is what kind of organization will likely become the controlling element in IDS/Ns—medical groups, hospitals, or MCOs. Medical group practice executives believe their medical groups will have less power and influence over IDS/Ns than will hospitals and MCOs. We expect that hospitals and MCOs and their executives will each control IDS/Ns at different times and places.

Some integration is better than no integration because integration can increase referrals from other providers and (possibly) provide quantity discounts in purchasing. However, although some integration is good, tightly coupled IDS/Ns may become strategic dinosaurs that are unable to change with the demands of the new century. Moreover, increasing structural integration must be completed through reinforcing tactical actions such as integration mechanisms if the potential benefits are to be achieved. Cultural integration of the various pieces of the system is also required.

When strategic intentions and tactical outcomes are combined to produce strategic types, we found that most medical practices have been Strategic Ostriches in the past. However, most intend to be either Strategic Engineers or Strategic Navigators in the future. When we compared the four strategic types in terms of organizational outcomes, we found that Navigators performed the best; Ostriches performed poorly. In terms of the cost-effectiveness and the profitability outcomes, Engineers performed well. It appears that successful organizations need to be both market-driven and operations-driven in their strategies and tactics.

Market-driven and operations-driven tactics were also examined. In the future, our executive respondents expect to implement significantly greater local market vertical integration along the continuum of care, shift their domain by substituting new markets and new stakeholders for old, and pursue national horizontal integration through contractual relationships with similar organizations in other markets.

In addition to expansion of these market-owned tactics, they also expect to increase their use of such operations-driven tactics as tightening controls on physician use of resources, differentiating themselves based on the technical quality of their services, and using the results of cost-benefit studies to consolidate services.

Web navigation skills are also important. Healthcare executives need to diagnose and manage their key stakeholders by differentiating whether each is internal or external to the organization and diagnose them in terms of their potential for threat and for cooperation. In the future, physicians in the organizational and system webs, patients, and IDS/Ns are viewed primarily as supportive and secondarily as mixed-blessing, whereas system and competitor hospitals and MCOs are primarily mixed-blessing. Navigators, large practices, and nonacademic practices view their stakeholders as more supportive than do Ostriches, small practices, and academic practices. Internal physicians will be managed primarily through involvement strategies; internal IDS/Ns and patients will be managed through involvement and collaborative strategies. Internal hospitals and MCOs will be managed primarily through collaborative strategies. All five key stakeholders will be managed through collaborative strategies when they are external to the organization. Strategic Web Navigators that simultaneously attempt to emphasize efficiency, quality, entrepreneurship, minimizing key stakeholder threats, and maximizing key stakeholder collaboration will be most successful.

Organizational outcomes were compared to local competitors along the dimensions of clinical quality, organizational survival, market share, fulfillment of stakeholder needs, service orientation, profitability, and cost-effectiveness. Our respondents envision a decreased emphasis on profitability and organizational survival in the future, together with increased emphasis on clinical quality, cost-effectiveness, and fulfillment of stakeholder needs. Relative to local competitors, they felt they did better in terms of clinical quality and organizational survival but worse in terms of cost-effectiveness and profitability. Nonacademic organizations and Strategic Web Navigators tended to perform better than their academic and Ostrich counterparts. In addition, larger organizations tended to perform better in terms of organizational survival and market share but worse in terms of service orientation relative to smaller organizations.

Finally, we examined the executive respondents' perceptions of their organization's skills and abilities relative to their local competitors. Not surprisingly, most respondents felt they were better or much better than their local competitors in terms of all of the managerial skills and abilities. The weakest area was information system skills and capabilities to support decision making. The organizations that were nonacademic, large, and Strategic Web Navigators had better skills than those who were academic, small, and Ostriches.

HOW MUCH INTEGRATION AND WHAT TYPE?

Medical practices will continue to face a turbulent environment in the years ahead, as consolidation of the industry continues. Yet, it is not obvious that tightly coupled, fully integrated systems are the wave of the future. This is because of the difficulty of managing a system that provides many different products or services in many different markets. It is impossible for managers of fully integrated systems to understand the different products and services and their markets. This is why tight coupling and high degrees of vertical integration have not been successful as corporations struggle to focus on their "core competencies." For example, USAir has been struggling since the merger of six different carriers between and 1968 and 1989 ("USAir to Reinvent Itself," 1996). The problem is that they have never been operationally and culturally integrated.

It is true that healthcare providers will need to be part of a larger organization that provides a wide range of consumer and employer choices, one-stop shopping, economics of scale, cost-effectiveness, clinical quality, and service quality. It is not true that the only way to achieve these goals is through participation in a fully integrated system.

The advantage of a fully integrated delivery system/network is that unified ownership allows for coordinated adaptation to changing environmental circumstances (Robinson and Casalino, 1996). In principle, vertical integration provides a unity of control and direction that allows the IDS/N to focus all of the energies of the subunits on the same goals and strategies. There is a single mission statement, hierarchy of authority, and financial bottom line. This unity of purpose is essential under managed care (as it is currently structured) and underlies the drive toward vertically integrated delivery systems that incorporate primary care physicians, specialty panels, hospitals, and MCOs.

The advantages of virtual integration through contractual relations (more loosely coupled systems) lie in the potential for autonomous adaptation to changing environmental circumstances (Robinson and Casalino, 1996). Organizational independence preserves the risks and rewards for efficient performance rather than replacing them with salaried employment. Coordination could be achieved through negotiated payments and performance guarantees rather than through managerial authority. However, they must involve collaboration (creating new value), a dense web of interpersonal connections based on trust, and partners willing to nurture the collaborative relationship itself rather than simply trying to control it. If vertical integration worked in practice the way it works in principle, markets and contracts would be rare (Robinson and Casalino, 1996). The healthcare system could be structured as one large administered bureaucracy with centralized planning, centralized resource allocation, a single purpose, and a single process. However, vertically integrated systems suffer from two weakness: incentive attenuation and influence costs. Vertical integration replaces the entrepreneurship of the owner-managed medical practice with administrative hierarchies where managers and clinicians are largely paid by salary. It also greatly increases influence costs, defined as the effects of internal struggles for control over resources by various incumbent constituencies (primary care physicians, specialists, MCOs, hospitals, system managers, and so forth). At the extreme, the vertically integrated IDS/Ns could come to resemble public bureaucracies with a civil service mentality.

Because hard evidence of the superiority of any one approach to structuring is practically nonexistent, it would be prudent to proceed with caution. Much of the activity we see in the industry today is imitation of the actions or the presumed actions of others. The downside of all the emphasis on new acquisitions, new enrollment, and restructuring has been that the consumer has been lost in the shuffle. In the future, consumer choice of providers should increase rather than decrease (Health Care Advisory Board, 1995). This means that systems not providing open access to plans and broad networks of providers will be at a competitive advantage.

In the future environment, it will be risky for providers to rely on exclusive partnerships because the winners and losers are unknown. Rather, the emphasis should be on patient satisfaction, patient retention, flexibility, more options for consumers, minimal paperwork, and multiple capitated contracts or partnerships for providers. Already, we are seeing cost-oriented providers like Humana shift to a user-friendly philosophy that emphasizes quality and patient satisfaction (Galuszka, 1996).

One model for the future is for large medical groups to contract with MCOs to provide the full spectrum of medical services to a defined population on a capitated basis. In California, these groups have been growing rapidly (Robinson and Casalino, 1995). The physician groups are part of a physician network but are not part of an IDS/N. In essence, they are a virtual network established by contract with no common ownership or merging of assets. These medical groups manage utilization through their own medical directors and physician committees. This fosters a cooperative rather than an adversarial relationship often found where outside MCOs monitor physician utilization and performance. Utilization in these networks is significantly below California and national benchmarks.

No one structure is necessarily the final answer. Individual market dynamics will determine the appropriate level and structure of integration. The process is evolutionary because it needs to meet the functional needs of all parties (Smith, 1994). The structure should be responsive to the needs and goals of the potential partners within the context of their local healthcare market.

Many possible paths could lead to increased integration and coordination of clinical services under managed care. Medical practices face a trade-off between the advantages of coordinated adaptation through vertical integration and the advantages of autonomous adaptation through contractual networks. The current uncertainty and lack of hard evidence makes it difficult to predict eventual outcomes. However, it also indicates the potential downside of giving up autonomy or making large capital investments in a vertically integrated (owned) system. The trend today, both inside and outside healthcare, is toward more contractual relationships and less vertical integration. Could it be that the market is telling us something?

STEPS FOR FORMULATING AND IMPLEMENTING STRATEGIC WEB NAVIGATION IN MEDICAL GROUPS

The steps we recommend for formulating and implementing strategic web navigation in medical groups include the following, supported by Toolkit 10:

- Using Tool 10.1, develop strategic priorities and plans. In particular,

  Classify your own organization as a Strategic Navigator, a Strategic Engineer, a Strategic Entrepreneur, or a Strategic Ostrich, based on your priority on strategic entrepreneurship, strategic engineering, or both.

  Strive to emphasize both engineering and entrepreneurship by becoming a Strategic Navigator in the future.

- Using Tool 10.1, develop web relationship priorities and plans. Specifically,

  Classify your own organization as a Web Navigator, a Web Optimist, a Web Pessimist, or a Web Ostrich in terms of relative emphasis on a priority to enhance cooperation, reduce threat, or both.

  Strive to both enhance cooperation and reduce threat by becoming a Web Navigator in the future.

- Using Tool 10.2, develop strategy implementation tactics. In particular,

  Reinforce strategic intentions with supportive tactical actions (combine how you think and act).

  Develop a management and clinical information system that allows the practice to define and document data on a range of outcomes.

  Communicate these data to all key stakeholders in all four webs.

  Consider the viewpoints of all internal and external key stakeholders before implementing new tactical actions.

- Using Tool 10.2, develop web relationship tactics. Especially focus on doing the following:

  Implement generic relationship navigation tactics that fit the nature of the web relationship: involve trustingly in the supportive relationship; collaborate cautiously in the mixed-blessing relationship; defend proactively in the nonsupportive relationship; and monitor efficiently in the marginal relationship.

  Implement these generic tactics by developing specific actions and programs for each tactic and relationship combination.

- Integrate—so they create synergy rather than undermine each other—and implement

  Strategic priorities

  Web relationship priorities

  Strategic navigation tactics

  Web navigation tactics

- Using Table 10.1, develop an agenda for the first retreat, focusing on the following leadership issues for Strategic Web Navigation:

  Strategy navigation issues

  Web relationship navigation issues

- Using Table 10.2, develop an agenda for the second retreat, focusing on the following operational issues:

  Strategy implementation issues

  Web relationship implementation issues

  Strategic navigation and web navigation integration issues

- Evaluate the success of the strategic web navigation process and implement changes as needed. In particular, be sensitive to suboptimal strategic navigation and web navigation assessments and actions. Ask whether suboptimal strategic and operational choices led to one of the following:

  Putting the organization at risk

  Missing opportunities

  Wasting resources on low-priority web relationships

As we have indicated, we believe medical group leaders need to rethink their strategic priorities and tactical actions as they face increasing, and potentially conflicting, demands for efficiency and effectiveness from the wide range of stakeholders in their strategic web. They must minimally satisfy the needs of stakeholders in marginal web relationships while they maximally satisfy the needs of those in key web relationships—at the same time they are meeting their own medical group's needs, including its need to survive.

TOOLKIT 10

Integrating Your Navigation of the Strategic Web

Tool 10.1. Checklist for Formulating Strategic Web Navigation in Medical Groups.

Instructions: Check all the processes and actions you have completed for your medical group. (Strategic leaders should set strategic priorities and develop strategic navigation, as well as web navigation strategies and tactics.)

Stage F-1: Develop Strategic Priorities and Plans

___ Create shared mission and values (determine who you are and what you do best).

___ Assess external environmental opportunities and threats.

___ Assess internal organizational strengths and weaknesses.

___ Classify your own organization as a Strategic Navigator, Strategic Engineer, Strategic Entrepreneur, or Strategic Ostrich based on your priority on strategic entrepreneurship, strategic engineering, or both.

___ Strive to emphasize both engineering and entrepreneurship by becoming a Strategic Navigator in the future.

___ Establish priorities to achieve high-quality, customer-focused, cost-effective patient care.

___ Explore entrepreneurial opportunities to develop and market new services.

Stage F-2: Develop Web Relationship, Priorities, and Plans

___ Devote a high level of economic resources, effort, and time to relationship assessment and reassessment.

___ Do continual environmental scanning of key internal and external relationships in all four strategic webs.

___ Identify all key external and internal relationships now and in the future. Key relationships are those relevant to the implementation of the strategic priorities and plans because they control economic or noneconomic resources needed by the organization.

___ Classify your own organization as a Web Navigator, a Web Optimist, a Web Pessimist, or a Web Ostrich in terms of relative emphasis on a priority to enhance cooperation, reduce threat, or both.

Tool 10.1. Checklist for Formulating Strategic Web Navigation in Medical Groups, cont'd.

___ Strive to enhance cooperation and reduce threat by becoming a Web Navigator in the future.

___ Assess each relationship in terms of its potential to form a supportive or non-supportive coalition with others.

___ Classify each key relationship as supportive, mixed-blessing, or nonsupportive based on its power to threaten or cooperate with the organization.

___ Link with organizations both inside and outside your IDS/N.

___ Determine which stakeholder resource inputs are vital to the medical practice and which have partial or total substitutes.

___ Shift dependence from nonsupportive to supportive stakeholders where feasible.

___ Become associated with a larger entity rather than remain totally independent.

___ Build a consensus toward integrating with other partners.

Tool 10.2. Checklist for Implementing Strategic Web Navigation in Medical Groups.

Instructions: Check all the processes and actions you have completed for your medical group. (Strategic leaders and operational managers together should set operational priorities and develop strategic navigation and web navigation implementation tactics.)

Stage I-1: Develop Strategic Implementation Tactics

___ Reinforce strategic intentions with supportive tactical actions (combine how your organization thinks and acts).

___ Reengineer internal systems to enhance customer value (high-quality, cost-effective patient care).

___ Use TQM/CQI processes and other techniques to measure, control, and improve physician and employee utilization of resources, as well as technical quality and service orientation.

___ Develop a management and clinical information system that allows the practice to define and document data on quality of care (outcomes), patient satisfaction, and cost-effectiveness.

___ Communicate these data to all key stakeholders in all four webs.

___ Carefully evaluate the performance of physicians in the medical practice against practice or external benchmarks in such areas as clinical quality, outcomes, patient satisfaction, complaints, cost-effectiveness, malpractice claims, and board certification.

___ Reward physicians based on their performance compared to the above dimensions.

Tool 10.2. Checklist for Implementing Strategic Web Navigation in Medical Groups, cont'd.

___ Allow physicians to be involved in the development of clinical protocols, as well as the measurement of the above dimensions.

___ Prepare and educate all staff concerning the changing market realities and the consequent need for collaborative relationships and cost-effective, high-quality patient care.

___ Manage patient satisfaction by enhancing employee commitment, motivation, and job satisfaction.

___ Model practice on service delivery in the better hotels.

___ Continually communicate with patients and employees, particularly during periods of major change.

___ Consider the viewpoints of all internal and external key stakeholders before implementation of new tactical actions.

___ Retain high levels of physician autonomy and independence.

___ Align physician incentives to be compatible with its medical practice and the parent IDS/N.

Stage I-2: Develop Web Relationship Tactics

___ View relationships as either supportive or mixed-blessing.

___ Perceive a higher potential for cooperation and a lower potential for threat.

___ Anticipate the goals of key stakeholders and then attempt to satisfy these stakeholders by offering appropriate inducements in exchange for essential contributions.

___ Implement generic relationship navigation tactics that fit the nature of the web relationship: involve trustingly in the supportive relationship; collaborate cautiously in the mixed-blessing relationship; defend proactively in the non-supportive relationship; and monitor efficiently in the marginal relationship.

___ Implement these generic tactics by developing specific actions and programs for each tactic and relationship combination.

___ Choose web partners who can bring resources to the relationship that are complementary to those of the organization.

___ Academic practices should align with primary care practice in the community.

___ Smaller practices should align with larger practices in order to gain market share.

___ Negotiate clinical and business issues with web partners.

___ Develop or contract for management skills to analyze, evaluate, and negotiate contracts with MCOs, IDS/Ns, hospitals, and other medical practices.

___ Link contract formation and coalition formation to group strategic goals and strategies.

___ Negotiate physician autonomy and control in medical practice when joining an IDS/N.

Tool 10.2. Checklist for Implementing Strategic Web Navigation in Medical Groups, cont'd.

___ Sign capitated contracts with MCOs that put the medical practice and its physicians at risk to preserve incentives for high-quality, cost-effective patient care.

___ Larger practices and those part of an IDS/N should explore capitated and noncapitated contracts with employers to provide specified services to a given cohort of employees.

___ Explore clinics without walls as the first step in medical practice integration.

___ Explore and select one of the following as a second step in integration: joint ownership with hospitals (MSOs), becoming part of a network of medical practices, joining an IDS/N, or selling out to a physician practice management company.

___ Avoic large capital investments in plants and equipment on new acquisitions.

___ Join a virtual network of providers.

___ Focus on a metropolitan area or region.

___ Emphasize acquiring many managed care contracts.

___ Focus on markets where the IDS/N can be first or second in market share.

___ Build relationships on a foundation of trust.

Stage I-3: Integrate and Implement Strategic Priorities, Web Relationship Priorities, Strategy Implementation, Tactics, and Web Relationship Tactics.

___ Plan and implement a strategic and an operational retreat on a periodic basis to formulate strategic and web navigation strategies and tactics.

___ Invite strategic leaders and operational managers to attend both retreats because implementation of reinforcing tactics is crucial to the success of strategic and web navigation strategies.

___ Determine which managerial and nonmanagerial employees should be involved in the implementation process.

___ Assign responsibility for specific managerial and nonmanagerial employees to implement specific strategy implementation tactics and web relationship tactics.

___ Hire additional managerial expertise or contract for it as necessary.

___ Evaluate the success of the strategic navigation process and the web navigation process.

___ Readjust the strategic navigation and the web navigation processes.

___ Seek cultural integration of disparate units around a few core values to be more compatible with market realities.

___ Establish a strong local or regional brand identity.

___ Market the medical practice or IDS/N to third-party payors by differentiating it from competitors in terms of location, physician credentials, operational systems and capabilities, willingness to accept risk, and other factors.

ABOUT THE STUDIES

Two studies, one quantitative and one qualitative, provided the data for this book. This resource describes the research methods used to collect the quantitative data, as well as the characteristics of the sample and of the case study that provided the qualitative data.

THE "FACING THE UNCERTAIN FUTURE" STUDY

The quantitative data used in this study are a subset of data obtained from a national survey of medical group physician and administrative executives. The study was entitled "Facing the Uncertain Future" (FUF). The FUF study was a jointly conducted project between the Center for Research in Ambulatory Health Care Administration (CRAHCA)—the research and development arm of the Medical Group Management Association (MGMA), Englewood, Colorado—and The Institute for Management and Leadership Research (IMLR), College of Business Administration, Texas Tech University, Lubbock, Texas.

MGMA's professional credentialing arm—the American College of Medical Practice Executives (ACMPE)—the faculty of Texas Tech University's Ph.D. and M.B.A. programs in health organization management (HOM), and faculty from the University of Alabama at Birmingham collaborated in this project. Abbott Laboratories, Abbott Park, Illinois, was the funding sponsor.

The FUF study consisted of two phases of data collection. The first phase was administered in mid-1994, with respondents answering questions about 1989,

1994, and 1999. In the second phase, respondents answered questions about 1995 and 2000. All the quantitative data used in this volume came from the second-phase FUF questionnaire, which consisted of 612 questions posed to two groups of health care executives: (1) medical group executives (including both physician executives and nonphysician executives); and (2) other health care industry executives. Respondents were asked to be informants about their own organizations rather than to answer questions about themselves.

A summary report of the results of the whole FUF project (Blair and others, 1995) offers extensive detail of the two-phase study, including both the expert and executive sampling phases. Only the executive study is used in this book.

Respondents and Respondents' Organizations

Of the original second-phase sample (of 3,233), 865 responded, resulting in a 26.8 percent response rate. Because this book focuses its analysis on medical group executives, only the 686 respondents who were classified as medical group executives were included. These executives had an overall high level of education (almost two-thirds had master's or doctoral degrees). They were typically the highest level of administrative personnel in their respective organizations.

Sampling Frame

The respondents in this study were asked to provide information about their organizations and were treated as "executive informants" for their respective organizations. None of the questions asked for the informants' opinions, although bias probably, to some extent, affected their perceptions about their organization, its stakeholders, and its strategies. In this study, the organization is the unit of analysis; individual responses were the unit of measurement.

The theoretical population for this study is all U.S. medical groups. However, the operationalized population is all U.S. medical group practices that are also members of MGMA. The sample selected for this study was defined earlier as all the members of MGMA's ACMPE, plus all the members of MGMA's Society for Physicians in Administration (SPA).

The sample is, therefore, not totally representative of the population of interest. If anything, it overrepresents the more proactive, informed executives from larger medical groups with more explicit strategic thinking and action.

THE "STRATEGY IN ACTION" STUDY

In addition to the survey, we enhanced and supplemented the theory-building aspects of our research by looking at the complexity of empirical reality—not easily captured in pencil-and-paper survey instruments—through qualitative observations and interviews.

The qualitative data used in this study, including the maps of the operational and strategic webs for Integrating System A and its composite System Medical Group A, are a subset of data obtained from a multiyear observation and qualitative data-gathering project entitled "Strategy in Action" (SIA). The SIA study was part of the Strategic Studies Program of the Institute for Management and Leadership Research at Texas Tech.

These complementary approaches facilitated our developing and extending the understanding of strategic management thinking and actions for integrating systems and for medical groups linked to such systems. The integrating system that was observed as it moved along the path of ever-further integration (which is not yet complete) was hospital-dominated. It started from a very large, urban tertiary care hospital. It then proceeded over a period of years from initial loose affiliations with rural hospitals, to the purchase of its own managed care organization, to the acquisition of multiple small physician groups and significant numbers of solo practitioner practices, to the formation of a new, composite medical group. Many of its challenges and choices are reported in this book, with the permission of its executives. Permission was obtained when the data were collected. Every attempt has been made to avoid compromising strategic secrets.

Integrating systems and networks represent the most complex organizations from strategic management and governance perspectives. They generally have the greatest number and variety of stakeholders and have the most complex strategic and operational webs. Hence, we have mainly focused on different aspects of those webs and the relationships to be identified, assessed, diagnosed, and managed—strategically—as part of gaining and sustaining competitive advantage or, at a minimum, competitive parity and survival.

Our data collection was designed to enhance the development of "strategic navigation" concepts, including the "strategic web" and was not intended to be a complete description and analysis of all aspects of integrating systems and networks. Thus, strategic theory and practice is informed by these qualitative data rather than systematically tested by them.

We encourage other researchers to test and extend the strategic approach presented in this book through both empirical and conceptual research. We also suggest that theoretical extensions of this approach should also address the implications for understanding emergent strategy (Mintzberg, 1988) and the broader organizational enactment of strategy (Weick, 1979).

Strategic navigation of their strategic webs represents a new way of thinking for many health care executives. Key stakeholders are critically important for overall business strategy formulation and implementation. Thus, successful implementation of stakeholder management practices should provide a competitive advantage in strategic web navigation. Our research indicates that health care executives should place *systematic and strategic* emphasis on the strategic navigation of their own webs.

REFERENCES

American Group Practice Association. *AGPA 2000: A Vision.* Alexandria, Va.: American Group Practice Association, 1992.

Appleby, C. "Doc Shopping." *Hospitals and Health Networks,* 1995a, *69*(14), 49–50.

Appleby, C. "Employers: Health Care's New Heavyweights." *Hospitals and Health Networks,* 1995b, *69*(9), 26–35.

Atkins, P. M., Marshall, B. S., and Javalgi, R. G. "Happy Employees Lead to Loyal Patients." *Journal of Health Care Marketing,* 1996, *16*(4), 12–19.

Autrey, P. and Thomas, D. "Competitive Strategy in the Hospital Industry." *Health Care Management Review,* 1986, *11*(1), 7–14.

Baliga, B. R., and Johnson, B. "Analysis of an Industry in Transition." *Health Care Strategic Management,* 1986, *4*(12), 5–15.

Barney, J. B. "Firm Resources and Sustained Competitive Advantage." *Journal of Management,* 1991, *17*(1), 99–120.

Bianco, A., and Schine, E. "Doctors, Inc.," *BusinessWeek,* Mar. 24, 1997, 204–210.

Blair, J. D., and Boal, K. B. "Strategy Formation Processes in Health Care Organizations: A Context-Specific Examination of Context-Free Strategy Issues." *Journal of Management,* 1991, *17*(2), 305–344.

Blair, J. D., and Fottler, M. D. *Challenges in Health Care Management: Strategic Perspectives for Managing Key Stakeholders.* San Francisco: Jossey-Bass, 1990.

Blair, J. D., Fottler, M. D., Lazarus, S. S., Paolino, A. R., and Rotarius, T. M. "Strategic Stakeholder Management: First Round Results From 'Facing the Uncertain Future.'" *Medical Group Management Journal,* 1995, *42*(3), 16–21.

Blair, J. D., Fottler, M. D., Paolino, A. R., and Rotarius, T. M. *Medical Group Practices Face the Uncertain Future: Challenges, Opportunities and Strategies.* Englewood, Colo.: Center for Research in Ambulatory Health Care Administration, 1995.

Blair, J. D., Rock, T. T., Rotarius, T. M., Fottler, M. D., Bosse, G. C., and Driskill, J. M. "The Problematic Fit of Diagnosis and Strategy for Medical Group Stakeholders—Including IDS/Ns." *Health Care Management Review,* 1996, *21*(1), 7–28.

Blair, J. D., and Whitehead, C. J. "Too Many on the Seesaw: Stakeholder Diagnosis and Management for Hospitals." *Hospital and Health Services Management,* Summer 1988, *33*(2), 153–156.

Borchardt, W. W. "Patient Perception of Quality in a Clinic Setting and Relevant Strategies for Improvement." *College Review,* Spring 1994, *11*(1), 72–97.

Chapman, T. W. "Challenges of Leadership in an Era of Health Care Reform." *Frontiers of Health Services Management,* 1993, *10*(2), 3–26.

Chrisman, J. J., Hofer, C. W., and Boulton, W. K. "Toward a System for Classifying Business Strategies." *Academy of Management Review,* 1988, *13*, 413–428.

Coddington, D. C., Moore, K. D., and Fischer, E. A. *Integrated Health Care: Reorganizing the Physician, Hospital and Health Plan Relationship.* Englewood, Colo.: Medical Group Management Association, 1994.

Coddington, D. C., Moore, K. D., and Fischer, E. A. *Making Integrated Health Care Work.* Englewood, Colo.: Center for Research in Ambulatory Health Care Administration, 1996.

Coile, R. S., Jr. *The New Governance: Strategies for an Era of Health Reform.* Ann Arbor, Mich.: Health Administration Press, 1994.

Counte, M. A., Glandon, G. L, Oleske, D. M., and Hill, J. P. "Total Quality Management in a Health Care Environment: How Are Employers Affected?" *Hospital and Health Services Administration,* 1992, *37*(4), 503–518.

Dearmin, J., Brenner, J., and Migliori, R. "Reporting on QI Efforts for Internal and External Customers." *The Joint Commission Journal of Quality Improvement,* 1995, *21*, 277–288.

DelaFuente, D. "Group Insurance: By Establishing Their Own Medical Groups and Provider Networks, Health Plans Hope to Assume Their Place in Healthcare Delivery." *Modern Healthcare,* 1994, *24*(24), 39–44.

Delmar, D. "Group Practices Are Being Buffeted by the Winds of Healthcare Change." *Physician's Financial News,* 1995, *13*(7), 54.

DeNelsky, S. J. "TQM and Low Cost, High Quality Healthcare." *Group Practice Managed Healthcare News,* 1994, *10*(12), 23–27.

Enthoven, A. E., and Singer, S. J. "Managed Competition and California's Health Care Economy." *Health Affairs,* Spring 1996, *15*(1), 39–57.

"Florida: Dermatologist Access, Doctor Report Card Become Law." *American Health Line,* June 4, 1997b, 5.

Ford, R. C., Bach, S., and Fottler, M. D. "Methods of Measuring Patient Satisfaction in Health Care Organizations." *Health Care Management Review,* Spring 1997, *22*(2), 55–70.

Fottler, M. D. "Health Care Organizational Performance: Present and Future Research." *Journal of Management,* 1987, *13*(2), 367–391.

Fottler, M. D. "The Role and Impact of Multiskilled Health Practitioners in the Health Services Industry." *Hospital and Health Services Administration,* 1996, *41*(1), 55–75.

Fottler, M. D., Crawford, M. A., Quintana, J. B., and White, J. B. "Evaluating Nurse Turnover: Comparing Attitude Surveys and Exit Interviews." *Hospital and Health Services Administration,* Sept. 1995, *40*(2), 278–295.

Fottler M. D., Hernandez, S. R., and Joiner, C. L. (eds.). *Strategic Management of Human Resources in Health Services Organizations.* (2nd ed.) Albany, N.Y.: Delmar, 1994.

Fottler, M. D., and Malvey, D. "Multiprovider Systems." In L. Wolper (ed.), *Health Care Administration: Principles, Practices, Structure and Delivery.* (2nd ed.) Gaithersberg, Md.: Aspen, 1995.

Fottler, M. D., Phillips, R. L., Blair, J. D., and Duran, C. A. "Achieving Competitive Advantage Through Strategic Human Resource Management." *Hospital and Health Service Administration,* 1990, *35*, 341–363.

Freeman, R. E. *Strategic Management: A Stakeholder Approach.* Marshfield, Mass.: Pitman, 1984.

Galuszka, P."Humana, Heal Thyself." *BusinessWeek,* Oct. 14, 1996, 73–76.

Golembesky, H., Malcolm, C., and Levin, S. "University Medical Centers: A Case Study of Town and Gown Integration." *Integrated Healthcare Reports,* Jan. 1994, *2*(1), 10–13.

Green, J. "Management for 80s Woes." *Modern Healthcare,* 1993, *23*(16), 3.

"Harris Poll: America, Land of the Shaken." *BusinessWeek,* Mar. 11, 1996, 64–65.

Hayes, P. "Top Growing Trends in Regional Buying Groups." *Healthcare Management Team Agenda,* 1996, *12*(6), 5–6.

Health Care Advisory Board. *Emerging From Shadows: Resurgence to Prosperity Under Managed Care.* Washington, D.C.: The Advisory Board Company, 1995.

Hedberg, B.L.T, Nystrom, P. C., and Starbuck, W. H. "Camping on Seesaws: Prescriptions for a Self-Designing Organization." *Administrative Science Quarterly,* 1976, *21*, 41–65.

Hibbard, J. D., and Jewett, J. J. "What Type of Quality Information Do Consumers Want in Health Care Report Card?" *Medical Care Research and Review,* 1996, *53*(1), 28–47.

Inkpen, A., and Choudhury, N. "The Seeking of Strategy Where It Is Not: Toward a Theory of Strategy Absence." *Strategic Management Journal,* 1995, *16*(4), 313–323.

"Intermountain Health Care: Utah Doctors Pull Out." *American Health Line,* May 28, 1994, 11.

Jaklevic, M. C. "Report Charts Integration Levels." *Modern Healthcare,* 1997, *34*(44), 57.

"JCAHO: Announces New Outcomes-Based Accrediting Component." *American Health Line,* Feb. 19, 1997, 11.

Johnson, B. A., and Schryver, D. L. "Positioning for Vertical Integration Through Clinics Without Walls." *MGM Journal,* May/June 1994, *41*(3), 81–84.

Kaluzny, A. D., and Zuckerman, H. S. (eds.). *Partners for the Dance: Forming Strategic Alliances in Health Care.* Ann Arbor, Mich.: Health Administration Press, 1995.

Kaluzny, A. D., Zuckerman, H. S., and Ricketts, T. C. III (eds.). *Partners for the Dance: Forming Strategic Alliances in Health Care.* Ann Arbor, Mich.: Health Administration Press, 1995.

Kaufman, H. "Competing in an Integrated Healthcare Market: Four Strategies for Success." *Healthcare Executive, 10* (13), 1995, 18–22.

Kotter, J. P. "Managing External Dependence." *Academy of Management Review,* 1979, 4(1), 87–92.

Kuttner, R. "Rewarding Corporations That Really Invest in America." *BusinessWeek,* Feb. 26, 1996, 22.

Larkin, H. "Welcome to the Machine." *American Medical News,* 1993, *36*(1), 27–28.

Lipson, D. J., and De Sa, J. M. "Impact of Purchasing Strategies on Local Health Care Systems." *Health Affairs,* 1996, *15*(2), 62–76.

Louis Harris and Associates. "Who Does the Best Job in Serving the Consumer?" *BusinessWeek,* Apr. 21, 1997, 6.

Lumsdon, K. "More Docs to Pick From." *Hospitals and Health Networks,* Dec. 5, 1995, *69*(23), 12..

"Managed Care: Connecticut Residents Divided on Benefits." *American Health Line,* Feb. 28, 1997, 7–8.

Mason, R. O., and Mitroff, I. I. *Challenging Strategic Planning Assumptions.* New York: Wiley, 1981.

"Massachusetts: Legislature Supports Physician Profiles." *American Health Line,* July 1, 1997, 6.

Matthews, M. A. "Direct Contracting Offers Hospitals Opportunity to Compete for Market Share." *Health Care Management Team Agenda,* 1997, *12*(11), 1–2.

McManis, G. L. "Leadership Perspectives: Evaluating and Choosing an Affiliation Partner." *Health System Leader,* July 1994, *1*(5), 20–25.

McManis, G. L., Pavia, L., Ackerman, F. K., and Connelly, I. "Opportunities and Issues for Medical Group Practices." *MGM Journal,* Sept./Oct. 1996, *43*(5), 30–39, 108.

McNamee, M. "Health Care Inflation: It's Back." *BusinessWeek,* Mar. 17, 1997, 28–30.

Merton, R. E. *Social Theory and Social Structure* (rev. ed.). New York: Free Press, 1957.

Miles, E. "How to Keep Your Publics Informed During Strategic Moves." *Health Care Management Team Agenda,* June 1996, *12*(3), 10.

Miles, R. E., and Snow, C. C. *Organizational Strategy, Structure, and Process.* New York: McGraw-Hill, 1978.

Mintzberg, H. "Patterns in Strategy Formation." *Management Science,* 1978, *24,* 934–948.

Mintzberg, H. "Opening Up the Definition of Strategy." In J. B. Quinn, H. Mintzberg, and R. M. James (eds.), *The Strategy Process: Concepts, Contexts, and Cases.* Englewood Cliffs, N.J.: Prentice Hall, 1988, 13–20.

Mintzberg, H. "The Design School: Reconsidering the Basic Premises of Strategic Management." *Strategic Management Journal,* 1990, *11*(3), 171–195.

Montague, J. "Precision Maneuvers." *Hospitals and Health Networks,* Jan. 5, 1994, *68*(1), 26–33.

Montague, J. "How One New York Hospital Is Moving to Head Managed Care Off at the Pass." *Hospitals and Health Networks,* Jan. 20, 1996, *70*(2), 22–23.

Montague, J., Nordhaus-Bike, A., and Sandrick, K. "How to Save Big Bucks!" *Hospitals and Health Systems,* Mar. 5, 1996, *70*(5), 18–24.

Morrall, K. "New Channels: Mammograms at the Mall." *Hospitals and Health Networks,* Nov. 5, 1995, *69*(21), 47.

Nelson, R. R. "Why Firms Differ and How Does It Matter?" *Strategic Management Journal,* 1991, *12*(10), 61–74.

Nerenz, D. R., Zajac, B. M., and Rosman, H. S. "Consortium Research on System Performance." *The Joint Commission Journal on Quality Improvement,* 1993, *19,* 577–585.

Ottensmeyer, D. J. "Governance of the Integrated Health Care System," *Group Practice Journal,* Jan./Feb. 1993, 21–24.

Phillips, K. "Stakeholder Rebellion: Employees, Consumers Demand Corporate Respect." *USA Today,* Mar. 7, 1996, *14*(122), 12A.

Pope, C. "Smart Practice Planning Means Acknowledging Larger Trends." *MGM Update,* 1996, *35*(8), 11.

Porter, M. E. *Competitive Strategy.* New York: Free Press, 1980.

Porter, M. E. *Competitive Advantage.* New York: Free Press, 1985.

Porter, M. E. "Toward a Dynamic Theory of Strategy." *Strategic Management Journal,* 1991, *12*(1), 95–117.

Porter, M. E. "What Is Strategy?" *Harvard Business Review,* 1996, *74*(6), 61–78.

"Prescription Drugs: HMOs Move to Further Limit Choice." *American Health Line,* Mar. 14, 1997, 10.

Ribnik, P. G., and Carrano, V. A. "Understanding the New Era in Health Care Accountability Report Cards." *Journal of Nursing Care Quality,* 1995, *10*(1), 1–26.

"The Rise of Group Practice." *American Medical News,* 1995, *38*(15), 5.

Robinson, J. C. "The Dynamics and Limits of Corporate Growth in Health Care." *Health Affairs,* 1996, *15*(2), 155–169.

Robinson, J. C., and Casalino, L. P. The Growth of Medical Groups Paid Through Capitation in California." *New England Journal of Medicine,* 1995, *333*(25), 1664–1687.

Robinson, J. C., and Casalino, L. P. "Vertical Integration and Organizational Networks in Health Care," *Health Affairs,* 1996, *15*(1), 7–22.

Rosenthal, G. E., and Harper, D. L. "Cleveland Health Choice: A Model for Collaborative Community-Based Outcomes Assessment." *The Joint Commission Journal on Quality Improvement,* 1994, *20*(6), 425–442.

Savage, G. T., Nix, T. W., Whitehead, C. J., and Blair, J. D. "Strategies for Assessing and Managing Stakeholders." *Academy of Management Executives,* 1991, *5*(2), 61–75.

Savage, G. T., and Purtell, D. "Transforming Health Insurance: Problems and Promises with State Reforms. " 1995 Southern Management Association Proceedings. Valdosta State College, 1995.

Savage, G. T., Taylor, R. L., Rotarius, T. M., and Buesseler, J. A. "Governance of Integrated Delivery Systems/Networks: A Stakeholder Approach." *Health Care Management Review,* 1997, *22*(1), 7–20.

Scott, L. "Communities Ask, What's in It For Us?" *Modern Healthcare,* Jan. 6, 1997, *27*(1), 39.

Sheldon, A. and Windham, S. *Competitive Strategy for Health Care Organizations.* Homewood, Ill.: Dow Jones-Irwin, 1984.

Sherer, J. L. "Managing Chaos." *Hospitals and Health Networks,* Feb. 20, 1995, *69*(4), 22–27.

Sherer, J. L. "The Human Side of Change: Managing Employee Morale and Expectations." *Healthcare Executive,* Jul./Aug. 1997, *12*(4), 8–14.

Sherman, S. J. "Will an Integrated Medical Delivery System Deliver?" *MGM Journal,* Sept./Oct. 1996, *43*(5), 6–12.

Shortell, S. M., Gillies, R. R., Anderson, D. A., Erickson, K. M., and Mitchell, J. B. *Remaking Health Care in America: Building Organized Delivery Systems.* San Francisco: Jossey-Bass, 1996.

Shortell, S. M., Gillies, R. R., Anderson, D. A., Mitchell, J. B., and Morgan, K. "Creating Organized Delivery Systems: The Barriers and Facilitators." *Hospital and Health Services Administration,* 1993, *38*(4), 447–466.

Shortell, S. M., Morrison, E. M., and Friedman, B. *Strategic Choices for America's Hospitals: Managing Change in Turbulent Times.* San Francisco: Jossey-Bass, 1990.

Shua-Haim, J. R., and Gross, J. S. "Decline in Hospital Utilization Forces Hospitals to Compete With Independent Physicians." *Healthcare Management Team Agenda,* Feb., 4, 1997, *12*(11), 4.

Signorelli, T. F. "Implementing and Managing Organizational Change in Medical Groups." *College Review,* Spring 1994, *11*, 5–24.

Slomski, A. J. "Maybe Bigger Isn't Better After All." *Medical Economics,* Feb. 27, 1995, *72*(4), 55–60.

Slovensky, D. J., Fottler, M. D., and Houser, H. "Developing an Outcomes Report Card For Hospitals: Case Study and Implementation Guidelines." *Journal of Healthcare Management*, 1998, *43*(1), 15–34.

Smith, B. J. "Physician-Hospital Integration: It's Not If or When, It's How." *Group Practice Journal*, May/June 1994, *43*(3), 40–44.

Snyder, M. "When Belief Creates Reality." In L. Berkowitz (ed.), *Advances in Experimental Social Psychology*, Vol. 18. New York: Academic Press, 1984, 247–305.

Sommers, P. A. "Preparing for 2000 and Beyond Through Physician Group, Hospital, Health Plan Integration." *Group Practice Journal*, Nov./Dec. 1994, *43*(6), 39–43.

"Texas Poll: Shows Satisfaction With Managed Care Plans." *American Health Line*, Mar. 11, 1997, pp. 10–11.

"Texas: Senate Approves Bill to Create HMO Report Cards." *American Health Line*, Mar. 14, 1997, p. 8.

Tokarski, C. "Medical Express." *Hospital and Health Networks*, 1995, *69*(23), 39–40.

Tokarski, C. "Finding the Optimal Service Mix in a Changing Marketplace." *Healthcare Executive*, 1997, *12*(3), 6–10.

Topping, S., and Fottler, M. D. "Improved Stakeholder Management: The Key to Revitalizing the HMO Movement?" *Medical Care Review*, 1990, *47*, 365–393.

"USAir to Reinvent Itself, Beginning with Name." *Birmingham News*, Nov. 13, 1996, p. 1.

Wagner, L. "Managed Care Plans Now Required to Disclose Physician Incentive Plans." *Healthcare Management Team Agenda*, June 1996, *12*(3), 1–2.

Wallen, E. "Merging Practices Often Help Physicians Gain Competitive Edge." *Physician's Financial News*, Sept. 30, 1993, *11*(16), 515.

Weick, K. E. *The Social Psychology of Organizing.* Reading, Mass.: Addison-Wesley, 1979.

Weick, K. E. "Management of Organizational Change Among Loosely Coupled Elements." In P. S. Goodman and Associates (eds.), *Change in Organizations: New Perspectives on Theory, Research, and Practice.* San Francisco: Jossey-Bass, 1982.

Weick, K. E. "Substitutes for Strategy." In D. J. Teece (ed.), *The Competitive Challenge: Strategies for Industrial Innovation and Renewal.* Cambridge, Mass.: Ballinger, 1987.

Whitehead, C. J., Blair, J. D., Smith, R. R., Nix, T. W., and Savage, G. T. "Stakeholder Supportiveness and Strategic Vulnerability: Implications for the HMO Industry's Competitive Strategy." *Health Care Management Review*, 1989, *14*(3), 65–76.

Zinober, J. W. "Alliances in Health Care: To Retreat or Not To Retreat." *Medical Group Management Update*, Feb. 1994, *33*(2), 14.

INDEX